W9-BRY-559

Historical Dictionary of Burundi

Third Edition

Ellen K. Eggers

The Scarecrow Press, Inc.
Lanham, Maryland • Toronto • Plymouth, UK
2006

SCARECROW PRESS, INC.

Published in the United States of America
by Scarecrow Press, Inc.
A wholly owned subsidiary of
The Rowman & Littlefield Publishing Group, Inc.
4501 Forbes Boulevard, Suite 200, Lanham, Maryland 20706
www.scarecrowpress.com

Estover Road
Plymouth PL6 7PY
United Kingdom

British Library Cataloguing in Publication Information Available

Library of Congress Cataloging-in-Publication Data

Eggers, Ellen K., 1955–
  Historical dictionary of Burundi / Ellen K. Eggers. — 3rd ed.
    p. cm. —
  Includes bibliographical references.
  ISBN-13: 978-0-8108-5302-7 (hardcover : alk. paper)
  ISBN-10: 0-8108-5302-7 (hardcover : alk. paper)
  1. Burundi—History—Dictionaries. I. Title. II. Series.

  DT450.68.E37 2006
  967.572003—dc22

                                              2006013959

For Paul

Contents

Editor's Foreword

Burundi, like its neighbor Rwanda, is a small, poor, and remote country that, along with the usual political, economic, and social problems, must cope with the most serious of all: ethnic divisions and friction. For some time, it seemed to have avoided the worst, until a prolonged period of warfare and sheer terror broke out, and it is only now, after 12 horrible years of bloodshed, that it seems to be getting back to "normal" and there is some hope for the future. Although small, poor, and remote, Burundi's situation is not without interest to others, especially its neighbors, but also Africa more generally and in some modest degree the world. For, if Burundi can overcome its handicaps, perhaps others can do so as well, and if it cannot, as history has shown, any troubles could spill over.

Admittedly, although there is a genuine attempt at reconciliation, nobody knows what the future will bring. Fortunately, this new edition of *Historical Dictionary of Burundi* offers some basis for at least evaluating the present and speculating more intelligently about the future. And it does so, among other things, by reaching back into the past to show how the state, previously a colony, and before that small kingdoms, has evolved. This is done first in the chronology, which, given the many twists and turns, is particularly useful. The introduction sets out a more general context. Then the dictionary, with many more entries than the previous edition, provides considerable information on important national figures, the political parties, and above all the army. Other entries deal with significant aspects of the economy, society, and culture. The bibliography, while hardly vast, suggests further reading on a country on which little exists in English (or even French) and thus helps the reader to round out the picture.

This was not an easy book to write, since it has been even harder than before to obtain reliable information on a country that, to begin with, was not that well researched nor—until the recent disaster—of much interest to the media. Thus, the author, Ellen K. Eggers, deserves special credit for having shed so much light on the current situation while also providing a good look at the past. At present Dr. Eggers teaches English and linguistics at California State University in Chico. She first got to know Burundi in 1985–1986 when she lived in Bujumbura and taught English and linguistics at the University of Burundi. Since then, she has followed the situation closely and also wrote the previous edition of *Historical Dictionary of Burundi*, which she has now substantially updated and expanded. This is her contribution to international understanding, and an important one for those who want to know more about this elusive country.

Jon Woronoff
Series Editor

Preface

Jan Vansina, an oral historian, says the following about Burundi:

> The political system did not favor historical memory. . . . It was in every-
> one's interest to forget the past, whether it was the *ganwa* who had taken
> the land, the subchief who had been dismissed, or the king himself who
> relied now upon one faction, now upon another. The former senior regent
> of the country told me that history was of no interest at the court so there
> were practically no historical accounts. The political system shows why.
> (1985, 115)

Vansina's view of the history of Burundi may very well be the correct one. Certainly, this is not the first historical work on Burundi to
quote him nor, in all probability, will it be the last. However, Vansina
speaks mostly of a country's oral tradition—a primary method by which
a country becomes familiar to the rest of the world, but not necessarily
the only method—and he seeks the truth. Perhaps the truth is something
that is never known precisely; historical truth, at least, is dependent
upon the givers and the receivers of it. Earlier, Vansina says of truth:

> Not all societies have the same idea as to what historical truth is. . . . In
> the Congo, "truth" is what has been transmitted by the ancestors as hav-
> ing really happened. . . . The Rundi have the same idea of historical truth,
> and as soon as something is accepted as a historical truth, they do not
> trouble to think whether it could have happened or not, or whether it re-
> ally happened in the way the tradition describes. In their eyes, analysis of
> a testimony is meaningless. ("Use of Process Models in African History,"
> 1964, 102–3)

It is difficult to ever know if what we learn of a people and of a culture is "true." Do those inside the culture have a better perspective, or
does the necessary objectivity come from outside? These questions may

never be answered to everyone's satisfaction, but they will still be asked as history continues and unfolds in the eyes of the world. A Burundi writer, David Niyonzima, points out that oral histories can be both accurate and inaccurate at the same time: accurate in that they are carefully transmitted from one generation to the next, but inaccurate because the storytellers can freely pick and choose from among the various accounts. Niyonzima also notes that blaming all of Burundi's problems on ethnic conflict is simplistic; conflicts based on territory and power often had nothing to do with ethnicity. He adds that *ethnicity* and *tribalism* are difficult to define in Burundi; much of what outsiders consider "ethnic" or "tribal" are really issues of class. Another writer on Africa has suggested that *Tutsi* and *Hutu* have become umbrella terms attempting to describe the complex situation. Finally, Burundi writer Edward Nyankanzi points out that there is, in Burundi, a "tendency to ignore the past."

This historical account of Burundi seeks to find facts rather than truth; unfortunately, the line between the two is not always as clear as we might like. The country and the region it inhabits, as well as probable future developments in its struggle to achieve and maintain peace, continue to be objects of the world's speculation.

Acknowledgments

I would like to thank the following colleagues whose generosity has been of great help during the writing of this dictionary. From the University of Nebraska–Lincoln: Learthen Dorsey, Dieudonné Kwizera, Paul Olson, Oyekan Owomoyela, and George Wolf. From the University of Burundi: Jacques Bacamurwanko, former Burundi ambassador to the United States. This project was partially supported by a Fulbright grant.

Reader's Note

LANGUAGE

The adjectival form of Burundi can be found alternatively as *Rundi*, *Burundi*, and *Burundian*. *Rundi* was generally preferred in earlier (precolonial and colonial) descriptions, while *Burundi* and *Burundian* are both used in modern descriptions; here it has been standardized to *Burundi*, unless the material is quoted. Also for the sake of standardization, the simplified terms *Hutu*, *Tutsi*, and *Twa* are used throughout to indicate the collective form of the ethnic groups as well as the adjectival form; this usage is not meant to ignore or diminish the complexities in the language or within each of the groups, but rather for ease of reference.

The verbal element in Kirundi is complex, as is characteristic of Bantu languages. It consists of a verbal root to which bound morphological elements are affixed. The basic prefixes of the verb are the subject prefix (obligatory, except in infinitives and imperatives), a tense marker, and optional focus and object markers, in that order. Basic suffixes include all reflexive, applicative (allowing an already transitive verb to take two objects), locative, and causative markers (optionally), and an obligatory aspect marker as the final syllable. Primarily relevant to these entries, however, is the infinitive marker. The basic infinitive in Kirundi is the prefix *ku-*. In some words, the *ku-* changes to *gu-* following the rules of Dahl's Law; this linguistic principle says that a morpheme beginning with a voiced consonant ([b], [g], [d], [z], [v], etc.) must precede one beginning with a voiceless one ([p], [k], [t], [s], [f], etc.). The verbs in these entries are listed by the initial letter of the word stem.

The noun is as complex in Kirundi as it is in other Bantu languages. The classification system (sometimes called a gender system, although it is not gender in the sense of the lay usage; rather, it is semantic categories) comprises 17 classes, most having current semantic as well as historical value. For example, classes 1 and 2, which are reserved for words designating humans, are *mu-* and *ba-*; therefore, *Murundi* means "Burundi person" and *Barundi* means "Burundi people." An entry such as this will be listed under the root—in this case, *-rundi*—with the relevant prefixes listed. However, if a word is used in only one form (such as *Kirundi*, "Burundi language," *ki-* being the prefix for language names), the full form will be listed. A single-vowel prefix is often added before the class prefix in discourse situations. For further information concerning the structure, sound system, and sound changes of Kirundi, which is beyond the intended scope of this historical dictionary, the reader will find numerous linguistic analyses listed in the bibliography.

NAMES

Kings (*bami*) of Burundi are listed under their better-known dynastic names, with a cross-reference to their birth names. In the case of Mwezi II, while his dynastic name is usually used, he is also known in some Western texts as, alternately, Kissabo, Kisabo, Gissabo, or Gisabo when his given name is used; that given name has here been standardized to Gisabo.

CROSS-REFERENCING

When a word is in bold print in an entry, it can be found elsewhere in the dictionary under its own heading.

Acronyms and Abbreviations

ACCORD	African Centre for Constructive Resolution of Disputes
AIDS	acquired immune deficiency syndrome
AMIB	African Mission in Burundi
APRODEBA	Association des Progressistes et Démocrates Barundi/Association of Barundi Progressives and Democrats
AU	African Union
CCB	Coopérative des Commerçants du Burundi/ Cooperative of Traders in Burundi
CEC	Centres Extra-Coutumiers/Extra-Customary Centers
CEPGL	Communauté Economique des Pays des Grands/ Economic Community of the Great Lakes
CNC	Conseil National de la Communication/ National Council of Communication
CNDD	Conseil National pour la Défense de la Démocratie/National Council for the Defense of Democracy
CNR	Conseil National de la Révolution/ National Revolutionary Council
CPJB	Coalition for Peace and Justice in Burundi
CSP	Conseil Supérieur du Pays/National Superior Council
DRC	Democratic Republic of the Congo
EAC	East African Community
EU	European Union
FDD	Forces pour la Défense de la Démocratie/Forces for the Defense of Democracy
FNL	Forces Nationales de Libération/National Liberation Forces

FOREAMI	Fonds Reine Elisabeth pour l'Assistance Médicale aux Indigènes
FRODEBU	Front Démocratique Burundi/Burundi Democratic Front
FTB	Féderation des Travailleurs du Burundi/Federation of Burundi Workers
FULREAC	Fondation de l'Université de Liège pour les Recherches Scientifiques au Congo Belge et au Ruanda-Urundi
GDP	gross domestic product
HIV	human immunodeficiency virus
IDP	internally displaced person
IMF	International Monetary Fund
ISABU	Institut des Sciences Agronomiques du Burundi/ Burundi Institute of Agronomic Science
JNR	Jeunesse Nationaliste Rwagasore/Nationalist Rwagasore Youth
JRR	Jeunesse Rwagasore Révolutionnaire/Rwagasore Revolutionary Youth
MIPROBU	Mission pour la Protection des Établissements Démocratiques au Burundi/Mission for the Protection of Democratic Institutions in Burundi
NGO	nongovernmental organization
NTRC	National Truth and Reconciliation Commission
OAU	Organization of African Unity
ONUB	United Nations Operations in Burundi
PALIPEHUTU	Parti pour la Libération du Peuple Hutu/Party for the Liberation of the Hutu People
PARENA	Parti pour le Redressement National/Party for National Recovery
PARMEHUTU	Parti du Mouvement de l'Émancipation d'Hutu/ Party of the Movement of Emancipation of Hutu
PDC	Parti Démocratique Chrétien/Democratic Christian Party
PDJTB	Parti des Jeunes Travailleurs du Burundi/ Young Workers of Burundi Party
PDR	Parti Démocratique et Rural/Democratic and Rural Party

PP	Parti du Peuple/Party of the People
PRP	Parti de la Réconciliation des Personnes/People's Reconciliation Party
RPA	Radio Publique Africaine/African Public Radio
RTNB	Radiodiffusion et Télévision Nationale de Burundi/ National Broadcasting and Television of Burundi
TANU	Tanganyika African National Union
UBU	Umugambwe wa'Bakozi Uburundi/Burundi Laborers' Party
UCJAB	Union Culturelle de la Jeunesse Africaine du Burundi/Cultural Union of the African Youth of Burundi
UDB	Union des Démocratique Barundi/Democratic Barundi Union
UFB	Union des Femmes Burundaises/Union of Burundi Women
UN	United Nations
UNB	Union Nationale du Burundi/National Union of Burundi
UNEBA	Union Nationale des Étudiants Burundi/National Union of Burundi Students
UNESCO	United Nations Educational, Scientific, and Cultural Organization
UNHCR	United Nations High Commissioner for Refugees
UNICEF	United Nations Children's Fund
UPRONA	Parti de l'Union et du Progrès National/Party of National Union and Progress
USAID	United States Agency for International Development

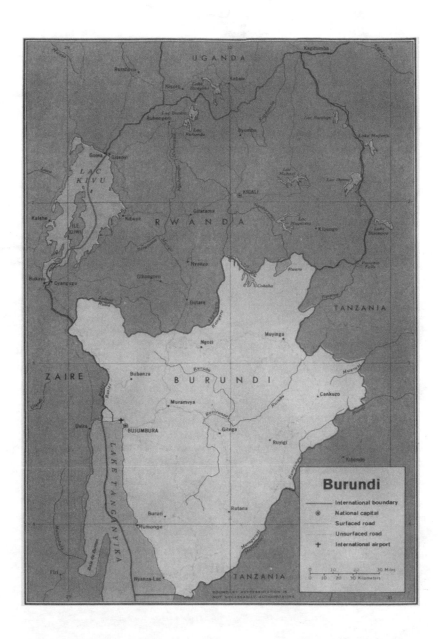

UGANDA

Rutshuru

Kisoro
Lake
Bunyoni
Kabale

Kagitumba

Ruhengeri
Lac Bulera
Edu
Muhondo

Byumba

Lac Hashiya

Lake Mutanda

Goma   Gisenyi

LAC
KIVU

KIGALI

Lac
Muhazi
Lac Ihema

Kalehe

Kibuye

R W A N D A

Gitarama

ILE
IDJWI

Lac
Mugesera
Kibungo

Lake
Rwanyakizinga

Bukavu
Cyangugu

Gikongoro

Nyanza

Butare

Cohoha

Ruera

Rusumo
Falls

TANZANIA

ZAIRE

Bubanza

Ngozi

B U R U N D I

Muyinga

Muramvya

Cankuzo

Uvira

BUJUMBURA

Gitega

Ruyigi

Kibondo

LAKE   TANGANYIKA

Bururi

Humonge

Rutana

Nyanza-Lac

TANZANIA

Burundi

—— International boundary
  ⊛ National capital
    Surfaced road
    Unsurfaced road
  ✛ International airport

0   10   20   30 Miles
0   10 20   30 Kilometers

Chronology

Note: Place names are listed in this chronology as they were known at the time. For example, the capital of Burundi is listed as Usumbura before the country's 1962 independence and Bujumbura after that date.

800–1000   Hutu farmers, who belong to the Bantu group, come to the area that is to become Ruanda-Urundi and establish their language and customs.

1300–1600   The Tutsi, who are said to be descendants of Nilo-Hamitic shepherd people, arrive from the north and achieve political and economic domination through their feudal system. They found Burundi's first kingdom early in the 16th century.

1675   The Tutsi king Ntare I builds a kingdom in what is now Burundi.

1858   Richard Burton and John Hanning Speke arrive together at Lake Tanganyika, the first of the European explorers. They hoped to find the source of the Nile River at the northern end of the lake.

1860   Mwezi IV Gisabo begins his reign as *mwami* (king).

1871   During their exploration of Lake Tanganyika, Henry Morton Stanley and Dr. David Livingstone reach a point approximately 16 kilometers (10 miles) from where Bujumbura lies today.

1879   An expedition of Cardinal Lavigerie's White Fathers arrives in Urundi, venturing along the eastern shore of Lake Tanganyika.

1881   A group of White Fathers is accused of befriending Arab slave traders and murdered in Rumonge.

1884   **8 November:** Germany recognizes the International Association of the Congo.

1885   25 August: Germany ratifies the boundaries described in the Declaration of Neutrality (of 1 August). This ratification has two parts: recognition of the neutrality of the Congo State and recognition of its borders.

1890   Often considered the end of the era of great explorations on the African continent, the Anglo-German partition of Africa occurs, after which explorations become inseparable from colonial administration.

1892   Oskar Baumann, an Austrian leading a Masai expedition of the German antislavery committee, is the first European to traverse the country from east to west.

1894   Negotiations between Germany and Britain concerning a "Cape to Cairo" corridor of communications culminate, leading to a delineation of borders for German East Africa, including Ruanda-Urundi.

1896   Two priests arrive in Urundi to found a Catholic mission and are forced to flee from the attacks of a chief named Musibiko. The first permanent Catholic mission is built at Muyaga. Richard Kandt leads an important expedition to make the first detailed maps of the region of Ruanda-Urundi.

1896–1897   Germans found the Usumbura military station.

1899   Following an attack against the Bethe column, the government of Germany decides to occupy Ruanda-Urundi. A second group of White Fathers settles at Mugera, the residence of Mwami Mwezi IV Gisabo.

1900   December: A German contingent led by Captain Herrmann surveys the islands in Lake Tanganyika, as well as the volcanic region. The result is the first reliable large-scale map of western Urundi and Ruanda, which confirms reports that Lake Kivu lies farther to the west than was indicated on earlier maps.

1903   The Germans demand passage of the Treaty of Kiganda, which stipulates that missionaries are allowed to work with total freedom. Father J. M. Van der Burgt publishes the first French–Kirundi dictionary.

1905   10 March: A governor's ordinance states that entry to the Ruanda-Urundi territories is permitted only from the military station of Usumbura and only with written permission from the district office.

This was in answer to what has become known as the *Inder Frage* or Indian Question.

1906 Military occupation of Ruanda-Urundi ends, and colonial administration begins. **26 May:** The Congo Free State and the Holy See sign a contract that adds education to the evangelical activities of the Catholic Church.

1908 Mwezi IV dies at the age of 63; Mutaga IV begins his reign. This begins a period regarded by the Germans as political chaos.

1909 A government school is established in Usumbura. In the first year, the school has 25 students, about three-fourths of whom are Rundi children; the others are children of foreign business owners and traders.

1910 Ruanda-Urundi becomes completely administered by Germany.

1912 The Kivu-Ruanda-Urundi vicariate is founded. The seat of the Urundi *residence* moves from Usumbura to Gitega.

1914 **18 September:** A German boat on Lake Kivu captures a Belgian boat, thus establishing German control of the lake.

1915 Mutaga IV ends his reign, and Mwambutsa IV, at the age of two, becomes the king of Burundi.

1916 Belgian troops enter Ruanda in two converging columns and, after successful battles, occupy all of Ruanda-Urundi.

1917 The arbitrary power of the *bami* and other native authorities is abolished.

1919 **30 May:** The Supreme Council of Allied Powers assigns the Ruanda-Urundi mandate to Belgium.

1923 Terms of the 1919 agreement are confirmed by the League of Nations. Domestic slavery in Ruanda-Urundi is abolished.

1924 Terms of the 1919 agreement are approved by the Belgian Parliament, which formally accepts responsibility for Ruanda-Urundi under the conditions established by the League of Nations.

1925 The Belgian Parliament passes a law joining Ruanda-Urundi in an administrative union with the Belgian Congo; a separate budget is maintained for the mandate territory, but the administration and monetary systems are combined with those of the Congo. Prince Leopold of Belgium visits Ruanda-Urundi; he repeats the visit in 1933.

1926 The triple hierarchy of native authorities—the chief of crops, the chief of pastures, and the chief of armed units—is abolished and replaced by a single authority. Archaeologists discover arrowheads and knives from the late Stone Age.

1932 Coffee, which is well suited to Burundi's higher elevations and is to become Burundi's largest export, is first introduced by the Belgians as a cash crop under a compulsory cultivation system.

1936 The native system of justice is completely reformed.

1938 Kurkhart Waldecker erects a pyramid at the southernmost source of the Nile River in what is today Burundi.

1945 At the end of the World War II, after four years of Ruanda-Urundi contributing to the war effort of the Allied nations, the United Nations makes it a trust territory, ending the mandate.

1946 3 December: The United Nations General Assembly approves the Trusteeship Agreement for the territory of Ruanda-Urundi. The agreement requires Belgium to work for the development of free political institutions and to assure the inhabitants of increased participation in administrative responsibilities.

1947 Prince Charles, regent of Belgium from 1944 to 1950, visits Ruanda-Urundi.

1948 The first Trusteeship Council mission visits Ruanda-Urundi, with visits to continue at three-year intervals; the first two missions report that social and political advancements are proceeding too slowly. The first Homemaking Center to promote the education of women opens in Usumbura.

1949 25 April: Belgium assumes responsibility for the political, social, and economic development of Ruanda-Urundi "in order to guide it to autonomy in good time." **14 August:** The vice governor-general of the trusteeship publishes an ordinance that formally recognizes the boundary between Ruanda and Urundi. This political boundary remains in effect today.

1951 Belgium institutes a series of economic and administrative reforms. The economic reforms are embodied in the Ten-Year Plan; administrative reforms involve reorganizing of indigenous political structures and instituting a limited degree of representative government.

1952 Belgium sets up the Ten-Year Development Plan for Ruanda-Urundi (1952–1961), the first significant step taken toward the economic improvement of the country. **1 May:** The resident governor legally abolishes polygamous marriages. **14 July:** A decree establishing the hierarchy of subchieftaincy, chieftaincy, territorial, and country councils inaugurates a new political organization.

1954–1955 The almost exclusively Tutsi kingdom councils in Ruanda and Urundi abolish cattle clientage.

1955 King Baudouin I of Belgium makes what has become known as a "triumphant tour" through his African territories.

1957 A General Council replaces the Council of the General Vice-Government, the highest consultative assembly of the territory. The new council extends representation.

1959 **November:** A serious outbreak of violence between Hutu and Tutsi occurs in Rwanda and augments tensions in Burundi.

1960 **October:** Two university departments are opened in Usumbura, one in philosophy and letters and social, economic, and administrative sciences, the other in various scientific and agricultural disciplines. More than 20 political parties are formed in a new period of political awakening.

1961 **September:** Legislative elections result in the widespread allegiance among both Hutu and Tutsi electorates to the Parti de l'Union et du Progrès National (UPRONA; Party of National Union and Progress) under the leadership of Prince Louis Rwagasore. **13 October:** Rwagasore, the prime minister–designate, is assassinated by a Greek national who was allegedly part of a conspiracy organized by a rival political faction. André Muhirwa succeeds him.

1962 **6 June:** A special United Nations commission recommends that the two territories (Ruanda and Urundi) be given independence as separate countries. **27 June:** The UN General Assembly unanimously decides to give full and separate independence to the Republic of Rwanda and the Kingdom of Burundi. **1 July:** Burundi becomes independent and separates from Rwanda. **18 September:** Burundi joins the United Nations. **21 December:** Mwami Mwambutsa IV of Burundi becomes the first African sovereign to visit Jerusalem in 2,900 years (when the Queen of Sheba visited King Solomon). The mwami and President Itshak Ben Zvi of Israel sign a treaty of friendship.

1963 15 January: Five men convicted of complicity in the murder of Rwagasore are hanged in Gitega in front of a crowd of 20,000. **June:** Pierre Ngendandumwe becomes the first member of the Hutu majority to hold the post of prime minister. Muhirwa, the outgoing prime minister, is accused of destroying national unity. **8 June:** The army and the gendarmerie are converted into secretariats of state and brought under the exclusive jurisdiction of the court. **29 July:** Belgium promises 19 million francs in aid to Burundi. **23 December:** When Rwanda and Burundi are unable to reach an agreement for sharing reserve currencies, Rwanda decides to sever its economic ties with Burundi. Burundi then establishes the Banque du Royaume du Burundi (Bank of the Kingdom of Burundi), which later becomes the Banque de la République du Burundi.

1964 23 January: By royal decree, the Université Officielle du Bujumbura is established. This decree transforms the former Collège du Saint-Esprit, established by the Roman Catholic Society of Jesus (the Jesuits) in Bujumbura in 1960, into a joint program of the church and the government. **March:** Tracts of mysterious origin circulate in Ngozi announcing the mwami's resolution to dismiss four members of the Cabinet, all Hutu. **31 March:** After dismissing the four ministers, the mwami asks Ngendandumwe to form a new government, but when agreement still cannot be reached on a new cabinet, Ngendandumwe resigns. **6 April:** The mwami calls on Albin Nyamoya, previously the minister of agriculture and minister of the interior, to form a new government. **28 April:** A Burundi delegation arrives in Peking for an official visit. **18 May:** Mwami Mwambutsa IV meets with U.S. president Lyndon Johnson. **19 May:** The national banks of Rwanda and Burundi, successors to the Banque d'Émission du Rwanda et Burundi, open in Kigali and Bujumbura. **17 August:** The Burundi foreign minister wires the secretaries-general of the Organization of African Unity (OAU) and the United Nations, informing them that the situation between Rwanda and Burundi is "very tense." **8 September:** The mwami signs two royal decrees proclaiming martial law and a state of emergency in some regions of the provinces of Bubanza and Ngozi. **8 October:** Prime Minister Nyamoya cables the chairman of the OAU ad hoc commission on the Congo, as well as the secretaries-general of the OAU and the UN, charging that Zairian military aircraft have bombed Burundi communities twice. **December:** A large quantity of arms and ammunition is discovered in the vicinity of Gitega, and rumors quickly spread of an impending coup sponsored by China.

1965 8 January: Mwami Mwambutsa dismisses the Nyamoya government and, five days later, asks former prime minister Ngendandumwe to form a new government. **15 January:** Ngendandumwe is assassinated by Tutsi extremists from Rwanda. **24 January:** Joseph Bamina, president of UPRONA, is appointed prime minister. **12 February:** The International Monetary Fund (IMF) approves a standby arrangement with Burundi that authorizes drawing up to $4 million during 1965. **10 May:** The first postindependence elections to the National Assembly result in a Hutu majority. **13 September:** Léopold Biha is appointed prime minister. **October:** The École Normale Supérieure, a second institution of higher education, is opened in Bujumbura to train secondary school teachers. **19 October:** A putsch by Hutu military personnel, led by Gervais Nyangoma, is thwarted by army loyalists under the command of Capt. Michel Micombero. Prime Minister Biha is wounded, and Hutu leaders are slaughtered in retaliation. **2 November:** Mwami Mwambutsa leaves for Europe.

1966 5 January: Diplomatic relations with Zaire, broken since August 1964, are resumed. **8 January:** The International Commission of Jurists reports in Geneva that 86 people, including all of the elected officers of both houses of Burundi's Parliament, have been executed following the abortive coup of October 1965. Another report lists the number executed at 23, all Hutu. **7 March:** The International Labor Organization (ILO) files a formal complaint with the UN Commission on Human Rights, charging the Burundi government with mass executions of political and labor leaders following the 1965 coup attempt. This is the first complaint ever lodged against a government as a UN agenda item. **24 March:** The mwami, while still in Europe, gives his son, Crown Prince Charles Ndizeye, substantial powers. **25 April:** Burundi's

UN ambassador states in Geneva that his country has been "judged and condemned unjustly." **8 July:** The crown prince deposes his father (who is still in Europe), dismisses Biha's government, and suspends the country's constitution. **11 July:** Prince Charles asks Micombero, the Belgian-trained army captain now serving as defense minister, to form a new government. **1 September:** Crown Prince Charles Ndizeye is installed as Mwami Ntare V. In Geneva, the deposed Mwambutsa IV claims that his son is being manipulated by extremist elements. The new mwami calls on the people to heal their ethnic divisions. **20 November:** Radio Burundi broadcasts a decree (dated 18 November) that restores the Biha government and abrogates the 8 July decree that had suspended it. **24 November:** A royal decree establishes UPRONA as the sole political party in Burundi. **28 November:** Micombero deposes Mwami Ntare V and proclaims Burundi a republic, of which he is the first president. The military coup is peaceful. **30 November:** The military regime confirms UPRONA's status as the sole political party. **6 December:** The National Revolutionary Council of military personnel announces that Micombero's term as president will be seven years and promotes him to the rank of colonel. **20 December:** Micombero announces that all governmental directives will be issued as presidential decrees, on the advice of ministers, and after consultation with the attorney general.

1967 **1 February:** The Burundi Ministry of Information and the Soviet news agency Tass sign an agreement under which Tass agrees to supply information equipment to Burundi at no cost and to provide news service at minimal cost. **10 February:** All of the country's youth organizations merge into one group, the Jeunesse Rwagasore Révolutionnaire (JRR). **March:** Micombero integrates the police into the national army. **20 March:** The presidents of Rwanda and Burundi disarm refugees on both sides of their common border. **1 December:** The East African Community (EAC) is formally inaugurated in a ceremony at EAC headquarters in Arusha, Tanzania. Presidents Jomo Kenyatta of Kenya, Julius Nyerere of Tanzania, and Milton Obote of Uganda attend. A Burundi delegation attends as guests. **16 December:** Burundi makes a formal application to join the EAC.

1968 **January:** Micombero dissolves the National Council of the Revolution. **March:** After meeting in January and February, an East

African negotiating team states that no new members will be admitted to the EAC for at least two years. **7 June:** President Johnson appoints George W. Renchard as U.S. ambassador to Burundi; the post had been empty since the expulsion of Donald Dumont in January 1966. **11 July:** The Burundi government announces that it is expelling (on 48 hours' notice) seven officers and an enlisted man from a 44-member Belgian military assistance group in Burundi.

1969 September: An abortive Hutu plot against the government is discovered. **11 October:** Burundi's foreign minister discloses that at least 20 people have been arrested in Bujumbura for plotting against Micombero's regime and says that the plot was financed by an embassy in Bujumbura. **17 December:** The Burundi government announces that 26 people, including three former cabinet members, have been sentenced to death for taking part in the September coup attempt and for planning a massacre of Tutsi; those sentenced are part of the new Hutu elite that emerged after the mass slaughter of Hutu leaders in 1965.

1970 November: Several operations are undertaken against Tutsi guerrillas operating against Rwanda from northern Burundi in the Burundi government's attempt to improve relations with the Hutu government of Rwanda. *Africa Report* prints an anonymous article entitled "Burundi: Political and Ethnic Powderkeg."

1971 Burundi sets up a 30-member Supreme Council of Revolution. **13 October:** China and Burundi restore diplomatic relations.

1972 March: Idi Amin of Uganda helps arrange a written guarantee of amnesty for Ntare so that the deposed king can return to Burundi as a private citizen. **30 March:** Ntare returns to Burundi and is flown to one of his father's former residences in Gitega to be detained. Hours later, the Voice of the Revolution Radio announces that Ntare has been arrested trying to lead West German mercenaries in an invasion; this was denied. **29 April:** Micombero dismisses his entire government and the executive secretary of UPRONA; the government radio station reports riots in Bujumbura. The radio also reports fighting in Gitega, where Ntare has been under house arrest, during which the former king was killed in an attempt to rescue him. **30 April:** Fighting is reported to be very heavy in the south with bands of Hutu attacking members of the ruling Tutsi. Micombero appoints military governors to each of Burundi's eight provinces. **3 May:** Zaire sends troops to Burundi. **4 May:** The Voice of the Revolution Radio reports that those responsible for the coup attempt have been arrested and that the whole country is calm. **5 May:** The radio report is repeated without the announcement of countrywide calm; scattered fighting is reported. **7 May:** The government radio station announces that an unspecified number of people have been executed for their part in the coup attempt. Diplomatic sources in Kampala, Uganda, say that the death toll in Burundi has reached several thousand and that about 10,000 refugees have fled to Tanzania and Zaire. **29 May:** The Belgian prime minister states that Burundi is faced with a "veritable genocide." **12 June:** U.S. senators Edward M. Kennedy and John V. Tunney call for international action to deal with the situation in Burundi; Tunney, referring to press reports estimating that more than 100,000 people have been killed, says that even if the conflict falls within the UN definition of a domestic matter, "the international community cannot escape its moral responsibility to act." **13 June:** Micombero denies that his government is engaged in a policy of genocide against the country's Hutu, reiterating that all of the 50,000 or more people said to have been killed by the rebels were Tutsi; he compares the attacks to previous unsuccessful coup attempts by the Hutu in 1965 and 1969. **21 June:** A telegram from the U.S. embassy in Burundi reports "selective genocide" and describes live burial and executions of the Hutu elite, as well as of villagers and refugees throughout the country. **4 July:** UN secretary-general Kurt Waldheim says the dead might number as high as 200,000. Burundi reacts angrily, and the United States reacts with silence. **August:** An American Universities Field Staff report on Burundi says there is only one Hutu nurse left in the entire country and that only a thousand Hutu secondary school students survived the massacre. **December:** The disaster relief office of the U.S. Agency for International Development concludes, "In human terms, Burundi was the worst disaster to occur in 1972."

1973 21 March: After a Burundi army patrol was ambushed near the Tanzanian border by a guerrilla band of Hutu on 16 March, Burundi responds with mortar fire and strafing; Tanzania protests that three villages are hit. **3 April:** Burundi extends a formal apology to the Tanzanian government, admitting the incursion and offering to pay compensation for loss of life and property. **August:** The UN Subcommission on the Prevention of Racial Discrimination and the Protection of Minorities names Burundi as a situation that possibly reveals a persistent pattern of human rights violations.

1974 Early this year, full diplomatic relations are resumed between the United States and Burundi in spite of persisting reports of the ruling Tutsi carrying out a policy of genocide against the Hutu. The United States plans to renew an aid fund for $100,000 that was suspended in 1972. A new constitution confirms Burundi as a one-party state. **2 February:** Burundi establishes diplomatic relations with Cuba.

1975 Former U.S. ambassador to Burundi Thomas Melady publicly criticizes the lack of UN action over the 1972 massacres.

1976 **1 November:** Micombero's government is overthrown in a bloodless military coup. UPRONA, Burundi's only political party, is dissolved. **6 November:** Voice of the Revolution Radio announces that the country has returned to complete normality, that a Supreme Revolutionary Council headed by Lt. Col. Jean-Baptiste Bagaza is embarking on a national and international campaign to explain its aims, and that Micombero, who has been under house arrest, will be imprisoned.

1978 **January:** The office of prime minister is abolished, and the president is made head of the government. The president chairs an 11-member Executive Committee, responsible to the newly formed Supreme Revolutionary Council of army officers.

1979 **June:** Fifty-two Protestant and Roman Catholic missionaries are expelled from Burundi, accused of encouraging rebellion against Bagaza's military government. **September:** Bagaza heads the delegation from Burundi to the 34th UN General Assembly in New York.

1980 **March:** The first national congress of the revived UPRONA Party, the only legal political party, chooses the head of state, Bagaza, as the only candidate for party president and head of the Central Committee, which has recently taken over from the Supreme Revolutionary Council of army officers.

1981 **November:** A new constitution, approved by a national referendum, provides for a national assembly to be elected by universal adult suffrage.

1982 **October:** The first elections under the new constitution are held. **November:** In a cabinet reshuffle, 11 new ministers are named, including, for the first time, two women.

1983   16 July: Micombero dies of a heart attack in Mogadishu, Somalia, where he has lived since shortly after the overthrow of his government and his arrest in 1976.

1984   31 August: Bagaza is reelected in the first presidential election since he gained control of the government in 1976. As president of UPRONA, he is the only candidate for the national presidency.

1985   August: More than 150 local priests are detained. The government cites defiance of a recent ban on church services between 7 A.M. and 5 P.M. as the reason.

1986 A new political party named Front Démocratique Burundi (FRODEBU; Burundi Democratic Front) is founded by Melchior Ndadaye.

1987   3 September: Pierre Buyoya leads a bloodless coup overthrowing Bagaza's government, suspends the constitution, announces the formation of a 31-member Military Committee for National Redemption, and dismisses all government ministers. Bagaza was attending a summit of Francophone countries in Canada at the time of the overthrow.

1988   5 August: A Hutu uprising occurs in Marangara when Hutu villagers demand the removal of four Tutsi civil servants and then panic when three military vehicles arrive. **6 August:** The Hutu arm themselves with arrows, spears, and machetes, fell trees across roads, and dismantle a bridge in order to block the army. **7 August:** When soldiers arrive with a chain saw to clear the road, several dozen Hutu, the first group of refugees, flee to Rwanda. **14 August:** In what is considered the flash point of the 1988 massacres, a wealthy Tutsi coffee merchant in Ntega refuses to pay a group of Hutu money that he owes them, taunting and killing five of them. In an enraged response, the Hutu mobilize, surround and stone his house, and besiege him for many hours. When he defends himself with a shotgun, they break in and kill him and his family. After this, pandemonium erupts in many areas of the country; the violence claims the lives of about 20,000 Hutu civilians as well as a number of Tutsi. **22 August:** In an open letter to the president, 27 Hutu intellectuals ask for an inquiry into the massacres and point to gaps in the official account. **6 October:** Buyoya presses on with reforms, creating a Consultative Commission on National Unity with 12 Hutu and 12 Tutsi members to investigate the recent massacres. **19 October:**

Buyoya reshuffles his cabinet, increasing the number of Hutu ministers from 6 to 12, now a majority. He also re-creates the position of prime minister and appoints a Hutu.

1990 19 October: Burundi ratifies the Convention on the Rights of the Child, part of the 1949 Geneva Conventions.

1991 1 February: The Charter of National Unity is adopted by 89.2 percent of the electorate in a national referendum. The document was written under the auspices of the ruling UPRONA Party and had been criticized by some opposition groups, including the new and now principal Hutu party, Party for the Liberation of the Hutu People (PALIPEHUTU).

1993 March: A new constitution that disallows political organizations that advocate "tribalism, divisionalism, or violence" and states that parties must be representative of both the Hutu and Tutsi is approved by over 90 percent of the electorate; this paves the way for multiparty democracy. **1 June:** The first free presidential election takes place, resulting in the election of Ndadaye with 64.7 percent of the vote, against 32.5 percent for the incumbent (and reportedly surprised) Buyoya. **29 June:** The first free legislative elections take place. **Late June:** Students and civil servants protest against what they call "ethnic inventory" in Burundi, which they claim the election became. **10 July:** Ndadaye takes over the office of the presidency. He is the first democratically elected president, as well as the first Hutu and the first civilian to hold that office. **18 July:** Ndadaye announces an amnesty for about 500 political prisoners, both Hutu and Tutsi. **21 October:** Ndadaye is assassinated in an attempted coup. **22 October:** Massacres against Tutsi begin with intensity across many provinces, including Bujumbura; thousands of Hutu and between 100,000 and 200,000 Tutsi are reported killed. Leaders of the attempted coup establish a Committee of National Salvation to run the country temporarily, sealing the borders, closing the airport, shutting down the Lake Tanganyika port, and cutting telephone service. **23 October:** Lt. Col. Jean Bikomagu, Burundi's chief of the army, says the troops who took part in the attempted coup are willing to surrender power in return for amnesty. From Rwanda, Jean Minani, the health minister, proclaims a government in exile. **24 October:** Prime Minister Sylvie Kinigi takes refuge along with seven other ministers in the French embassy; she says the remaining ministers known to be alive are hiding in the city or have fled the country. **26 October:** The army leadership urges government ministers to come out of hiding and resume control. The government, led by Prime Minister Kinigi, refuses to give amnesty to soldiers involved in the coup and refuses to negotiate until the soldiers disarm and return to their barracks. **15 November:** Dozens of Hutu villagers are killed by the military in Kiganda district. Despite such reports, the military claims that the country is calming down and that the troops have remained neutral.

1994   January: Cyprien Ntaryamira is appointed Speaker by the National Assembly; the appointment is challenged in the Constitutional Court by the opposition. **February:** Amnesty International receives reports that more than 40 civilians have been killed and many homes destroyed since 31 January. **3 February:** The government and opposition parties meet in the capital and agree that Ntaryamira will take the oath of office, reinstate the Constitutional Court judges, and appoint a new prime minister from among the ranks of the opposition on 5 February. **4 February:** The Coalition for Peace and Justice in Burundi is formed by a group of Barundi in Ithaca, New York. **5 February:** Ntaryamira is inaugurated and, during the ceremony, says the main goals of his government will be "to do everything possible so that peace, tranquility, and mutual trust return among Burundians." **5 March:** Missionary and Amnesty International reports claim that several hundred people have been killed in Bujumbura in the continuing ethnic conflict set off by the October coup. **12 March:** Relief agencies, including the Office of the United Nations High Commissioner for Refugees (UNHCR), say that the fighting since the October coup may have forced as many as a million people to flee to neighboring countries, where dozens are dying each day from disease and starvation in makeshift camps. The United States suspends its $16 million aid program to Burundi and later rejects an appeal to send troops there as part of a UN peacekeeping mission. **6 April:** Ntaryamira and Rwandan president Juvenal Habyarimana are killed when their plane crashes near the airport in Kigali, Rwanda; Rwanda's UN ambassador tells the Security Council that the crash was not an accident but an assassination; the plane was hit by rocket fire. This incident sparks massive and widespread violence in Rwanda, while Burundi remains relatively calm (pockets of fighting and killing have been reported in Burundi continually since the October coup attempt). **24 April:** Fighting intensifies in the Bujumbura suburb of Kamenge; more ethnic clashes are reported in the countryside. Most of Bujumbura is now segregated into Tutsi and Hutu neighborhoods. **7 August:** Tutsi opposition leader Mathias Hitimana is arrested, bringing Bujumbura to a two-day standstill and sparking clashes by his followers that leave up to 15 people dead. **11 August:** A grenade from an unknown source is thrown into Bujumbura's main market, injuring at least seven people. **10 September:** A coalition government, comprising members of the country's 13 political parties, is set up. Under an agreement achieved with UN help, it is decided that the prime minister must be a member of UPRONA. **12 September:** Gun battles break out in the suburb of Kamenge; military officials say gunmen attacked troops in Nyabiraba, 18 kilometers (11 miles) from Bujumbura, and five attackers were killed. **October–November:** Hundreds of people in Burundi are killed by Hutu extremists and army reprisals. **1 December:** Minani, a Hutu and former exile in Rwanda, is elected Speaker of the National Assembly. **21 December:** About 20 people are killed in two days of ethnic attacks that bring Bujumbura virtually to a standstill; a 7 P.M. curfew in Bujumbura is initiated in an attempt to curtail the violence in the city. **22 December:** The UN Security Council calls for a halt to violence in Burundi, fearing a repeat of the ethnic mass killings in Rwanda earlier this year. **23 December:** UPRONA withdraws from the coalition government for as long as Minani remains Speaker of the National Assembly; the party accuses Minani of inciting Hutu against Tutsi following Ndadaye's murder.

1995   29 January: U.S. envoy to Burundi Robert Kruger announces that scores of people have been killed in a new outbreak of violence between Hutu and Tutsi; local villagers blame the killings of Hutu on Tutsi army personnel. **4 February:** Opposition leader Charles Mukasi threatens to topple the fragile coalition government, but backs off, saying he never intended to use violence to achieve his aims. **8 February:** Bujumbura is virtually shut down for six days under a general strike called by UPRONA to press for the resignation of Prime Minister Anatole Kanyenkiko; Kanyenkiko says he will not resign until the two parties agree on a successor, while the UPRONA chairman says the strike will continue until Kanyenkiko's government collapses. **11 February:** In a radio broadcast, U.S. president Bill Clinton urges Burundi to "say no to violence and extremism" and seek peace. **16 February:** Kanyenkiko resigns; shooting and grenade blasts break out in Bujumbura. **22 February:** President

Sylvestre Ntibantunganya appoints a new prime minister, Antoine Nduwayo. **6 March:** Twenty-nine Hutu are slain by Tutsi near the provincial capital of Muyinga, about 130 kilometers (80 miles) northeast of Bujumbura. **9 March:** A seven-person mission that had been dispatched to Burundi by the UN Security Council in February calls for an increased UN presence to help the Burundi government strengthen its legal system and train civilian police. **11 March:** Mines and Energy Minister Ernest Kabashemeye is shot in downtown Bujumbura; following the shooting, gunfire and grenade explosions can be heard in Bujumbura, and young Tutsi militia members begin congregating on street corners. **13 March:** Tutsi government official Lucien Sakubu is kidnapped, allegedly by Hutu militants. **14 March:** President Ntibantunganya asks the international community to help his country avert genocide. **15 March:** The mutilated and crucified body of Sakubu is found; Tutsi riot to avenge the killing, attacking Hutu with grenades and knives. **19 March:** Two Burundi soldiers and three Belgians are killed outside Bujumbura by a Hutu gang. **20 March:** The killings set off fighting in Bujumbura's market in which five people are reported killed. Minani, head of the FRODEBU Party, says he wants the attackers tracked down quickly and punished to make them an example. **26 March:** Burundi Radio reports that the FRODEBU Party headquarters in Bujumbura has been burned down. As many as 50,000 residents flee Bujumbura following a night of fighting between security forces and Hutu. **27 March:** Ntibantunganya says he fears genocide has started in Burundi. **28 March:** Amnesty International says that Burundi is "poised on the brink of another cycle of horrific slaughter." **29 March:** A United Nations Children's Fund (UNICEF) study of 2,769 (of the more than 14,000) children orphaned by ethnic killings since October 1993 finds that 58 percent had been personally attacked, 77 percent of those knew their attacker, and in 81 percent of those cases, the attacker was a neighbor. **31 March:** President Ntibantunganya and Prime Minister Nduwayo sign an agreement to pursue stability, protect lives, and encourage the return of about two million refugees living in camps. **1 April:** Tanzania closes its borders to Burundi and Rwandan refugees. **3 April:** About 150 people, mostly Hutu women and children, are reported killed in the district of Gasorwe in northeastern Burundi; survivors say their attackers wore army uniforms. **4 April:** More than 60 civilians are killed in ethnic fighting in northern Burundi, bringing the number of deaths reported in the last two weeks to more than 500. **18 April:** Hutu gunmen (reported to be from

Rwanda) kill two soldiers in an assault on an army post in Gasorwe in northeastern Burundi; five of the attackers also die. **25 April:** Two soldiers and at least 10 other people are reported killed during fighting between security forces and Hutu militia members in Bujumbura; the fighting begins when security forces search the Kamenge district of Bujumbura for five young members of a Tutsi militia known as Sans Echec ("Without Fail") who had been kidnapped the day before allegedly by "Hutu elements." **26 April:** Burundi Radio says that, in fact, 24 people were killed in the latest violence. **1 May:** The international group Reporters without Borders urges President Ntibantunganya to close six newspapers that have "stirred up for many months, in a blatant and deliberate way, ethnic hatred." **5 May:** Unidentified gunmen attack a bus with guns and grenades in northern Burundi, killing 18 and wounding 13 others; 36 people are reported injured by a grenade thrown into Bujumbura's central market. **9 May:** According to the United Nations High Commissioner for Refugees (UNHCR), Burundi breaches the 1951 UN refugee convention by denying asylum to 317 Rwandan refugees and expelling them back to their country. **15 May:** Foreign relief groups suspend all but essential humanitarian assistance in Burundi for one week in reaction to the death of a Catholic Relief Services (CRS) aid worker. **19 May:** The main market and most shops in Bujumbura close for a peaceful protest against the arrival in Burundi of Rwandan Hutu blamed for the previous year's genocide in Rwanda; UPRONA organizes a march of about 10,000 people through the capital. **22–24 May:** Unidentified extremists successfully close down Bujumbura for three days with gunfire, grenade blasts, and barricades. **30 May:** An Organization for African Unity (OAU) peace mission arrives in Burundi seeking to promote reconciliation between Tutsi and Hutu; the team is to meet with former president Bagaza, who currently leads the radical Tutsi Party for National Recovery (PARENA), the only political party not part of an agreement to share power. **2 June:** Gunfire continues in Hutu areas of Bujumbura; the casualty total remains unknown because soldiers have banned reporters and other outsiders from entering Kamenge. **6 June:** Prime Minister Nduwayo orders the army to prepare to move into Kamenge; he also urges civilians to evacuate Kamenge and offers them refuge at a soccer stadium, but as of late afternoon, no one has taken the offer. **7 June:** At dawn, 13 hours before the end of the interval that the civilians had been given to flee, army troops begin pushing into Kamenge in armored vehicles. **8 June:** The bodies of at least 25 children, women, and elderly are reportedly found after the army offensive against militiamen; a Tutsi soldier claims that Hutu militiamen killed their own people in order to implicate the army. **9 June:** The United Nations calls for an investigation by the Burundi government into the massacre of Hutu civilians. **12 June:** At least 13 Hutu students are killed at the Matanga campus of Bujumbura University when Tutsi students throw grenades into dormitories. **14 June:** Gunmen ambush a convoy between the villages of Rusenda and Bukinanyana in the province of Cibitoke near the Zaire border in northwest Burundi, killing an OAU observer from Burkina Faso and wounding another observer and six Burundi soldiers. **15 June:** Amnesty International reports that immediate international action is necessary to stop Burundi's army and other armed groups from killing civilians. **18 June:** In an attempt to lessen ethnic violence, President Ntibantunganya announces a nationwide 5 P.M. to 9 A.M. curfew, a requirement for travel documents and special permission to travel outside of one's home province, and bans on political meetings, demonstrations, and broadcasts. **21 June:** Tutsi militants murder a Hutu professor and director of research, Ruzemza Stanislav, at Bujumbura University. Prime Minister Nduwayo says that civilian casualties in the current fighting in Bujumbura are inevitable because Hutu guerrillas are using civilians as shields. **24 June:** Foreign ministers of the OAU pass a resolution in Addis Ababa, Ethiopia, urging countries bordering Burundi to stop the flow of illegal arms into the country. **29 June:** Fifteen FRODEBU members of the National Assembly flee the country and go into hiding amid death threats following their defeat of the president's proposal giving the government extra emergency powers to curb the ethnic violence. **30 June:** Heavy gunfire in Bujumbura forces between 30,000 and 50,000 Hutu to move farther into the hills surrounding the capital. **1 July:** Tutsi and Hutu celebrate Independence Day peacefully but separately, with President Ntibantunganya leading celebrations in Gitega, which is mostly Hutu, and Prime Minister Nduwayo leading festivities in Bujumbura, now almost completely Tutsi. **12 July:** The president of FRODEBU says that when all reports are added up, the daily death toll is approximately 100. An OAU team leaves Bujumbura after failing to persuade Tutsi opposition parties to participate in peace talks in Addis Ababa. **3 August:** Two South African peacemakers leave Burundi, saying that they found little commitment to peace during their six-day visit and that they were "worn out by taking on so much ethnic hatred." **19 August:** FRODEBU's Minani says that nine high-ranking Hutu officials have been killed or have survived assassination attempts in the previous two weeks. **28 August:** The UN Security Council creates a commission of five jurists to probe the 1993 death of President Ndadaye and to "address the violations of international humanitarian law in Burundi." **9 September:** Prime Minister Nduwayo censures the U.S. ambassador over allegations that the army was involved in the killing of civilians. **14 September:** UN sources say that North Korean military experts are training the Burundi army in the use of heavy weaponry in the northwestern regions of Cibitoke and Bubanza. **19 September:** Pope John Paul II appeals to refugees from Burundi and Rwanda for an end to the "terrible tragedy" in the two countries. **21 September:** The OAU welcomes former U.S. president Jimmy Carter's plan to discuss with African leaders how to end conflicts in Burundi and Rwanda. **27 October:** President Ntibantunganya says he wants Carter to convene a conference to deal with the crisis in Burundi; Carter, former Tanzanian president Julius Nyerere, and South African archbishop Desmond Tutu are to serve as mediators. Burundi's defense minister vows to wage a "merciless war" against both Hutu and Tutsi extremists. **October and December:** Nyerere makes visits to Burundi to assure himself that all sides are ready to engage in mediation. **November:** The OAU formally requests Nyerere to act as mediator between groups in Burundi. **27 November:** The Burundi army steps up its military campaign against suspected Hutu rebels; diplomats say the strategy is likely to cripple peace prospects. **8 December:** The U.S. State Department strongly condemns the reported massacre of 430 civilians, 90 percent of them women and children, by the Burundi military. **15 December:** The Red Cross suspends all activities in Burundi, citing too much danger for its workers. **19 December:** International Action against Hunger also suspends activities in Burundi, following the wounding of two of its workers in a grenade attack on their residence in Gitega. **20 December:** Two prominent Hutu Burundi politicians of FRODEBU are murdered in Bujumbura.

1996 1 January: President Ntibantunganya says that Burundi is on the brink of collapse. Doctors without Borders estimates that the death toll in Burundi in 1995 was 15,000. **April–May:** Nyerere holds two meetings between UPRONA and FRODEBU, the two parties represented in Parliament. **25 June:** Burundi asks for international aid to avoid escalation of fighting. **July–August:** At least 4,050 unarmed civilians are extrajudicially executed by government forces in Gitega. **25 July:** Buyoya leads a bloodless coup and, with the help of the army, retakes the presidency. **26 July:** The European Union announces it will withdraw development programs from Burundi. South Africa pledges it will not recognize any government brought about through the force of arms. **31 July:** African regional leaders formally impose a blockade on all trade with Burundi. **25 August:** Buyoya's government fails to send a delegation to a peace summit in Tanzania despite his indications to the contrary; he also refuses permission for other Burundi political parties to attend.

1997   6 June: The Burundi government and the National Assembly sign a transitional government agreement that replaces the 1992 constitution and the statutory order of 13 September 1996. **12 June:** A new government, comprising 22 ministers, is appointed by the president. **15–17 June:** The first round of talks of the Arusha negotiations brings together 17 delegations from Burundi. **20 July:** This date had been set for a cessation of all hostilities in Burundi, but the fighting continues. **20–29 July:** The second round of talks occurs with no significant progress. **October:** By this time, 540,000 Barundi are displaced within the country and in neighboring countries. Buyoya begins peace talks with Hutu and Tutsi opposition groups. **19 November:** Amnesty International reports there are continued wide-scale massacres perpetrated against unarmed civilians by the Burundi army.

1998   January: Regional heads of state lift trade sanctions on Burundi, but arms sales to the army and rebel groups remain banned. **14 May:** François Ngeze, who assumed the presidency after the murder of Ndadaye, is acquitted of the murder. **October:** Nyerere dies; he had remained at the center of the Burundi peace process up until his death. **December:** Government troops kill 40 civilians in Gitega.

2000   11 May: A church-sponsored radio station, Ivyizigiro (Radio Hope) begins to broadcast; its programming focuses on peace initiatives and youth and women's issues. **28 August:** Arusha Accord (Peace and Reconciliation Agreement), brokered by Nelson Mandela, is signed. **September:** Government troops kill 20 civilians in Kamenge. **30 November:** National Assembly ratifies the peace agreement, proposing extensive reforms of the security forces, the judiciary, and political institutions; the Forces Nationales de Libération (FNL; National Liberation Forces) is threatened with sanctions by a regional summit if it fails to enter negotiations.

2001   May: Government introduces new taxes "to create a fund to finance urgent security requirements." **23 July:** President Buyoya and Vice President–Designate Ndayizeye meet in Arusha and sign a document outlining conditions for a smooth transition. **October:** Mandela secures an agreement from South Africa to deploy South African troops as peacekeepers in Burundi; the Conseil National pour la Défense de la Démocratie-Forces pour la Défense de la Démocratie (CNDD-FDD; National Council for the Defense of Democracy–Forces for the Defense of Democracy) rejects its leader, Jean-Bosco Ndayikengurukiye, and declares Pierre Nkurunziza its new leader. **November:** Buyoya takes over as transitional leader for 18 months with a Hutu vice president whose signature is required on all presidential texts pertaining to security and the armed forces; a 26-member power-sharing government is sworn in to oversee the three-year transition.

2002   March: Voluntary return program for Burundi refugees in Tanzania begins. **28 May:** Conseil National pour la Défense de la Démocratie-Forces pour la Défense de la Démocratie (CNDD-FDD) restates its commitment to a negotiated settlement, but says it will only talk to Burundi's army, which, it claims, holds the real power in the country as opposed to the transitional government. **10 October:** The IMF approves the credit of $13 million postconflict aid for Burundi's reconstruction and economic recovery. **December:** Cease-fire agreement signed between the government and the three main rebel groups; FDD lays down its weapons and joins government.

2003   27 January: The government and the three rebel groups sign a memorandum of understanding, establishing a Joint Cease-fire Commission. **21 February:** Conseil National pour la Défense de la Démocratie-Forces pour la Défense de la Démocratie (CNDD-FDD) announces suspension of its cease-fire talks, citing continued hostilities and the blockage of humanitarian aid. **24 April:** Buyoya, who has achieved power twice by coup, promises he will never again seek to obtain power by force. **1 May:** Under the terms of the Arusha Accord, Buyoya (defying his doubters) steps down as president in favor of his vice president, Domitien Ndayizeye; this handover from a Tutsi to a Hutu is a symbolic moment for the country and the region. **15–16 September:** Regional summit is held with the objective of an agreement between the government and Nkurunziza's CNDD-FDD; this 22nd attempt by regional heads of state to find a solution to Burundi's conflict fails. **8 October:** Ndayizeye and Nkurunziza announce a new agreement to implement the cease-fire deal reached in January. **30 December:** Gunmen kill Archbishop Michael Aiden Courtney, Burundi's papal nuncio.

2004 January: Ndayizeye meets Forces Nationales de Libération (FNL) officials in Amsterdam; they agree on the need to stop violence, but fighting resumes within days. Burundi government publishes a national program for the rehabilitation of refugees and internally displaced persons. **7 January:** Government soldiers and Forces pour la Défense de la Démocratie (FDD) rebels begin fighting on the same side against the FNL. **February:** An international conference on landmine clearance convenes in Bujumbura; this serves as the stimulus for the army and Conseil National pour la Défense de la Démocratie-Forces pour la Défense de la Démocratie (CNDD-FDD) to agree to work together to map affected areas. **12 February:** Burundi independent radio station Radio Publique Africaine (RPA) is suspended by the National Council of Communication, accused of "offending public morals" by reporting on the rape of an eight-year-old girl, and Burundi's private news agency, Net-Press, is banned for seven days following libel complaints. **4–12 April:** Following talks with Tanzanian government officials, FNL, Burundi's lone remaining rebel group, pledges to enter peace talks, but is told by the chief of the UN Mission in Burundi (United Nations Operations in Burundi [ONUB]) that they first must renounce terrorism. **21 April:** FNL announces its decision to suspend hostilities against the transitional government. **1 June:** ONUB begins its mission to oversee the disarmament of former rebels and help cement the multiparty power-sharing agreement. **15 July:** Fifteen civilians are massacred by the FNL 48 kilometers (30 miles) south of Bujumbura. **19 July:** A group of South African and Burundi women gather in South Africa to discuss the peace process in Burundi. **26 July:** Six Tutsi political parties boycott a meeting with Jacob Zuma, South African deputy president and a mediator in Burundi's peace process. **August:** More than 10,000 Barundi return home as part of the United Nations High Commissioner for Refugees' (UNHCR) voluntary repatriation program. **13 August:** Between 150 and 180 ethnic Tutsi Congolese, mostly women and children, are slaughtered in the Gatumba refugee camp. **22 August:** Burundi issues international arrest warrants for Pasteur Habimana and Agathon Rwasa (spokesperson and leader, respectively, of the FNL) for war crimes and crimes against humanity, following the killings in the Gatumba camp. **17 September:** African Development Bank resumes cooperation with Burundi after a five-year break brought about by Burundi's debt arrears. **24 September:** Two Burundi trade union leaders are detained by police for criticizing the government at a labor meeting. **10 October:** Nurses in hospitals and health centers across Burundi begin a two-day strike demanding better working conditions. **29 October:** Cholera epidemic strikes the town of Rumonge, with at least 140 cases and one death reported over the next two weeks. **November:** FDD joins transitional power-sharing government under the terms of the peace accord, giving it 15 seats in Parliament. **1 November:** New interim constitution, based on the Arusha Accord, takes effect. **14 November:** President Ndayizeye accuses Vice President Alphonse Kadege of undermining efforts to end civil war by failing to support the constitutional referendum and dismisses him. **December:** Law is enacted to set up a 25-member National Truth and Reconciliation Commission (NTRC). Demobilized combatants begin retraining for a new national police force intended to be split equally between Hutu and Tutsi. **11 December:** A new vice president, Frederic Ngenzebuhoro, from the UPRONA (Tutsi) Party is appointed.

2005   9 January: Forces pour la Défense de la Démocratie (FDD) formally transforms itself from a rebel group to a political party. **1 February:** Forces Nationales de Libération (FNL) agrees for the first time to hold unconditional talks with the government. **2 February:** Governor of Bubanza Province is ambushed and assassinated by men believed to be members of FNL. **16 February:** About 18,000 ex-fighters from FDD voluntarily give up their weapons. **26 February:** About 800 Barundi, including 200 Twa, flee to Rwanda in fear of political intimidation. **28 February:** In the first democratic poll in 12 years, a new constitution is overwhelmingly approved. **14 March:** Army accuses FNL of killing four people in the hills outside Bujumbura; the rebels deny involvement. **17 March:** Aude Ndayizeye, Burundi's first lady, launches Burundi's chapter of African Synergy, an initiative of African first ladies on an HIV/AIDS training program for doctors, nurses, and social workers. Its primary goal is prevention of mother-to-child HIV infection. **29 March:** Belgian defense minister arrives for talks on financing the reform of Burundi's new security forces. **21 April:** Burundi army attacks Hutu rebel positions north of Bujumbura after two people are killed by rebels at a highway roadblock. **25 April:** FDD suspends participation in the power-sharing cabinet in protest against what it calls delays by Ndayizeye in appointing an FDD member as interior minister. **1 May:** National Truth and Reconciliation Commission (NTRC) is established.

6 May: Nkurunziza, leader of FDD, accuses Burundi's president of being "the biggest threat to peace in Burundi." **11 May:** Ndayizeye appoints an FDD member as new interior minister. **15 May:** Burundi president signs truce with FNL, the last remaining Hutu rebel group still fighting the government. **17 May:** United States welcomes agreement on an immediate cease-fire and congratulates Burundi and regional participants. **20 May:** In a setback to the truce agreement, an army commander orders a helicopter attack on an FNL stronghold in the Rukoko Forest west of Bujumbura. **31 May:** UN Security Council extends its mandate of the UN Operation in Burundi until 1 December 2005. **1 June:** Burundi government troops kill 17 fighters from FNL. **3 June:** FDD wins absolute majority in local elections; voter turnout is between 70 and 80 percent. **7 June:** Voting in local elections is delayed in six districts after overnight attacks blamed on FNL. **11 June:** FNL launches attacks on army on outskirts of Bujumbura just hours after opening peace talks with the government. **17 June:** Eight people are killed and seven wounded in several attacks by rebels, including one on a church near Bujumbura. **18 June:** Campaigning begins for legislative elections. **19 June:** Three members of Front Démocratique Burundi (FRODEBU) are killed and five wounded in two grenade attacks on a bar in Bujumbura. **20 June:** Two candidates (members of FRODEBU) die in grenade attack. **3 July:** Legislative elections are held. **6 July:** Demobilization of police officers with the payment of allowances begins; process is suspended on 29 September for lack of a reliable list of affected individuals. **29 July:** Senatorial elections are held. **31 July:** The monitoring and implementation commission of the Burundi Peace and Reconciliation Agreement signed in August 2000 ends its duties. **1 August:** At least 30 people are injured in a grenade attack on a nightclub in Gitega. **16 August:** Immaculée Nahayo is first woman to be elected Speaker of Burundi's lower chamber of Parliament. **17 August:** FNL launches mortar attack in the hills north of Bujumbura two days before scheduled presidential election. **19 August:** Presidential selection by communal councils dominated by FDD; FDD candidate Nkurunziza wins election. Hundreds of thousands of primary school students line up to enroll for the first time in school, promised by the new president to be free. **26 August:** After an almost four-year transitional government ushers in democratic elections, Nkurunziza is sworn in as Burundi's president for a five-year transition period. **30 August:** UN Security

Council acknowledges Nkurunziza's election, saying it marks "the welcome final step of the transitional process." **22 September:** A hundred members of FNL call on the United Nations and African Union to prevail on the movement's leader, Rwasa, to put an end to hostilities. **2 October:** Government troops kill 17 FNL rebels in western Burundi. FNL retaliates for previous day's attack by looting and burning houses and ambushing vehicles; one person dies, nine are wounded, and thousands of civilians flee their homes. **3 October:** Belgian government grants Burundi two million euros to pay civil servants' salaries and help boost the country's stability. **12 October:** Rwasa is expelled as FNL leader. **18 October:** South Africa announces that Burundi will receive its 2005 Africa Peace Award in honor of Burundi's peaceful elections and transition to the new government. **21 October:** Burundi army denies allegations by Burundi human rights group Iteka that the country's soldiers have committed atrocities against civilians. **December:** The UN Security Council votes to extend the UN Operation in Burundi until June 2006; at the same time, the council approves a proposal by the Burundi government for a gradual withdrawal of UN peacekeeping forces.

Introduction

Some of the earliest European explorers alternately referred to the area where Burundi is located as the "Switzerland of Africa" and the "Mountains of the Moon." These names describe the rustic, physical beauty of the country. However, they do not indicate anything of its long history of internal troubles, which include interethnic struggles as well as class struggles between the country's aristocrats and others. These conflicts and their manifestations as decades of internal fighting and ethnic massacres have helped to prevent strong economic, educational, and health advances. While the situation seems, of late, to be getting better, it is impossible to know the direction the country will take. In spite of the internal difficulties of the country that have existed for more than 40 years since its independence, Burundi remains little known and even less understood by the majority of the Western world.

LAND AND PEOPLE

Burundi is located in east central Africa just south of the equator, between 2° and 4° south latitude and between 29° and 31° east longitude. It is landlocked, which is probably part of the reason that European and Arab explorers and Christian missionaries came fairly late to the region. Burundi is bordered to the north by Rwanda, a country similar in history, ethnic makeup, and topography. The two countries were once colonized (by Germany and Belgium) and then administered (by Belgium) together under the name of Ruanda-Urundi. The Kagera, Kanyaru, and Ruwa rivers, flowing east to west, now mark the border between the two republics, set by the United Nations prior to their independence. On its western border, Burundi is separated from the Democratic Republic of the Congo by the Ruzizi River and Lake Tanganyika. In the east and southeast, the Burundi-Tanzania border was established by both countries early in the 20th century; the border follows the Mwibu, Ruvubu, Rumpungu, and Muragarazi rivers, with the southern border ending at Lake Tanganyika.

In spite of its near-equatorial location, Burundi does not have a typically tropical climate. The terrain is mountainous and the elevation varies considerably. The lowest elevation is 772 meters (2,533 feet), and the highest is 2,670 meters (8,760 feet) in the mountains dividing the Congo and Nile river basins. Temperatures average around 23°C (73°F) in the lower regions and around 19°C (66°F) in the higher ones. Rainfall averages between 102 and 153 centimeters (40–60 inches) per year, with the heaviest rainfall in March and April and the least in June, July, and August.

Burundi is one of the smallest African countries, with a total area of approximately 27,830 square kilometers (10,745 square miles), 25,650 square kilometers (9,903 square miles) of which is land. By comparison, it is slightly smaller than the state of Maryland. Burundi's population is estimated at approximately seven million. Accurate census counts are difficult for a variety of reasons, particularly because of the large number of citizens who have been internally displaced in the country as well as those who have become refugees outside of the country. It is estimated that as many as 550,000 of the people—that is, between 8 and 9 percent of the total population—have been displaced. Another difficulty in taking an accurate census is the large number of people affected by HIV/AIDS, which has lowered the life expectancy and raised the infant mortality rates (currently about 71 deaths to 1,000 live births). At approximately 206 people per square kilometer (534 per square mile), however, this makes Burundi one of the most densely populated countries on the African continent.

The land occupied by Burundi has some natural resources, such as nickel, uranium, peat, cobalt, copper, and platinum, but these resources are largely untapped. Due to excessive deforestation and soil erosion, only about 44 percent of the land is arable; Burundi exports coffee and tea and, to a smaller degree, sugar, cotton, and hides, with the coffee crop accounting for approximately 80 percent of foreign exchange earnings. Almost 90 percent of the population depends on subsistence farming.

The literacy rate of the country is only about 50 percent. The national language is Kirundi, which is spoken by all members of the population.

Swahili, the primary *lingua franca* of the East African region, is spoken in the major trade centers, and French is the international language used in many government documents and in higher education.

Burundi is divided into 17 provinces. In 2000, the urban province surrounding the nation's capital, Bujumbura, was divided into two: Bujumbura Rural and Bujumbura Mairie (French for "municipal administration"). The other 15 provinces are Bubanza, Bururi, Cankuzo, Cibitoke, Gitega, Karuzi, Kayanza, Kirundo, Makamba, Muramvya, Muyinga, Mwaro, Ngozi, Rutana, and Ruyigi. These regions are further divided into 114 districts, which are then divided into communes. Because of the hilly geography of the region, there are few villages in the traditional sense; rather, extended families live on the steep hillsides in small groupings. The "hill" (*chanyo* in Kirundi or *colline* in French), then, is a common description of the smallest administrative unit. There are few cities of significant population; after Bujumbura, with its population of approximately 300,000, Gitega has the next largest population, approximately 17,000. Each province has a governor. The provinces are, generally, ethnically mixed, except for Bujumbura Mairie, the population of which is almost completely Tutsi. Travel throughout the country is possible, but there have been long periods of armed rebel activity in Bubanza, Bujumbura Rural, Bururi, Cibitoke, and Makamba, sometimes making travel perilous.

During the last 10 to 12 years, there has been a significant change in the population profile of the country. Due to civil unrest, thousands of people were forced into guarded camps. It is estimated that about 800,000 more fled the country to neighboring Congo, Rwanda, and Tanzania—mostly to Tanzania. Following the signing of cease-fire agreements between the government and several rebel groups in 2003, thousands of refugees and internally displaced people have returned home. The United Nations estimates that more than half of the displaced people (estimates range from 280,000 to 550,000) had returned home by mid-2004. At the same time, however, more people were displaced around the Bujumbura area.

The population of Burundi is unusual in many respects relative to other African countries. It comprises three primary groups of people: the Hutu (approximately 85 percent), the Tutsi (approximately 13 to 14 percent), and the Twa (approximately 1 percent); the expatriate population, which consists mostly of South Asians, makes up about 1 percent.

What makes Burundi unusual is that the indigenous people are not divided in the typical tribal manner. All people of the country speak the same language, have the same religious practices, and share traditional beliefs and kinship systems. While most people of all ethnic groups maintain some of the traditional animistic religious beliefs, nearly 67 percent of the population has converted to Christianity (62 percent Roman Catholic and 5 percent Protestant), and between 5 and 10 percent have converted to Islam. Nevertheless, at least since independence, the Hutu and Tutsi have been in conflict, the result of which has been numerous deadly civil conflicts. The Tutsi, in spite of their relatively small population, have long held political, military, and economic power in the country; the majority Hutu have struggled through several massacres that targeted their intellectual leadership.

Burundi is a very poor country (among the 10 poorest countries in the world) with a gross domestic product of approximately $3.78 billion, divided into agriculture (47.4 percent), light industry (19.3 percent), and services (33.3 percent). The poor condition of the country became even worse in 1996 when the export economy (largely based on the export of coffee and tea) was seriously damaged by an embargo imposed by neighboring countries. The per capita gross domestic product is only about $120; this is down from about $200 in the early 1980s, according to the Ministry of Development and Reconstruction. More than half of the population lives below the poverty line. More than 90 percent of the labor force works in agriculture.

HISTORY

Precolonial History

The kingdom of Burundi was founded between approximately 1675 and 1680. By that time, the Hutu had been in the region for a very long time—some say between six and eight centuries; they were typically farmers, and they established their language and customs in the area. The Twa, a Pygmy group, had been in the region even longer; it is possible that they were the original inhabitants. The Tutsi arrived in the region from the north between 1300 and 1600; they were typically shepherds and are said to be descendents of Nilo-Hamitic people originally from the region that is now Ethiopia. The Tutsi were the ones who founded the first kingdom, dominating the Hutu through a feudal system. For more than 200 years, this system was upheld; unusually, in spite of their political and economic dominance, the Tutsi adopted the language and many of the customs that had long been established in the region by the Hutu. When one examines the language of Burundi, the many words indicating feudal patronage are apparent. The Tutsi lords gave the Hutu protection from outside enemies and permission to care for Tutsi cattle. In return, the Hutu servants or serfs did the farming; it is said that the early Tutsi considered farming to be beneath their dignity.

In these very early days of Burundi's history, the Tutsi chiefs ruled only small areas, perhaps only one or two hills; power and control were measured in terms of how many hills and head of cattle a chief possessed. The first real king (*mwami* in Kirundi, the plural being *bami*) united a number of small chiefdoms. His dynastic name was Ntare I, and he was the first of nine kings of Burundi; all of these kings came from one of four dynasties: Mwambutsa, Ntare, Mwezi, and Mutaga. In theory, Burundi was an absolute monarchy, but in reality the bami shared power with members of the aristocracy known as the *ganwa*. Very little is known about Burundi in these early days; much of the general information that we have comes from the oral court histories from Rwanda, a country that shares much of the history of Burundi.

In fact, until relatively recently, the people of Rwanda were the only foreigners who knew anything about Burundi. Until the end of the 19th century, foreigners rarely entered Burundi. Many people suspected that the source of the Nile River was located in this unknown region, and this idea brought some explorers to the area. Most famous among these were Dr. Stanley Livingstone and Sir Richard Burton, who described the people of Burundi as "inhospitable." Even though the southernmost source of the Nile was, indeed, found to be in Burundi, this land is still one of the least known areas of the continent of Africa. Having heard about Burundi's difficult terrain and the negative reputation of its people, Arab traders from Zanzibar often circumvented Burundi and went beyond it to the area that is now the Democratic Republic of the Congo.

Colonial History

Probably the first Europeans to settle in Burundi were a Roman Catholic missionary group known as the White Fathers. Although many of them were killed shortly after their initial arrival, the church established a long residency in the country at the end of the 19th century. In 1885 at the Berlin Conference, the European governments agreed that Burundi and Rwanda would be a German "sphere of interest," meaning that they had the option to colonize and develop the area. The Germans did not really begin to explore the area until several years later, however. They arrived in Burundi in 1892 during the reign of Mwami Mwezi IV Gisabo, and their arrival lessened the security of a monarchy that was already in difficulty because of rival groups of ganwa, the ruling class. The Germans thought that, by controlling the mwami, they could control the population. In 1899, Germany made Burundi and Rwanda part of German East Africa (which already included a large part of Tanganyika, now Tanzania). That same year, they established a military post in Usumbura (now Bujumbura).

In 1916, six months after Gisabo's death and the coronation of his infant son Mwambutsa IV, the territories of Burundi and Rwanda came under the control of the Belgians, who already had firm control over the Belgian Congo (currently the Democratic Republic of the Congo) with almost 8,000 troops there. Belgium was, by all accounts, not so committed to keeping Ruanda-Urundi as part of its territories; it was ready to give the region up to another European power following World War I, but that plan did not work. Instead, in 1923, Ruanda-Urundi became a mandated territory of the League of Nations and Belgium was put in charge of it. The Belgians were obliged, according to their agreement with the League of Nations, to maintain peace in the region as well as to provide modern education and health care and to promote the progress of the indigenous population. In 1925, Belgium began to administer Burundi and Rwanda as part of the Belgian Congo; in fact, many foreigners came to think of Burundi and Rwanda only as two provinces of the Congo.

After World War II, the League of Nations was replaced by the United Nations. Burundi and Rwanda were made a UN Trust Territory under the name of Ruanda-Urundi, and Belgium continued to administer the territory. Belgium's responsibilities grew under the auspices of the United Nations. In addition to maintaining peace and promoting the well-being of the people, it was now required to work toward ridding the countries of their feudal ways and preparing Burundi and Rwanda for self-government. The Belgians and the United Nations often disagreed on the administration of the territory; Belgium believed that economic and social progress should take priority, while the United Nations pressed for more political development. In the early 1950s, the Belgian government introduced a 10-year plan to improve schools and living conditions. It also began to allow advisory councils at all levels of the government with some representatives elected by the people.

By the end of the 1950s, some people in Burundi were taking a very real part in the political action. Between 1959 and 1962 when the country became independent, nearly two dozen political parties were formed. The dominant party was the Parti de l'Union et du Progrès National (UPRONA; Party of National Unity and Progress), led by Prince Louis Rwagasore. Rwagasore became the first prime minister–elect, and he carefully chose a balance of Hutu and Tutsi for his government. Two weeks after his election, however, he was assassinated by members of an opposing party, which left the country in a state of political chaos. It was in this state that the country became independent in July 1962.

Independence

Rwagasore's UPRONA Party broke into several rival groups, many of which were carryovers from precolonial *ganwa* rivalries. These disputes continued for years, and the UPRONA Party remained the only viable political party for nearly 30 years. In addition to the competition among the ganwa, the conflict between Hutu and Tutsi escalated during this period of political chaos. In 1965, a Hutu attempt to overthrow the government was put down by the army, and the mwami left the country for Europe. The country declared itself a republic in 1966. Many consider this period to be a turning point in Hutu–Tutsi relations, with mistrust between the two groups reaching a new level. This mistrust continued, and the Tutsi maintained control over the government and the military for most of the next 30 years. During this time, there were several more ethnic uprisings, one of the largest coming in 1972 when it is estimated that approximately 80,000 Hutu were killed or forced into exile; this included almost all Hutu who were educated beyond primary school. It is not known exactly how many Hutu fled the country at this time, but the number was in the thousands.

From the time of independence, the government of Burundi has changed many times. Until 1993, none of these governmental changes involved democratic elections. The head of state (prime minister, then president) has changed more than 15 times; a few resigned, but most were overthrown or killed while in office. In 1993, the country held its first democratic election for president, which was won by a Hutu, Melchior Ndadaye. A representative of the majority population ruled the country at last; however, this lasted only a few short months before he was assassinated during a coup attempt, once again throwing the country into a long period of chaos and interethnic killing.

Since then, there have been more elections and coalition governments; there has also been some diplomatic intervention from Western and other African countries. After more than 12 years, the country has once again became relatively peaceful, although there are still pockets of ethnic killings and other human rights abuses throughout the country. Some of the rebels who were once fighting against Burundi's government soldiers were, however, as of January 2004, fighting side-by-side with them. Under terms of a peace agreement signed late in 2003 by the Burundi government and the rebel Forces pour la Défense de la Démocratie (FDD; Forces for the Defense of Democracy), the Hutu rebels were integrated into the national army. In his New Year's Day speech, the president at that time, Domitien Ndayizeye, announced that by 7 January 2004, 40 percent of the army's leadership would be made up of former FDD rebels. The FDD welcomed the move as a crucial step for the beginnings of a new army.

There have been many observed and reported abuses of human rights in Burundi since its independence. A Burundi human rights group, Iteka, recorded 667 killings and 1,657 rapes in 2004 despite the decrease in violence because of peace accords to end the country's civil war. In May 2004, Save the Children named Burundi as being among the five worst conflict zones in the world for women or children. Unfortunately, according to the United Nations Operation in Burundi (ONUB), there has been no significant improvement in the human rights situation since November 2004; ONUB recommends that all parties identify and address the root causes of human rights violations, which requires the support of both military and civilian authorities. With the help of peacemakers from other African countries, as well as some from Burundi, the country is developing a National Truth and Reconciliation Commission (NTRC). The NTRC, according to its planning charter, will be charged with "establishing the truth about acts of violence committed during the cyclical conflicts that have plagued Burundi since July 1, 1962, the day of independence, establish and identify those responsible, and identify the victims." This commission is based on the South African model from the 1990s.

It is impossible to know where Burundi will go in the future in terms of its ethnic conflict. A coalition government drafted a new constitution, which has been approved by the voters. Under this new constitution, the government branches include a better mix of Hutu and Tutsi than ever before (60 percent Hutu, 40 percent Tutsi—and within those numbers, 30 percent women), as does the military. The power-sharing agreement requires the 30,000 troops in the national army and the 20,000 officers in the government police force to be evenly divided among Hutu and Tutsi. In August 2005, Burundi held a democratic election, the second in its history. Voter turnout was large, and the current government vows to work toward a lasting peace.

Many analysts of African politics and history are optimistic about Burundi's future. In spite of a relatively sudden switch to a democratic system, it is clear that Burundi's new government and the voters are working toward a permanent peace or, at least, a peaceful resolution to decades of internal ethnic strife. The Burundi peace process was carefully brokered and then watched by regional leaders in Africa as well as the United Nations and individual world leaders. The country that had long been characterized as a model of unrest is now cautiously being watched as a model for its region of what is possible when all sides are tired of fighting and collectively interested in a government that offers equal rights to all of its citizens.

The Dictionary

– A –

ABADASIGANA. This was the original Kirundi name for the **UPRONA** Party, meant to evoke elements of tradition. It derives from *dasigana*, the personal entourage of a *mwami*, especially **Mwezi IV**. The **Parti Démocratique Chrétien**, during the period just preceding Burundi's 1962 independence, called itself Amasuka u'Mwami, which refers traditionally to the same category of royal officials. This name, however, is more closely associated with Mwami **Ntare II** (Rugaamba), giving it a pro-**Batare** meaning, rather than the pro-Bezi connotation of the Abadasigana.

ABASAPFU. *See* MUSAPFU.

ACTION SOCIALE. This program for **women** was inaugurated in 1949 and was taught by **White Sisters** and European women (often wives of colonial officers and workers). The purpose was to teach women of Burundi skills that would raise them "to the level of their husbands" (according to the program's charter). These skills included sewing, knitting, home management, and gardening. The classes were open only to women with families. At the onset of the program, the enrollment was 244 women; it rose to 2,332 by 1957.

AFRICAN UNION (AU). The **Organization of African Unity (OAU)** was transformed into the African Union in July 2001. This had first been proposed in 1999 by Libyan leader Moammar Gadhafi as a more effective institution for increasing prosperity throughout the region. The AU had a deep involvement with the conflict in Burundi; since 1993, Burundi had been unable to achieve peace and security,

1

and the international community had been noticeably absent from the procedure. The involvement of **Tanzania** and **South Africa** by 1998 resulted in the signing of two agreements, and the deployment of international peacekeeping forces became necessary to monitor the cease-fire and facilitate the peace-building process. The African Union took the lead in the deployment of peacekeepers and special forces and was the first to provide a visible international presence in the country, in the form of the African Mission in Burundi (AMIB). This peacekeeping force remained in Burundi until 2003 when the **United Nations** peacekeeping force took over.

AGRICULTURE. Except for a very few small industries, Burundi's **economy** has, for the most part, been based primarily upon agriculture at a subsistence level. The ratio of arable land to population was documented in the early 1960s around the time of independence at 1.18 acres per capita; since then, it has become even smaller due to population growth and spread as well as erosion of the soil. Generally, however, except for occasional periods of severe drought, Burundi has been self-sufficient in terms of food until recently. Arable land and land used for permanent crops accounts for 49 percent of Burundi's land area. The main subsistence crops have been sorghum, corn, millet, beans, peas, potatoes, cassava, tobacco, peanuts, and various fruits such as bananas and papayas. Honey is also popular and is gathered throughout the country. Additionally, coffee and cotton have become the most important commercial agricultural products and the main sources of foreign exchange.

The **Belgians** introduced coffee to Burundi in 1932 because the crop was very well suited to the country's higher elevations. From the beginning, the system of coffee production was not structured beneficially for the people of Burundi; large Belgian companies developed and operated the coffee plantations and controlled the export and marketing process. People were forced to work on the plantations with little or no compensation, and later the government required property owners to plant and care for coffee on their land and neglect the production of their basic food necessities. Under this government edict, the farmers were allowed to keep the proceeds from selling the coffee.

AID. *See* INTERNATIONAL AID.

AIDS. *See* HIV/AIDS.

ALBERT, ETHEL. A linguistic anthropologist, Albert did extensive research in Burundi in the late 1950s and early 1960s. Her research cast some new light onto many social practices of the Barundi; it also provided linguistic insight into the class structure of the country. Albert noted that

> speech is explicitly recognized as an important instrument of social life; eloquence is one of the central values of the cultural world view; and the way of life affords frequent opportunity for its exercise. . . . Argument, debate, and negotiations, as well as elaborate literary forms are built into the organization of society as means of gaining one's ends, as social status symbols, and as skills enjoyable in themselves. ("Rhetoric, Logic, and Poetics," 1964)

Albert also observed that the formal speech of the **Tutsi** and the **Hutu** differs; Tutsi men receive formal training in the practice of eloquence, while Hutu men are taught that the production of eloquent, "aristocratic-type" speech before a "superior" is tactless. She has said that caste stereotypes prevent members of the upper caste from raising their voices or allowing anger or other emotions to show. In her words, "The Batutsi herders prefer to bear a grudge silently and to take revenge when opportunity permits, even if it comes 20 years after the affront has been suffered."

AMASUKA U'MWAMI. *See* ABADASIGANA.

ANGLO-CONGOLESE AGREEMENT. This agreement was important in eventually deciding the borders of Ruanda-Urundi in 1894 and after. Between 1890 and 1894, Cecil Rhodes popularized the notion of a "Cape to Cairo" line of British communication. The difficulty was that the telegraph would have to pass through German East Africa, which included Ruanda-Urundi. The **Germans** protested against the British corridor although, at that time, European trade in the Ruanda-Urundi area was nonexistent. To the Germans, the Cape-to-Cairo route was a symbol of British domination of the African continent—something the Germans wanted to prevent at all costs. Ironically, this corridor was originally subordinate to other parts of the 1894 agreement and was included—some say accidentally—as Article III. The original objectives of the 1894 agreement were quite similar to those of an 1889 agreement concluded by the Imperial British East Africa Company and the Congolese state: both allowed for a British corridor to Lake Tanganyika through Ruanda-Urundi, but the later agreement focused on the prevention of French advancement to the Nile. By June 1894, the British were convinced that the Germans were targeting Article III and that they wanted it completely withdrawn. All of this, including the withdrawal of Article III, led to further exploration and delineation of the European and Congolese claims in the region of Ruanda-Urundi.

ARMY. The army of Burundi has long been a source of controversy. Since 1965, members of the army have carried out or attempted at least six coups. At first, around the time of independence, it was closely controlled by the government. In the months immediately following independence, for example, all non-**UPRONA** officers were weeded out of the corps. The army started out as ethnically neutral, but by around 1965 this was no longer true, and it was increasingly dominated by **Tutsi**, especially among officers.

Gradually, the number of **Hutu** army officers has lessened until mid-1990s, when there were fewer than 5 percent Hutu in the army at any level. This helped to retain the atmosphere of controversy and distrust for more than 30 years after independence; many said that a Hutu president would be unable to control the Tutsi-dominated army, and in fact the first elected Hutu president, **Melchior Ndadaye**, was assassinated by the army. He was also the first civilian head of state in three decades. However, his predecessor, President **Pierre Buyoya**, had also been plagued by a disgruntled army, including a group that plotted in 1989 against the regime. The assumption remains that the purpose of that coup was to return President **Jean-Baptiste Bagaza** to power, although that has never been proven.

Ndadaye's assassination was the catalyst of a civil war that lasted 12 years. The army remained a powerful force and was faced with resistance from a number of armed rebel militia groups. During the civil war, the government forces and the rebel forces were all accused of violent acts against one another; unfortunately, however, the vast majority of violent acts and **human rights** violations were committed against unarmed civilians. For several years, for example, when a rebel group (mostly Hutu) attacked the army (mostly Tutsi), the army would retaliate against Hutu villagers; the rebel groups did the same against Tutsi civilians.

When the process of achieving peace began, all involved parties knew very well that the ethnic distribution in the army was one of the most important issues to address. Although there had been various half-hearted attempts to include Hutu in the army, it remained primarily Tutsi. The **Arusha Accord**, the peace agreement that eventually ended the civil war, specifically addresses the ethnic population of the army, assuring that Hutu make up 50 percent of the troops, including officers. Many, if not most, of these Hutu had been members of the armed rebel militias. By 2005, the general who was second in command of the national army was, indeed, a former commander in the rebel forces of the **Forces pour la Défense de la Démocratie (FDD)**.

ARTS AND CRAFTS. In the visual arts, Burundi is undeveloped by Western standards. As with much of East and Central Africa, decorative art tends more toward geometric motifs, consisting of lines and circles, than toward other types of nonrepresentational designs. Sculpture and figure painting are not popular forms of expression, but the geometric designs painted on otherwise utilitarian basketry and pottery are unique and quite beautiful. In some regions, the ancient art of copper smelting and working continues in traditional ways; often, special songs accompany different stages of the work.

Burundi still has a rich tradition in crafts. Once made for purely functional uses, such craft items as papyrus baskets, pottery, shields, masks, and drums are now more often created for tourists; the dye used to color these products comes from natural plant extracts. The **Twa** are known to be the potters and basket weavers in the country. There is an artisan center in Giheta and an art school in **Gitega**.

Bujumbura houses the Living Museum (established in 1977), and Gitega has been home to the National Museum since 1955. Many of the country's traditional arts and crafts can be seen in these two locations. *See also* MUSIC AND DANCE; QUINCUNX.

ARUSHA ACCORD. After more than 40 years of ethnic conflict that resulted in hundreds of thousands of deaths, warring parties signed this peace agreement in August 2000 in Arusha, **Tanzania**. In August 1995, the **United Nations** Security Council adopted a resolution "to address the violations of international humanitarian law in Burundi" and requested an international commission to investigate the assassination of President **Melchior Ndadaye** and the violence that followed it. At the beginning of the peace process, such international leaders as former **United States** president Jimmy Carter and former Tanzanian president Julius Nyerere were instrumental in bringing Burundi's factions into the process. Later, after Nyerere's death in 1999, other regional leaders of Africa, most notably, Nelson Mandela of **South Africa**, continued the process of brokering Burundi's peace.

The agreement was signed in the presence of international observers by the government, which was dominated by **Tutsi** at that time; the **political parties**; and most **Hutu**-dominated militias. It provided for a process of transition toward democratic elections; amendments to Burundi's National Assembly; judicial reform, partly to decrease Tutsi domination; military reform, also to decrease Tutsi domination but also to integrate rebel armed forces into the national **army**; the establishment of a **National Truth and Reconciliation Commission (NTRC)**; an international military force to assist in the transition; and an independent investigation into crimes of genocide. The initial stage of the agreement permitted **Pierre Buyoya** (a Tutsi) to remain as president for 18 months with a Hutu vice president; at the end of this period, the Hutu vice president was to take over leadership of the country and to administer with a Tutsi vice president. This transitional government was to conclude with a series of democratic elections.

Everything that has happened in Burundi since 2000 has happened with the Arusha Accord in the background. There were many bumps in the road, including several delays and refusals on the part of some rebel groups to participate, but eventually this process did occur. Many political analysts now see Burundi's peace process as a model for other warring nations in the region such as **Rwanda** and the **Democratic Republic of the Congo**. *See also* HUTU AND TUTSI, RELATIONS BETWEEN.

ASSOCIATION DES PROGRESSISTES ET DÉMOCRATES BARUNDI (APRODEBA)/ASSOCIATION OF BARUNDI PROGRESSIVES AND DEMOCRATS. In the very early days of independence, several **Hutu** politicians were supported in their quest for democratic rule by some **Belgian** functionaries. Two of the most enthusiastic were *Resident* de Fays and the court inspector F. L. Asselman. These two actively participated in the launching of the pro-Hutu APRODEBA; when the organization's vice president later joined **UPRONA**, the two Belgians gave their full support to the **Parti du Peuple**.

– B –

BACAMURWANKO, JACQUES. As ambassador to the **United States** in 1994, Bacamurwanko wrote extensively of his views of the crisis that plagued Burundi since the assassination of President **Melchior Ndadaye**. In his unpublished document "Burundi: Which Way Out? (Perspective of the Crisis)," he wrote about the need for security throughout the country as well as for elected officials. He also discussed reforming the **army** to correct the notable lack of **Hutu** soldiers; in fact, he stated that the "biggest threat to Burundi's emerging democracy has been, still is, and will ever be the configuration of the army." Bacamurwanko proposed long-term plans for peace and democracy, which included improved security forces, an independent judiciary, an independent legislature, a more solid civilian society, viable **political parties**, a free press, civilian control of the military, self-support of the military, an increase of small enterprise, and a more competitive **educational** system.

BAGAZA, JEAN-BAPTISTE (1946–). Lieutenant Colonel Bagaza, a **Tutsi-Hima**, deputy **army** chief of staff, and member of the "**Family Corporation**" under President **Michel Micombero**, overthrew Micombero's government in a bloodless coup in November 1976. Bagaza charged that the "clans of self-interested politicians" had used their office to gain personal wealth. In the aftermath of the coup, the new government's first appointments included Bagaza as president and Lt. Col. **Edouard Nzambimana** as prime minister. As well, a special executive council led by Bagaza would conduct the administration, with a 30-member Supreme Revolutionary Council, consisting exclusively of army officers. Micombero, who had been under house arrest, was imprisoned. Just five days after the coup, Burundi's **Voice of the Revolution** radio stated that the country had returned to complete normality and the supreme council had embarked on a nationwide and international campaign to explain its aims.

Although the period of Bagaza's presidency was outwardly relatively peaceful, it was nevertheless full of ethnic and **religious** strife. For example, in June 1979, a group of 52 Protestant and Roman **Catholic** missionaries was expelled from Burundi after being accused of encouraging rebellion against the military government. A report from Bagaza's office stated that the missionaries had been urging young people to flee the country by telling them that a civil war was about to break out. The incident was one of many in a series of tensions between Bagaza's government and the church in Burundi. The month before this incident, Bagaza had issued a decree limiting Catholic masses to Sundays only; the church bishops protested the move in a letter questioning the restrictions of their religious freedom, to which Bagaza responded with a statement accusing the bishops of spreading antigovernment propaganda and contributing to the division of the population.

From 1985 to 1987, Bagaza continued his attempts to diminish the influence of the church in Burundi. The government charged that the missionaries injected politics into their **health** and **education** work by supporting the **Hutu**. Religious colleges were taken over by the government, and new measures were imposed to close catechism classes in primary schools, ban instruction based on religious texts, and outlaw Catholic **youth** movements. From 1980 until the end of Bagaza's presidency, more than 450 foreign missionaries were forced to leave Burundi, and several other members of the clergy were detained for varying periods of time. The government also shut down the Catholic radio station and newspaper, prohibited religious gatherings without prior approval, and closed a network of church literacy groups that taught an estimated 300,000 children and adults in rural regions.

In a move to boost the national **economy** in the 1970s, Bagaza arrested 70 former officials on charges of misappropriating public funds. To try to keep the country's meager wealth from going abroad, Bagaza then forbade any Burundi national from holding foreign investments and any company owned by Barundi from using overseas bank accounts or acquiring foreign property. In 1980, the first national congress of **UPRONA**—the Party of National Union and Progress, Burundi's only legal **political party** at that time—chose Bagaza as the sole candidate for party president and head of the **Central Committee**. In July 1984, Bagaza was overwhelmingly reelected as the president of UPRONA. Under the constitution, the party leader was the only candidate for the national presidency. The following month, Bagaza won 99 percent of the 1.7 million votes in the first presidential **election** since he had seized control of the country. This election was a step in Bagaza's efforts to reestablish a measure of democratic rule in Burundi; he had promised upon taking over the government to restore civilian rule and to ease the deep animosities and long-standing ethnic rivalries partly caused by the violence in 1972.

Among the indications of ethnic strife in Burundi during this period was, paradoxically, the total denial of ethnic strife. Bagaza is said to have believed that by not mentioning the division between Hutu and Tutsi citizens, the problems would cease to exist; foreign nationals working in Burundi during this period were forbidden by their embassy officials to even use the words "Hutu" and "Tutsi" in public for fear of expulsion from the country.

Bagaza promised to heal the ethnic strife and to promote policies of national reconciliation when he seized power. According to some past critics of Burundi's treatment of the Hutu, who had become newly hopeful, he toured the country to promote reconciliation and urge officials to facilitate the return of as many as 150,000 Hutu **refugees** who had fled during the years of repression; he declared land reforms to help Hutu acquire more property and desegregated the national university to encourage more interchange between Hutu and Tutsi. In fact, however, these few reforms to counter the existing institutionalized discrimination against the Hutu were not enough. In September 1987, Bagaza's government was overthrown in another bloodless coup led by **Pierre Buyoya**. Bagaza found refuge in Uganda, where he was granted temporary asylum. He said that the coup had been carried out by "young boys without a great deal of political experience," and he vowed to return home. In November of that year, however, when he attempted to fly to Burundi, the government refused the plane permission to land in **Bujumbura**. After being denied permanent asylum in Uganda, he took up exile in **Belgium**.

In the early 1990s, Bagaza returned to Burundi. In 1993, he was accused of masterminding the coup in which **Melchior Ndadaye** was killed, but he denied involvement, and there was never any proof. He did, however, found the radical Tutsi **Parti pour le Redressement National (PARENA)/Party for National Recovery**, which was one of the political parties that did not, at first, join the process of the power-sharing peace accord. His actions led to his house arrest, but the eventual government under the power-sharing government allows for National Assembly seats for all living former presidents.

BAMBUTSA AND BATAGA. While the **Batare and Bezi** were the central figures in the conflicts around and after Burundi's independence in 1962, the two other dynastic families, the Bataga and the Bambutsa, were not sufficiently important in terms of influence or numbers to make a significant contribution to the conflicts. The Bataga were represented by Mwami **Mwambutsa IV** and his late brother **Kamatari** almost exclusively; the Bambutsa, who were descendents of Mwami Mwambutsa II, were still quite young at the time of independence, while their distant cousins, descendants of **Mwambutsa I** (*mwami* from 1765 to 1795), had long been absent from the political scene.

BAMI. See MWAMI.

BAMINA, JOSEPH (1925–1966). After **Pierre Ngendandumwe's** death in 1965, the *mwami* appointed Bamina as prime minister. Bamina was a university-educated **Hutu** considered to be from a high-status lineage and married to a **Tutsi**. Bamina had briefly served as a compromise president of **UPRONA** in late 1962; he was acceptable at that time to both Tutsi and Hutu. At the time of his appointment as prime minister, it was thought that Bamina's strength lay in his unique position as a Hutu who had been a prominent member of the **Casablanca** Group and that his racial origins would enable him to rally the support of many in the Monrovia Group as well. Finally, his political ties should have made it possible for him to extract concessions from the Tutsi minority. Bamina was one of 23 people (all Hutu) found guilty of leading the abortive coup of October 1965; all 23 were executed in January 1966.

BANDWA (MU-, BA-). These are initiates or participants in ceremonies honoring **Kiranga**. The verb that corresponds to this noun, *kubandwa*, means to invoke Kiranga. Kiranga then communicates with the living through intermediaries known as *bishegu*. R. Bourgeois traced the roots of this religious practice to the arrival of Bantu-speaking people in **Rwanda** and Burundi, because it seemed to be more popular among the **Hutu** than among the **Tutsi**. Others have argued that the practice of worshipping Kiranga probably predates the arrival of the Tutsi.

BANGEMU, FRANÇOIS. Just before—and while—an almost entirely new cabinet was being formed in November 1967, a series of firings and arrests took place, ridding the country of many left-wing elements to whom the **army** had become averse. Among these were Bangemu, known to be a **Jeunesse Nationaliste Rwagasore (JNR)** zealot and, at the time of his arrest, the director-general in the ministry in charge of party affairs. He was arrested for the 1965 assassination of Prime Minister **Pierre Ngendandumwe**, but was later acquitted for lack of evidence along with the other accused conspirators.

BANGIRICENGE. *See* MWAMBUTSA IV (BANGIRICENGE) (1913–1977).

BARAHINDUKA, JEAN. A brother-in-law of **Michel Micombero** and a member of the "**Family Corporation**," Barahinduku became the governor of Muyinga Province in 1972.

BARANKITSE, MARGUERITE. A humanitarian worker from Burundi, Barankitse founded the nongovernmental organization Maison Shalom (House of Peace) and was honored with the 2005 Nansen Refugee Award "for her tireless efforts." The award is a $100,000 grant for a **refugee**-related project. During the massacres in Burundi, primarily in 1994, she saved many orphaned children in Ruyigi, a town in the east of Burundi. At that time, there were 25 children in the home; the number grew in one year to 100, and now it is more than 10,000. Maison Shalom provides a home for orphans and children separated from their families, including former child soldiers. Barankitse and her team now run four "children's villages" around the country as well as a center in **Bujumbura**. The children, along with female-headed families, are taught about **health** and hygiene, especially **HIV/AIDS** prevention and treatment, how to manage a household, how to tend livestock, how to run income-generating projects, and how to benefit from apprenticeships. Many of the children in the villages are thought to be children conceived after their mothers were raped; many of them are HIV-positive. In Ruyigi, they also manage a cinema, a public swimming pool, a restaurant, a hairdressing salon, and a guesthouse. In November 2005, Barankitse called on the international community to show more generosity toward Burundi refugees.

BARANYANKA. Great-grandson of Mwami **Ntare II** and once the personal secretary of Richard Kandt, the first **German** diplomatic *resident* in Ruanda-Urundi, Baranyanka became a chief during the early years of **Belgian** colonial rule. Known for his very Western outlook, Baranyanka was one of the most eminent representatives of the **Batare** family. The Belgians thought him to be brilliant and so chose him to rule over one of the largest chiefdoms; at the height of his career, he almost surpassed the *mwami*'s (**Mutaga II**) prestige in the eyes of the Belgian administration and was regarded by the Bezi as a threat to the monarchy. Baranyanka became the protégé of several later *residents* of Burundi, most notably *Resident* Robert Schmidt (1944–1954), who demonstrated a systematic policy of favoritism toward the Batare. For example, Schmidt gave an important chiefdom to **Jean Ntitendereza**, Baranyanka's eldest son. Baranyanka was the founder of the **Parti Démocratique Chrétien (PDC)** and thus helped to carry on the family politics of his clan.

BARIBWEGURE, JOACHIM. In late 1962, young **Tutsi** militants affiliated with the **Jeunesse Nationaliste Rwagasore (JNR)** made threats against **Hutu** trade unionists and politicians. Baribwegure, then president of the **Parti du Peuple (PP)** was an object of these often violent threats.

BATARE AND BEZI. Before independence in 1962, the primary political problems still reflected conflicting interests and goals of several princely families associated with a class of traditional **Tutsi** rulers known as *baganwa*. The most important of these were the Batare and Bezi families, the descendants of whom were associated around the time of independence with, respectively, the **Parti Démocratique Chrétien** (PDC)/Democratic Christian Party, with whom the **Belgian**

administration identified, and the Parti de l'Union et du Progrés National/Party of National Union and Progress, better known universally as **UPRONA**. At that time, both of these Tutsi-led parties vied for support of the **Hutu** majority.

The roots of the Batare-Bezi conflict lie in the distribution of power that characterized the traditional politics of Burundi, where political competition often took the form of periodic struggles among the different dynastic segments of the royal line. During the time of independence, the authority of the Bezi grew at the expense of the Batare, their immediate rivals, but complete elimination of the Batare from the political arena was a process that was slow and, in fact, according to many historians, incomplete. The Batare continued to be vital and resourceful, at least limiting the Bezi sphere of influence somewhat. It was these traditional princely feuds that caused cyclical tensions within the political system of the early 1960s, which led to a dispersal of power between the factions as well as within each of them. At the time that **Mwezi IV** Gisabo was *mwami* in the 19th and early 20th centuries, his primary preoccupation was to evict his predecessor **Ntare II**'s descendants (the Batare) from their positions, to the profit of his sons (the Bezi).

This struggle, which was so much an established policy as to become institutionalized, continued quietly during the colonial period and intensified in the months preceding independence. By then, the Bezi had established themselves as dominant, with the Batare holding a position clearly inferior in power. Eventually, the links between the mwami and the Bezi family created a network of mutual obligations that continued to influence royal policies long after independence; in fact, according to Chief Barusasyeko, who was interviewed by René Lemarchand, the Bezi managed to "persuade **Mwambutsa** [**IV**] that he was of Bezi origins." Lemarchand himself believed that the mwami was "fully aware of his **Bataga** origins but deliberately chose to align himself with the Bezi because they were the only ones whom he could trust to solidify his rule." *See also GANWA.*

BAUMANN, OSKAR. In 1892, this Austrian became the first European to traverse Burundi from east to west. Leading a Masai expedition of the **German** antislavery committee, he claimed to have received a friendly welcome from the **Hutu**, who thought of him as a liberator from **Tutsi** domination.

BELGIUM, RELATIONS WITH. Belgian plans for the territories conquered in 1916 involved using them as pawns in postwar negotiations. The Belgians hoped to cede Ruanda-Urundi to Great Britain; they then hoped the British would cede a portion of **German** East Africa to Portugal and that the Portuguese would cede the southern bank of the lower Congo River to be joined to Belgium's Congo colony. First, however, Belgium's claims to the possession of the conquered territories needed to be recognized by the Allied Council, consisting of the **United States**, Great Britain, France, and Italy.

In August 1919, the council recognized Belgium's claims to Ruanda-Urundi. With approval by the League of Nations following shortly, Ruanda-Urundi became a mandated territory of the League of Nations under the supervision of Belgium. A law joining Ruanda-Urundi in an administrative union with the Belgian Congo (formerly Zaire; currently **Democratic Republic of the Congo**) was passed by the Belgian Parliament in 1925. The seat of the colonial administration was in Brussels; the chain of command passed to the governor-general in Léopoldville (Kinshasa), and from there to the Usumbura-based governor of Ruanda-Urundi, who held the title of vice governor-general of the Belgian Congo. Many officials in Brussels began to consider the territory another province of the Belgian Congo.

The residency of Burundi was then divided into nine territories, each under a Belgian territorial administrator. The country's traditional political organization of approximately 36 chiefdoms under the *mwami* was subordinated to the Belgian administration. All chiefs and subchiefs were subject to the approval of the administering authority.

The government **education** policy during the early years of the Belgian administration was geared toward the training of the sons of the *ganwa* and other lesser **Tutsi** chiefs. As with the German administration, the intent was to equip these boys and young men to fill positions in the administration and civil service. For the rest of the population, emphasis was placed on primary education, mostly carried out through subsidizing the **Catholic** missions. This goal of the predominance of upper-caste elements in the higher councils was achieved and raised anxieties among the **Hutu**.

After the **United Nations** was formed in 1945, Ruanda-Urundi was made a trust territory. This new arrangement encouraged the political development of the people and the development of a democratic system—things not present in the League of Nations mandate.

Since Burundi's independence in 1962, Belgium's intervention and involvement has been sporadic. It has given **international aid** and technical assistance to a degree. In 1987, when President **Jean-Baptiste Bagaza** did not renew residency visas for missionaries, Brussels "reviewed" its technical assistance program in Burundi, and there was a strong anti-Belgian campaign in Burundi's news media. Also, since independence and primarily beginning with the massacres of 1972 (and continuing until the present), Belgian imperialism has often been cited as the cause for the ethnic divisions in both Burundi and **Rwanda**. However, there are many analysts who disagree with this or consider it too simplistic an explanation of the ongoing difficulties between the groups.

Edward Nyankanzi accuses the Belgian embassy in **Bujumbura** of being instrumental in the 1972 and 1993 massacres. Belgium remains one of the most consistent financial supporters of Burundi, recently granting Burundi two million euros to pay civil servants' salaries and help boost the country's social stability.

BEZI. *See* BATARE AND BEZI.

BIGAYIMPUNZI, PIERRE. A *ganwa* of Bezi origin, Bigayimpunzi founded the **Parti Démocratique et Rural (PDR)/Democratic and Rural Party** in 1961 during the time when many of the old **UPRONA** (Parti de l'Union et du Progrès National) chiefs were severing their ties with the party. He, along with **Léopold Biha**, was a member of the *mwami*'s inner circle, but his favored position was not sufficient to gain votes, and he and his party finally had to concede defeat. Later, however, possibly because of this favored status, he was appointed to the post of director of the Institut des Sciences Agronomiques du Burundi (ISABU). In 1972, as a member of President **Michel Micombero**'s **Family Corporation** (he was the uncle of Micombero's sister-in-law), he became minister of **agriculture** and often chaired cabinet meetings in Micombero's absence. *See also* BATARE AND BEZI.

BIHA, LÉOPOLD (1919–2003). Chief Léopold Bihumugani, who became popularly known as Biha, was the founder of **UPRONA**, the Parti de l'Union et du Progrès National, in 1957. A favored member of the *mwami*'s inner circle, he eventually conceded defeat to the prime minister designate, Prince **Louis Rwagasore**, for the party's leadership. Rwagasore's return to Burundi from Europe coincided with the beginnings of UPRONA. After several years of political turmoil, often influenced by the strife between **Hutu** and **Tutsi**, Biha, still a leading Bezi courtier (and the mwami's personal secretary), was named interim prime minister on 13 September 1965. As the Hutu had won an electoral majority in the National Assembly in May of that year, the Hutu parliamentarians concluded that the mwami intended to deny them the fruits of their victory.

On 18 October, a group of Hutu **army** and gendarmerie officers tried to take over the royal palace, but encountered too much resistance from the mwami's personal guard. As this attempted takeover was occurring, another group attacked Biha at his home, injuring him severely. On 20 November, although Biha was still recovering and physically incapable of performing his duties, the mwami restored the Biha government, which had been suspended during the emergency. In August 1966, after Mwami **Ntare V** had taken over from his absent father, Biha was arrested and, along with others who had been ministers of state under the previous regime, lost his title and all of the political power he had enjoyed for nearly a decade. *See also* BATARE AND BEZI.

BIKOMAGU, JEAN. As **army** chief, Lieutenant Colonel Bikomagu, who had been called the leader of the 1993 coup attempt that resulted in the death of President **Melchior Ndadaye**, both denied that he had had a hand in the activities and, shortly after the violence began, designated himself as a mediator. Since the 1992 **PALIPEHUTU** attack, Bikomagu had acquired a distinguished **human rights** record. He also claimed that he managed to bargain for the lives of the president's wife and children during the uprising. In the role of mediator, Bikomagu announced on a Burundi radio station that the soldiers who had seized power were ready to give up in return for amnesty. At this time, he also said, "The government must have confidence in its army. I control the entire army. Everything is now in order. But as for civil war, everything now depends on the government." A government spokesman, Jean-Marie Ngendahayo (a **Tutsi** and the minister of **communications**) replied, "How can I trust the army?" In 1994, several weeks after President **Cyprien Ntaryamira** was killed along with the Rwandan president, Bikomagu claimed to have foiled an attempt by Tutsi paratroopers to oust the interim government of President **Sylvestre Ntibantunganya**.

BIMAZUBUTE, GILLES. In 1959, while a student in Lubumbashi (then Elizabethville), Bimazubute, along with another student, Prime Nyongabo, founded the **Union Culturelle de la Jeunesse Africaine du Burundi**, later known as the **Jeunesse Nationaliste Rwagasore**. While still a student abroad, he was the principal spokesman for the **Union Nationale des Étudiants Burundi** student organization. His criticisms were at first directed against specific characteristics of the monarchy's policies, later against people closely involved with the *mwami*, and finally against the mwami himself. In one of his tracts, he stated that he was speaking on behalf of the "millions of citizens, abandoned to their fate, the intellectuals bullied by their elders who claim to be more deserving, and the young . . . who are no longer naïve enough to balance their interests against those of a crown that has become ever more tarnished." He added, "Let there be no mistake—*we* are the rebels."

Later Bimazubute became the assistant secretary of the cabinet; in this capacity, he publicly commented on the ethnic nepotism that had been occurring in government organizations. In January 1967, he was made secretary-general to the presidency, yet his sympathies for left-wing causes were not diminished; March of that year brought a major reshuffling of the cabinet, after which Bimazubute was appointed to the post of director-general in the Ministry of Information. He held that post until he was put in prison in May 1967 on President **Michel Micombero**'s orders under suspicion of being involved in a coup attempt. Bimazubute was a member of the Abasapfu clan. However, in 1968, he became secretary-general of **UPRONA**, as well as the secretary of the interior and the secretary of civil service. He was killed in the coup attempt of October 1993 that also resulted in the death of President **Melchior Ndadaye**.

BIMPENDA, GERMAIN. Like **Léopold Biha**, Bimpenda was a descendant of the princely Bezi clan. After independence, they were among the most important personalities at the court and used their kinship affinities with the royal family to strengthen their leverage on royal decisions. *See also* BATARE AND BEZI.

BIROLI, JOSEPH. Son of **Baranyanka**. Some historians, for example, René Lemarchand, note that the historical conflicts and antagonisms between the **Batare and Bezi** families flared up with renewed strength as independence and self-government approached. In addition to this, however, were other factors that reinforced these traditional rivalries. The president and one of the founders of the **Parti Démocratique Chrétien (PDC)**, Biroli (Batare) and Prince **Louis Rwagasore**, the leader of **UPRONA**, disliked each other personally and intensely, a fact that was not concealed from the public eye during this time. Biroli was known to be a brighter student than Rwagasore at the Institut Universitaire des Territoires d'Outre-Mer in **Belgium**, and he attended Oxford and Harvard universities before going to work for the European Common Market organization. He was highly regarded in European circles, and his social graces tended to make Rwagasore appear awkward and backward by comparison. Political convictions notwithstanding, Biroli received greater sympathy and support from the European administration.

Apparently well established are the facts surrounding the death of Rwagasore just prior to independence. The gunman, **Jean Kageorgis**, was a tool in the hands of the PDC leaders, and the assassination was the result of a political conspiracy organized by Biroli and his brother **Jean Ntitendereza**. The aim was to create disturbances throughout the country that would be exploited by the PDC; their actions were actively encouraged by some Belgian officials. Although the case was tried by judicial authorities of the Belgian administration, a retrial was ordered after independence. In the new trial, Biroli, who had previously been sentenced to penal servitude, was sentenced to death. On 14 January 1963, the sentence was carried out in front of an estimated 10,000 witnesses. According to Lemarchand (and others), although the crime was due to a combination of motives both political and personal, it was also a settling of "old scores" between two rival dynasties.

BIRU (MU-, BA-). Historically, these were the guardians of tradition and the royal counselors. The *ubwiru* was the ritual code of the monarchy and the *abiru*, the interpreters of the code.

BITEYAMANGA. This was the name of the court jester, who was always with the *mwami* even in his travels. Some sources say that the jester was traditionally a dwarf; others maintain that the occupation was filled by members of the **Twa** ethnic group. The jester was responsible for the expected performance activities such as reciting silly speeches and poems, gesturing wildly, and generally playing the fool.

BOMUNZU. Clans are subdivided into lineages, the descendants of a grandfather or great-grandfather. These are called *bomunzu* or *abo bunzu imwe*, "those in one household," or people living in one *rugo* presided over by an elder (*umujuru*). The council that makes a group decision is generally composed of lineage heads who speak with authority for all members of their group.

BUDUDIRA. The spirit of the traditional family. Bududira represents an orientation of all members to the lifelong welfare of the whole. Plural marriage was traditionally preferred because it made possible an estate system in which property could be kept in the family more easily. Therefore, the nuclear family comprising the spouses and their children could be quite large.

BUJUMBURA. The capital of Burundi, Bujumbura has a population that varies between 300,000 and 350,000. It is located on the north shore of Lake Tanganyika and is the center of business, trade, industry, **transportation**, **education**, medicine, and culture, in addition to being the seat of government. Bujumbura is also Burundi's main port for passenger and freight traffic. As the most industrialized area of Burundi, the capital has many factories, a brewery, several textile plants, and one of the country's main coffee factories. As the seat of government, Bujumbura houses embassies, ministries, the Supreme Court, one of the country's courts of appeals, and the National Assembly. As the business center, Bujumbura houses the Central Bank (Banque de la République de Burundi), several commercial banks, and a development bank.

Under the **German** and **Belgian** occupations of Burundi, the city was called Usumbura; it became the capital while Burundi was under Belgian administration as a **United Nations** trust territory. The name was changed to Bujumbura when the country became independent in 1962.

The population of Bujumbura continues to be in flux because of the many years of ethnic strife and civil war. Today, the city is primarily

Tutsi (with the surrounding rural province primarily **Hutu**); however, due to extreme deforestation and drought in other parts of the country, the government is attempting to encourage urbanization. The feeling is that with fewer people in the rural areas depending on the country's natural resources, farming and planting programs can be encouraged and expanded. *See also* GOVERNMENT SYSTEM.

BUNGERE (MU-, MI-). Amulets and charms (*iviheko*) used to bring good fortune and ward off evil were a very important part of Burundi tradition. These particular amulets carried by **women** to ensure good fortune during their pregnancy were made of a hollow tube (often a reed) with a piece of quartz set into it. The quartz represented the unborn infant.

BURURI. Just before the aborted **Hutu** revolt in 1972, the southern **Tutsi**, known as the Bururi group, were on the verge of a violent clash with Tutsi from central and northern Burundi (known as the **Muramvya** and **Ijenda** groups, respectively). This conflict had historical roots; the southern Tutsi had been kept out of the political system in traditional Burundi, and for more than 60 years of European colonial rule, these same southern Tutsi were kept from the more important posts. In 1966, when the **army** seized control of the state, its commander (**Michel Micombero**) and many officers and regular troops were from various southern districts, which put the Bururi in a position of advantage.

BURYENDA. This special house was traditionally built in the *mwami*'s compound for the purpose of guarding the **Karyenda**.

BUTANYERERA. After finishing his studies at the Institut Universitaire des Territoires d'Outre-Mer in Antwerp, Prince **Louis Rwagasore** returned to Burundi and was given this chiefdom to administer. Not satisfied with this power alone, Rwagasore virtually took control of the newly founded **UPRONA** Party in 1958.

BUYOYA, PIERRE (1949–). In 1967, Buyoya went to **Belgium** for secondary and university education in social science. He then did military training before returning home to become commander of the local armored squadron; this was followed by further military training at Cavalrie, France, from 1976 to 1977. Upon this second return home, he was again made a commander of an armored battalion and became the chief training officer for the **army** chief of staff. Buyoya also pursued political interests, being an important member of **UPRONA** (Parti de l'Union et du Progrès National), and was elected to the **Central Committee** of the party in 1979 and reelected in 1984. In the meantime, he continued his military training at the West German War School from 1980 to 1982.

In September 1987, while President **Jean-Baptiste Bagaza** was attending a Canadian summit of Francophone countries, Major Buyoya led a bloodless coup, overthrowing Bagaza's government. Since Buyoya was formerly chief of operations and training in the defense ministry and was a Central Committee member of the ruling UPRONA Party, he was a natural leader for the country. The change in government was welcomed by many Barundi as well as by the country's Roman **Catholic Church**. Buyoya immediately suspended the constitution, announced the formation of a 31-member Military Committee for National Redemption, and dismissed all government ministers. Several of Buyoya's colleagues who had previously helped Bagaza overthrow **Michel Micombero** in 1976 were named to the new ruling committee, including the government's second in command and new army chief, Col. Edmond Ndakazi. Although Bagaza had pledged to heal the ethnic strife, there were few reforms to counter the existing institutionalized discrimination against the Hutu. When Buyoya took over, three-quarters of the cabinet and National Assembly, about two-thirds of all university students, 13 out of 15 provincial governors, all army officers, and 96 percent of all enlisted soldiers and police were **Tutsi.**

In his takeover speech, Buyoya emphasized that his reasons for the coup were almost identical to those of his predecessor: "We could, almost word for word, trace them in the declaration which 11 years ago justified the fall of the First Republic. These statements denounced the acquisition by one person of all party and state powers, blocking of all institutions, constant violation of the constitution . . . and an incoherent economic policy." He concluded, "We are unfortunately forced to note that just a few years later, the regime of the Second Republic had fallen into the same errors." Also according to Buyoya, a major factor that encouraged the coup was Bagaza's clampdown on political dissent in the country and more specifically, repression of the Roman Catholic Church. As a result, one of his first moves as president was to release several hundred political prisoners whom, he alleged, Bagaza had jailed "without justification and without trial," and to promise a more conciliatory policy toward the church.

In August 1988, there were again ethnic massacres in the countryside of Burundi that apparently escalated from a local event that got badly out of hand. Western diplomats did not think that the atrocities were ordered by the president, nor did they think that they were centrally planned by Buyoya, considered a sincere moderate. Nevertheless, his regime, seemingly committed to reform, was somewhat tarnished.

In October 1988, Buyoya re-created the position of prime minister and named a Hutu, **Adrien Sibomana**, to the post. At the same time, pressing on with reform, he created a consultative Commission on National Unity with 12 Hutu and 12 Tutsi members to investigate the massacres. Perhaps even more importantly, he reshuffled his cabinet, increasing the number of Hutu ministers from 6 to 12, now forming a majority.

The Buyoya government worked very hard to lay the groundwork for multiparty, nonethnic politics to take hold in Burundi. In February 1991, the **Charter of National Unity**, a document that transcended all laws, including the constitution, was adopted. The reforms were unprecedented and widely welcomed by Barundi as well as Western **international aid** donors. In June 1993, Buyoya was defeated in a democratic election by **Melchior Ndadaye**. He was reported to be gracious in defeat and remained fully supportive of the change in government. He continued to be an important spokesperson for Burundi under several administrations.

In July 1996, Buyoya again seized power, from **Sylvestre Ntibantunganya**, in a military coup. The day after the coup, the European Union announced it would withdraw development programs from Burundi, and **South Africa** said it would not recognize any government brought about through force of arms. Other countries in the region adopted economic sanctions against Burundi because of the nondemocratic power structure. Some of the sanctions appeared to have pushed the Buyoya government into moderating certain policies. Buyoya managed to bring the Tutsi militia under control, partly by incorporating many of their members into the national army. However, not all groups joined the army or the government. Former president

Bagaza was one of the leaders of criticism against Buyoya; Buyoya countered his opposition by placing Bagaza under house arrest. Opposition against Buyoya came to a head in May 1997 when it became public knowledge that Buyoya's regime was in the process of talking to members of Hutu rebel groups while in Europe. In 1998, Buyoya reformed the constitution to create a transition government and began talks with both Hutu and Tutsi opposition groups. Buyoya continued the peace process, bringing Burundi to Arusha for meetings on a lasting peace. He was instrumental in bringing many dissident groups together and became one of the transitional government leaders. When his transitional term ended, he again stepped down as promised and passed the presidency to a Hutu. Buyoya remains active in Burundi's government and has been given a seat in the newly elected National Assembly. *See also* ARUSHA ACCORD.

– C –

CASABLANCA AND MONROVIA GROUPS. Upon the death of Prince **Louis Rwagasore**, his dream of a truly nationalist **political party** unifying all people of Burundi was also lost. **UPRONA** broke into factions competing for control of the party, one led by André Muhirwa, a **Tutsi** *ganwa* who succeeded Rwagasore as prime minister, the other by **Paul Mirerekano**, a **Hutu**, sometimes described as a merchant and mystic. The two factions took on very different ideological orientations. The Tutsi-led faction, which came to be known as the Casablanca Group, was strongly anti-Western, partly because of the active role played by **Belgium** in support of the Hutu revolution against the Tutsi rule in **Rwanda** in 1959. The Casablanca Group was divided between traditionalists and modernists, monarchists and republicans, civil servants and politicians. The Hutu group became known as the Monrovia Group and was generally neutral or pro-Western in its orientation.

The two names derived from two conferences of African states, one held in Casablanca, Morocco, and the other in Monrovia, Liberia, and the two major African blocs that resulted from them. Other than their generally anti- and pro-Western sentiments, there was no direct connection between the factions in Burundi and these two blocs. The original Casablanca Group reflected the views of participants at the conference in Casablanca in 1961 that resulted in the African Charter of Casablanca, affirming that its signatories were determined to liberate and unify all of Africa. The Monrovia Group participated in a conference later the same year, where participants agreed on five principles. Among them was noninterference in the affairs of other African states.

By March 1963, the Monrovia Group was under the leadership of National Assembly President **Thaddée Siryuyumunsi**; the group made a series of attacks against the policy of the government and applied enough pressure on the court to have the minister of the interior removed from office. The effect of this was short-lived, however. Prime Minister Muhirwa arrested three Monrovia Group leaders, including Siryuyumunsi, on the grounds that they were conspiring against the security of the state. The *mwami* then intervened and ordered the three released, a short time later dissolving the Muhirwa government and appointing as the new prime minister **Pierre Ngendandumwe**, a Hutu of the Monrovia group.

Nearly a year later, under pressure from the Casablanca Group, the mwami issued a decree that restricted the powers of the government and centered greater control in himself and a few of his close associates. Instead of stabilizing the situation, this entrenchment of the traditional elements of the royal court made opposition to the monarchy more pronounced than it had been, and both factions of UPRONA considered the mwami an obstacle to their political control. In March 1964, the mwami dismissed four Hutu members of the cabinet; when Ngendandumwe was unable to replace them, the mwami gave the job to **Albin Nyamoya**, a member of the Casablanca Group, former minister of **agriculture**, and veterinarian. The anti-Western orientation of the Casablanca Group and the Nyamoya government resulted in the establishment of close ties with the Communist **Chinese** government as well as with other Communist bloc nations. These moves were meant to provide additional leverage against the monarchy, which continued to be supported by some Western nations.

In late 1964, political tension in the country was rising; at this time a cache of arms was discovered, and fears spread of an impending coup allegedly supported by pro-China elements. In reaction, the mwami dismissed the Nyamoya government and reappointed Ngendandumwe as prime minister; three days later, Ngendandumwe was assassinated. The assassination confirmed the mwami's fears of an impending coup; the Chinese ambassador, Liu Yi-feng, and other members of the Chinese embassy were expelled from the country, diplomatic relations were broken, a number of politicians from the Casablanca Group were arrested, and the leftist labor union **Fédération des Travailleurs du Burundi** and the **youth** wing of UPRONA, **Jeunesse Nationaliste Rwagasore**, were ordered to suspend their activities. **Joseph Bamina**, chair of the UPRONA **Central Committee** and a Hutu who had maintained political ties with the Casablanca Group, was named prime minister, but the mwami continued to restrict the powers of the government.

CATHOLIC CHURCH. An estimated 60–70 percent of the Barundi have been converted to Christianity, most of these to Roman Catholicism. The Catholic clergy (**White Fathers**) came to Burundi in the mid- to late-19th century and were accompanied by the **White Sisters**. The two groups established missionary centers and in 1900 began to set up schools.

The church has had a great deal to do with the conflict between **Hutu** and **Tutsi**. Although there are now many Tutsi priests and bishops in the church, it is said that the majority of Tutsi have ambivalent feelings toward Christianity. This is partly due to the belief that the church in **Rwanda** was closely connected to Hutu leaders of that country. In the postcolonial years, in fact, the church attracted more rural Hutu than Tutsi for literacy training.

President **Jean-Baptiste Bagaza** had shaky relations with the church. His successor, **Pierre Buyoya**, attempted to normalize relations somewhat by repealing most of the restrictions on church-sponsored activities. *See also* RELIGION.

CENTRAL COMMITTEE. In 1980, the first national congress of the only **political party** then legal in Burundi, UPRONA, chose **Jean-Baptiste Bagaza**, the head of state, as both the only candidate for party president and also as head of the Central Committee, which had taken over power from the Supreme Revolutionary Council of **army** officers earlier that year.

CENTRES EXTRA-COUTUMIERS (CEC)/EXTRA-CUSTOMARY CENTERS. In 1941, the Belgian residency set up two extra-customary centers, known as "Belge" and "Village des Swahili," in the vicinity of **Bujumbura**. This represented an extension of a royal decree of 1934, which made possible the creation of CECs in the urban centers of the Congo; as in the Congo, these later CECs were administered by a *chef*, assisted by an *adjoint* and an advisory council, all picked by the administration. According to **Léopold Biha, UPRONA** was founded in 1957 in protest against the decision of the administration to reintroduce a system of CECs in Bujumbura, **Gitega**, Nyanza Lac, and Rumonge. Such a system would have removed these areas from the jurisdiction of the crown and would have deprived the *mwami* of opportunities for patronage. While earlier administrations once thought the system of CECs was an imaginative initiative of the Belgian administration, the chiefs who sat on the **Conseil Supérieur du Pays** now saw it as an attempt to interfere with the mwami's traditional role and prerogative.

CHANYO (I-). The French equivalent, *colline*, meaning "hill," is the more commonly used word even in the writing of modern Barundi; however, it is a complex notion and crucial to an understanding of the traditional as well as the modern social system of Burundi. Because of the geography of the country, there are few villages of the type familiar to other African countries and to Westerners. Instead, socioeconomic communities are built around the series of hills scattered throughout the countryside, often isolated or hidden by banana trees. On each of the hills is a group of *urugo*, the inhabitants of which collectively use the surrounding pastures (*ubunyovu*).

Following Burundi's civil war that began in 1993, people have gradually begun to return to their hills and work in their fields during the day. Until 2004, however, at night, the **women** and children from each hill were required to gather in one home, while the men from each hill were organized into groups to patrol the area. Anyone who failed to show up at the designated site was beaten and fined; they also ran the risk of being killed as suspected rebels. *See also RUGO; SOZI.*

CHARTER OF NATIONAL UNITY. On 5 February 1991, the Charter of National Unity was adopted by 89.2 percent of the electorate in a national referendum, although the document, written under the auspices of the ruling **UPRONA** Party, had been highly criticized by opposition groups, including the externally based and then principal

Hutu party, **PALIPEHUTU** (Party for the Liberation of the Hutu People). **Jacques Bacamurwanko**, Burundi ambassador to the **United States** in 1994, wrote in his tract "Burundi: Which Way Out?" that the time spent on the "ritualization" of the concept and the symbols of national unity could have been utilized more usefully and economically. He saw the Charter of National Unity as an opiate concocted by President **Pierre Buyoya** to keep a firm grip on Burundi's fluid politics for a long time to come.

CHINA, RELATIONS WITH. Burundi was attractive to China as a base for Communist penetration in Africa because of its location close to the **Democratic Republic of the Congo** (formerly Zaire), the 1963–1964 revolutionary activities of which were an important reason behind the Chinese involvement. At independence in 1962, unofficial contacts had already been established between certain Barundi politicians and Chinese diplomats, but it was not until December 1963, after the *mwami* yielded to the pressures of the **Casablanca Group**, that mainland China received official recognition. The deterioration of the Congo situation at this time caused the mutual courtesies to crystallize into an alliance of sorts. Beijing was determined to take full advantage of what Chou En-lai described as "an excellent revolutionary situation" in reference to the Congo. The motives that inspired Chinese policies in Burundi were clearly formulated by defector **Tung Chi-ping**:

> Because it is the gateway to the Congo, this small, underdeveloped, overpopulated nation is important to Mao's long-range plans to dominate as much of Africa as he can. Before I went to Burundi, I had been thoroughly briefed on the progress being made there and the plans for the future. Again and again my superiors repeated Mao Tse-tung's statement: "When we capture the Congo, we can proceed to capture the whole of Africa." Burundi is the stepping stone for reaching the Congo.

Initially diplomatic relations between Burundi and China were shaky. After relations were established in December 1963, they were "temporarily" suspended in early 1965 by Mwami **Mwambutsa IV**, who was aware of China's use of Burundi to contact revolutionaries in the Congo. At this time, China also lost its contacts with **Rwandan** exiles who had been training in Burundi under Chinese experts in the hope of returning to Rwanda and seizing power. The suspension occurred two weeks after the assassination of **Hutu** moderate Prime

Minister **Pierre Ngendandumwe**, an act that escalated a crisis between Hutu and **Tutsi**. Although no specific charges were made against China at that time, there had been speculation that the Chinese were involved. Burundi's new prime minister said that China had interfered with internal affairs, but had had nothing to do with the assassination; he stressed that relations would resume when the political situation was clarified. In fact, diplomatic relations remained suspended until 1971.

COALITION FOR PEACE AND JUSTICE IN BURUNDI (CPJB). Organized in February 1994 by a group of Barundi gathered in Ithaca, New York, the CPJB is a nonprofit organization. In March 1994, the CPJB produced a response to the tract written by **Jacques Bacamurwanko**, then ambassador to the **United States**. It accused the ambassador of using statistics taken from a 1934 survey of ethnic populations in Burundi in a modern context. It also criticized some of the ambassador's other ideas, for example, recognizing that the **army** needed to undergo changes, but disagreeing with the ambassador's suggested methods. Finally, the coalition accused the ambassador of relaying false information.

In the CPJB's first newsletter in April 1994, the following were listed as its organizational goals:

- to strengthen the relationship between its members in order to partake in the restoration and maintenance of peace and justice in Burundi
- to facilitate discussions between its members on any question related to peace and justice in Burundi
- to reflect upon and express the opinion of its members on any issue capable of compromising peace and justice in Burundi
- to make a lasting contribution to the maintenance of peace and justice
- to call upon appropriate institutions any time that peace and justice may be compromised in Burundi
- to organize and participate in debates having to do with peace and justice in Burundi

In this same newsletter, the organization's president also called upon

all extremists in the country and outside to come back to their senses so as to avoid another bloodbath that would consummate the split among the Burundian population. This way, we can guarantee peace and justice not only for ourselves, but also for younger generations whose future is being gambled by a power struggle between the **Hutu** and **Tutsi** political elites.

COMMITTEE OF NATIONAL SALVATION. After the coup attempt of 1993 and the assassination of President **Melchior Ndadaye**, **François Ngeze**, the minister of interior in **Buyoya**'s government and one of the rare **Hutu** who held a position of power from 1965 to 1993, was made head of this new ruling committee and claimed that he had been forced to support the coup.

COMMUNICATIONS. Methods of communication have been sparse, sporadic, undependable, and expensive in Burundi. In the entire country, there are only about 24,000 land-line telephones. Since 2000, Barundi have begun to use more dependable cellular phones; approximately 64,000 are in use. In the late 1990s, there was only one Internet service provider (ISP) operating in Burundi, but since 2003, many more ISPs have begun operations; by 2005, there were 22 ISPs and more than 14,000 Internet users. *See also* MEDIA.

CONSEIL NATIONAL DE LA RÉVOLUTION (CNR)/NATIONAL REVOLUTIONARY COUNCIL. When Prime Minister **Michel Micombero** deposed the absent Mwami **Ntare V** in a peaceful coup in November 1966, he proclaimed a republic with himself as president. Micombero dissolved the government, replaced the eight provincial governors with **army** officers, and established a provisional 12-man National Revolutionary Council of military officers. He said the CNR would rule until a new government had been formed, "probably within two months." The council's first task would be drafting a new constitution; the *mwami* had suspended the former constitution earlier that year when he dismissed Prime Minister **Léopold Biha**. In December 1966, the CNR announced that Micombero's term as president would be seven years, and they promoted him to colonel.

Although set up as a provisional unit, until its dissolution in 1968 the CNR functioned as a supreme advisory body, influencing all nominations to the upper levels of the administration, including the appointment of army officers. The CNR was opposed by leftist members of the **Union Nationale des Étudiants Burundi** (later **Jeunesse**

Nationaliste Rwagasore). In 1967, Micombero dismissed Maj. Albert Shibura, a member of the council, from command of the army; when he announced the change, he said that "a small group of irresponsible men" had found accomplices in the judiciary and army in efforts to "take advantage of the Republic."

CONSEIL NATIONAL POUR LA DÉFENSE DE LA DÉMOCRATIE (CNDD)/NATIONAL COUNCIL FOR THE DEFENSE OF DEMOCRACY. A former minister of the interior, Leonard Nyangoma, has led this group, which was known to be one of the extremist groups involved in the ethnic killings following President **Melchior Ndadaye**'s assassination. Nyangoma claims responsibility for attacks on military and police posts. *See also* FORCES POUR LA DÉFENSE DE LA DÉMOCRATIE (FDD)/FORCES FOR THE DEFENSE OF DEMOCRACY.

CONSEIL SUPÉRIEUR DU PAYS (CSP)/NATIONAL SUPERIOR COUNCIL. In 1952, a **Belgian** decree provided for the establishment of representative bodies at every level of the administrative hierarchy; it was the first hint of democracy in local administration. Advisory councils were set up at the subchiefdom, chiefdom, district, and territorial levels and were called, respectively, "conseils de sous-chefferie," "conseils de chefferie," "conseils de territoire," and "conseils supérieurs du pays." In Burundi in 1953, **Tutsi** controlled 80.7 percent of the seats in the conseil supérieur du pays. The situation did not change markedly in 1956 with the advent of universal male suffrage. In 1957, the CSP strongly protested the administration's decision to institute a system of **centres extra-coutumiers (CECs)**, almost unanimously urging the *resident* to reverse the decision, citing the historical claims of the crown and the sacred character of kingship. The CSP members addressed a petition to a **United Nations** visiting mission; the text of the petition was nationalistic and pro-monarchy. *See also* GOVERNMENT SYSTEM.

COOPÉRATIVE DES COMMERÇANTS DU BURUNDI (CCB)/COOPERATIVE OF TRADERS IN BURUNDI. During the preindependence period, Prince **Louis Rwagasore** established cooperatives in order to build up support for his **UPRONA** (Parti de l'Union et du Progrès National). The Cooperative of Traders in Burundi was set up in the hope of using it to enlist support of the so-called Swahili population of **Bujumbura**. The CCB hardly got off the ground due partly to mismanagement and partly to the administration's refusal to extend its financial backing to the cooperative, which it considered a "front organization." The CCB initially received about six million Burundi francs from various European firms in Bujumbura, but by 1958 most of the money had vanished. According to a report by the **Conseil Supérieur du Pays**, almost two million francs had been lent to another cooperative, 450,000 francs to "an influential TANU [Tanganyika African National Union] personality," the rest "to a number of businessmen who failed to observe the terms of reimbursement."

COREKE (IN-, IN-). This term generally means "servant" or "follower," but the word (used with nonhuman prefixes) was traditionally used to refer to the *mwami*'s concubines. They were considered grand ladies who remained with the mwami even during his travels. They helped in teaching the ancient religious beliefs and practices to the royal children. *See also GACOREKE.*

CUMA (I-, I-). Literally translated as "iron," this word was used in the sense of gifts surrounding a marriage. It could be anything from beer (*terekera*) to cattle (*inka*). Even after the marriage, the *icuma* might continue as a sign of good relations between the principal families. After the marriage, the gift was almost always beer, but money for the new couple's house was also often offered.

CUTI (BU-, IN-). A very close relationship, usually beginning with two people or families needing each other economically and coming to appreciate the partnership. It is variously described as kinship, an in-law relationship, friendship, neighborliness, and trade partnership.

– D –

DASIGANA (MU-, BA-). In traditional usage, *abadasigana* refers to a group of individuals who formed the personal entourage of a *mwami*, but more specifically it refers to the entourage of **Mwezi IV** Gisabo.

It is usually translated by the Barundi as "the followers of Mwezi"; because of its attachment to the Bezi family, it implies a strong attachment to the crown as well.

DEMOCRATIC REPUBLIC OF THE CONGO (DRC), RELATIONS WITH. Although Ruanda-Urundi and the DRC (formerly Belgian Congo and then Zaire) were both colonized and administered by the **Germans** and later the **Belgians**, the Congo has been, for the most part, separate both politically and culturally. However, in 1963–1964, repercussions of the Congo Rebellion in the DRC were felt in Burundi when the **Chinese** embassy in **Bujumbura** became a major source of arms and equipment of the Armée de Libération Nationale (ALN) in the DRC. Congolese militia groups have also been accused of supporting other uprisings in Burundi and **Rwanda**.

As the postcolonial years passed, the DRC became a country of refuge for displaced Barundi, beginning particularly during and after the 1972 massacre. Today, many **refugee** camps exist in the Congo; in November 1995, DRC president and dictator Mobutu Sese Seko, who had threatened to expel all Burundi and Rwandan refugees from the uprisings over the previous two years in both countries, relaxed his deadline. He was thought to be sympathetic to **Hutu** militia members if not to the rest of the refugees. Having threatened to expel the refugees by 31 December 1995, Mobutu instead asked that the **United Nations High Commissioner for Refugees** do more to encourage repatriation. As conflicts continued in Burundi and Rwanda, they also escalated in the DRC. In all of the cases, the combatants were Hutu and **Tutsi** (or groups sympathetic to or related to these two groups); political analysts of the region believe that Burundi's peace process will serve as a model for other countries in the region. In addition, Burundi's peace is expected to alleviate the ongoing exchange of refugees in both countries.

DEUXIÈME MANIFESTE DU PARTI POLITIQUE. In the days shortly before independence, **UPRONA** made an effort to identify with the crown, but also tried to live up to the "Unity and Progress" of its name. Prince **Louis Rwagasore**, therefore, made it clear that his support of the monarchy was conditional. In the party's second manifesto, he said that his party was prepared to "endorse a monarchic regime only insofar as this regime and its dynasty favored the genuine emancipation of the Murundi people." The manifesto further stated the following:

> UPRONA notes that the Burundi monarchy is *constitutional*, and wishes to see the constitution of the realm adapted to a *modern state*. UPRONA favors the democratization of institutions . . . and will firmly and tenaciously combat all forces of social injustice regardless of the system from which they may come: *feudalism, colonialism*, or *communism*. . . . UPRONA favors the election of the chiefs and subchiefs by the population, and will combat with all its forces those who seek to destroy the *unity* of the country.

DIRIMBO (IN-, IN-). This popular type of song was traditionally performed by one person or a very small group and was considered appropriate for the expression of personal feelings. *See also* MUSIC AND DANCE.

DONGORANYWA (IN-, IN-). In addition to the bride price (*inkwano*) paid by the groom to the bride's family, the bride's family also gave this dowry. The parents of the bride traditionally provided in some way for the new couple's home and furnishings. In fact, the dowry could be small livestock, farming implements, or money. The primary purposes of the dowry were to ensure an alliance between the two families by consolidating the bonds between them. If the husband died, the *indongoranywa* went to his legitimate heirs, rather than back to the wife's family. *See also* KWANO.

DORSINVILLE, MAX H. At its 15th session in 1960, the **United Nations** General Assembly endorsed the UN Trusteeship Council's statement that the "best future for Ruanda-Urundi lies in the evolution of a single, united, and composite state with such arrangements for the internal autonomy of Ruanda and Urundi as may be agreed upon by their representatives." The General Assembly established a three-member commission headed by Dorsinville, the Haitian UN ambassador, to supervise the **elections** in the two countries. In December of that year, the permanent representative of **Belgium** to the UN told the secretary-general that a conference of **political parties** of Ruanda-Urundi—based on the results of communal elections, which gave eight delegates to the **Front Commun** and two to **UPRONA**—would be held in Ostend, Belgium, on 6 January 1961 and that the UN was invited to send observers.

At the conference, the Belgian government announced that elections would be held in Burundi on 18 January and in **Rwanda** on 23 January. On behalf of the UN, Dorsinville protested this as an attempt to circumvent the UN resolution. On 21 January, the Belgian government announced that it had agreed to follow the recommendations of the UN and that the elections would be postponed until the Dorsinville Commission had the opportunity to carry out its work of supervising the arrangements. The commission registered strong objections to the Belgian actions in general. It stated that democracy had not been strengthened in Burundi in spite of Belgium's indication of its desire to cooperate with the UN. Instead, according to the commission, the Belgian administration had simply favored "one feudal group over another."

DUMONT, DONALD. On 10 January 1966, the Burundi government ordered the expulsion of this **United States** ambassador and two other U.S. embassy officers on grounds that they were "rightly or wrongly" suspected of involvement with opposition "conspirators." The order emphasized that relations with the United States were not being broken; in fact, the statement from the Foreign Ministry stated that the relations between the two countries were going to improve after the recall of the three diplomats. However, Washington retaliated the following day by calling **Leon Ndenzako**, the Burundi ambassador to the United States, to the State Department, handing him a note that contained a strong protest against the expulsion of the diplomats from **Bujumbura**, and ordering his expulsion. On 12 January, Burundi filed a counterprotest. In a news conference, Foreign Minister **Marc Manirakiza** explained that his government suspected that Dumont and the others had abetted the abortive coup of October 1965. He emphasized again that Burundi's action was aimed only at the three individuals and did not signify a break with the United States.

– E –

EAST AFRICAN COMMUNITY (EAC). The EAC was formally inaugurated in December 1967 in a ceremony in Arusha, **Tanzania**. It was attended by presidents Jomo Kenyatta of Kenya, Julius Nyerere of Tanzania, and Milton Obote of Uganda. Guests included a delegation from Burundi, which also made formal application to join the EAC. This did not happen, and the EAC was dissolved in 1977 due to political and economic differences among the member states. In 1999, Kenya, Tanzania, and Uganda revived the EAC; its purpose is the establishment of a common regional market. In addition, the countries involved envision a monetary and political union, which they say could take up to 20 years to establish. Burundi and **Rwanda** have both expressed interest in joining the EAC.

ECONOMIC COMMUNITY OF THE GREAT LAKES/ COMMUNAUTÉ ECONOMIQUE DES PAYS DES GRANDS LACS (CEPGL). In September 1976, Burundi joined **Rwanda, Tanzania,** Zambia, and the **Democratic Republic of the Congo (DRC)** (formerly Zaire) in this organization, which was formed in order to work closely with the Economic Commission for Africa of the **United Nations** to develop the economic potential of the basins of Lakes Kivu and Tanganyika. This turn toward neighboring states for help in achieving economic progress was also a temporary turning away from the internal ethnic rivalries that plagued the country.

In 2004 the European Union commissioner for development and humanitarian aid, Louis Michel, called for the revival of the CEPGL, which had collapsed in 1998 due to political unrest in the region. The new CEPGL will have multiple purposes, including the safety of member states, the creation and development of activities of public interest, and the establishment of cooperation in all domains of the political, economic, and social life of the region.

An EU spokesperson said that the commissioner was encouraging this revival because political conditions are "ripe" following successful elections in Burundi and Rwanda and a large voter registration in the DRC. Regarding Burundi, the spokesperson also said that President **Pierre Nkurunziza** was showing an effort to meet with development partners. Nkurunziza has sent "all the positive signals . . . including the holding of free and fair **elections**, his **woman**-friendly government, and his policy priorities of **education** and reconciliation."

ECONOMY. Burundi is one of the 10 poorest countries in the world, with a gross domestic product (GDP) of approximately $3.78 billion, divided into **agriculture** (47.4 percent), light industry (19.3 percent), and services (33.3 percent). In the early 1980s, annual per capita income was about $200; with civil unrest, hundreds of thousands of internally displaced people, economic sanctions, drought, deforestation, and disease, that figure had dropped to less than $125 by 1999, according to Burundi's Ministry of Development and Reconstruction. For example, in 2004 alone, military expenditures exceeded $38 million, a disproportionately large percentage of the entire GDP.

A large portion of the national economy has been based on subsistence-level agriculture. Coffee and cotton are the most important commercial agricultural products and the primary sources of foreign exchange. The **United States** has been the primary buyer of Burundi's coffee bean crop (most of it purchased by the Folger's Company); **Belgium** and Luxembourg have been the primary buyers of cotton. Mineral resources include gold, bastnaesite, cassiterite, nickel, tungsten, and columbium, but ore reserves are very small, and many of the mines remain untapped.

The monetary unit is the Burundi franc, created in 1964 after the economic union between **Rwanda** and Burundi ended. The Bank of the Republic (Banque de la République du Burundi) is the central bank.

Currently, there are no records or statistical data available on the distribution of income between **Hutu** and **Tutsi**. However, many claim that the so-called ethnic division is, in fact, an economic one with "Tutsi" representing the upper caste and "Hutu" representing the lower ones. It should be noted that there are poor Tutsi as well as wealthy Hutu, but the above description remains dominant.

The government's ability to deal with extreme poverty has been lessened by the recent devaluation of the Burundi franc, which lost almost 30 percent of its value against the dollar between 2001 and 2002. The immediate consequence of this is a steep rise in inflation. This, in turn, increased the already high level of international debt, which, in 2002 represented 178 percent of Burundi's GDP.

EDUCATION. Today, Burundi's literacy rate is just over 50 percent, an increase from 1998, which might be explained by the return of many **refugees** and educated **Hutu** who had lived in exile for many years. Most of the precolonial education of the Barundi was provided in the home. Later, the bulk of the formal education was in mission schools administered by the **Catholic** and Protestant churches and subsidized by the government. In the early postcolonial years, primary education was provided almost exclusively by these mission schools. Between 1925 and 1949, missionaries established more than 500 primary schools. Secondary education remained based on the **Belgian** system. Many modern analysts point out that these European-style schools undermined traditional values and the authority of village elders. The use of French as the medium of instruction meant the use of books printed in Europe, thus eliminating mention of African history and culture. Some even say that the role of the European educator was to separate students from their history and traditions, instead guiding them toward capitalism, competition, and individualism.

Burundi's primary education comprises six years, leading to a Primary Studies Certificate. Secondary education is divided into lower and upper secondary: lower secondary is four years and available to those who pass the National Entrance Examination. When lower secondary is completed, students take a test, the results of which are sent to the National Orientation Commission, a body that decides whether or not students will continue to upper secondary; those who complete the three-year upper secondary program earn the State Diploma.

The national university (Université Officielle de **Bujumbura**) was founded in January 1964, and the postsecondary teacher training school (École Normale Supérieure de Bujumbura) in October 1965. Many students also study in other countries on various grants and scholarships. In the 1980s, four more institutions of higher learning were founded; these are schools of journalism, commerce, city planning and development, and **agriculture**. By 1989, all of these had been integrated into the national university, which today has 11 faculties, including medicine. In 1985, the position of director of research was created, and the coordination of research efforts has increased the contribution of university researchers to the socioeconomic development of the country. However, there are few criteria for evaluation of pedagogical skills, teaching methods, or syllabus design quality.

There was formerly a great deal of ethnic discrimination in secondary and higher education; as a result, the bulk of the bureaucratic posts went to **Tutsi**. Under the **Jean-Baptiste Bagaza** administration, there was a movement of "Kirundization," which insisted on the use of Kirundi as the sole **language** of instruction in primary and secondary schools. This is not an unusual nationalistic move, but in Burundi it perpetuated the ethnic discrimination. Access to French, the international and elite language, was restricted to privileged families whose members already spoke it, and Tutsi continued to dominate the bureaucratic posts.

By 1986, fewer than one-third of the students at the national university were Hutu. As of 1988, only a fraction of the Hutu population was qualified for employment in the modern sectors of the **economy**. Of these, from a population already decimated by the 1972 massacres, many were killed or forced into exile during the 1988 and 1991 massacres; many more Hutu fled the country following the 1993 onset of a 12-year period of civil unrest. Moreover, a secondary education is necessary to serve in the national **army**, and many Hutu families could not afford to send their children to secondary school, thus perpetuating the disproportionate dominance of the Tutsi in the army.

As Burundi emerges from a long period of civil war, the government and **international aid** donors recognize the need for far-reaching reform in the country's educational system and recognize the connection between education and a lasting peace. To that end, several measures have been taken. The **United Nations** Children's Fund (UNICEF), for example, has built temporary schools and recruited teachers for entire communities that have been displaced; it also provides for primary-level schooling in refugee camps. Tanganyika Christian Refugee Services funds the only secondary school in the Kanembwa refugee camp in Tanzania. Several international nongovernmental organizations have promoted education for peace and reconciliation, creating programs to help children regain a sense of nationalism, rather than ethnic division.

The biggest and most comprehensive move to increase educational opportunities in Burundi, however, has come from its newly elected transitional government, with international support. President **Pierre Nkurunziza**, after only three weeks in power, announced the waiving of all school fees for primary schools; the immediate reaction of the country was an increase of primary school enrollment from about 250,000 children to more than 550,000, overwhelming the already depleted educational resources. This breaks down to about 59 percent of school-age boys and 48 percent of school-age girls. Only about 8 percent of the relevant age group is currently enrolled in secondary schools, however. By 2008, Burundi hopes to add at least 350 new schools to its neglected educational infrastructure; the government has already allocated 110 million Burundi francs (almost $100,000) to be used for fees formerly paid by the students' families. UNICEF has pledged more than $4 million for the purchase of uniforms, school renovation and rebuilding, and teacher training.

Many analysts have pointed out that Burundi can hope to progress into a developed, democratic society when there is equal opportunity in education. Unlike some other countries that have had long conflicts between groups of citizens, however, this task in Burundi does not require the changing of laws that discriminate; since there have never been specific laws denying education to Hutu, any change will require a change of deep-seated attitudes.

ELECTIONS. Burundi has seen very few elections in its 45-year history since independence. Its first democratic, multiparty election was in 1993, when the people elected the country's first **Hutu** president, **Melchior Ndadaye.** Ndadaye's assassination just months after the election was one of the primary catalysts of a 12-year civil war. August 2005 saw the second democratic election in the country, the result of a lengthy peace process brokered in part by leaders of other African countries in the region. This most recent election, however, shows more promise than the previous one because the country's leaders are well aware of the difficulties that could exist when democracy comes too quickly and without the support of the national **army.** Many were surprised by the results of the 2005 election, which saw the leader of a recent rebel group, the **Forces pour la Défense de la Démocratie, Pierre Nkurunziza** elected as the country's president with 58 percent of the votes. Nkurunziza, in spite of his background that includes participation in alleged **human rights** atrocities, is committed to maintaining the fragile peace in the country.

ENVIRONMENT. Burundi has a larger proportion of arable land (almost half its total surface area) than almost any other country in Africa. Rainfall is plentiful, and two rainy seasons a year allow two harvests a year. Historically, the land has provided Burundi with basic necessities. Unfortunately, recent droughts have added to long years of overcultivation, overgrazing, soil erosion, and deforestation, which are all exacerbated by long years of conflict, disorder, and the constant movement of **refugees.** *See also* LAKES AND RIVERS.

– F –

FAMILY CORPORATION. Capt. **Michel Micombero**, who was named prime minister in 1966 and later named himself president, appointed a great many friends and relatives to his cabinet, thus securing his grip on power. Micombero's wife was an aristocrat and became his link to many in this group. Among these people, some of whom later overthrew Micombero's government, were **Pascal Kashirahamwe**; **Pierre Bigayimpunzi**; **Athanase Gakiza**; Col. **Sylvère Nzohabonayo**; Col. **Jean-Baptiste Bagaza**, second in command of the armed forces and a close neighbor of Micombero; and **Jean Barahinduka**. This group, often called the "family corporation," controlled the **economy**, the **army**, and the judicial system.

FASONI (MU-, BA-). See GANWA.

FÉDÉRATION DES TRAVAILLEURS DU BURUNDI (FTB)/ FEDERATION OF BURUNDI WORKERS. Around and just after the time of its 1962 independence, Burundi, like much of Africa, had an emerging, activist counterelite. In the case of Burundi, this counterelitism often manifested itself as antimonarchy. The FTB was made up of a handful of trade union leaders, but despite the efforts of the organization's secretary-general, **Augustin Ntamagara**, to build up a mass following, it never became a major force in the politics of the country. In spite of the small number of members, however, the FTB developed into a very vocal group that was clearly Marxist in its outlook. According to its own organizational statements circulated in 1964, it was committed to the liquidation of "colonialism, neocolonialism, imperialism, reaction, and feudalism." It was thought that two potential allies of the **Casablanca Group** would be the **army** and the trade unions; however, the FTB did not build up enough grassroots support among the people to be a strong backer of the Casablanca Group. When Prime Minister **Ngendandumwe** was assassinated, Mwami **Mwambutsa IV**'s fears of an impending coup were escalated, and the FTB was ordered to suspend its activities.

FONDATION DE L'UNIVERSITÉ DE LIÈGE POUR LES RECHERCHES SCIENTIFIQUES AU CONGO BELGE ET AU RUANDA-URUNDI (FULREAC). The Foundation of the University of Liège for Scientific Research in the Belgian Congo and Ruanda-Urundi sent a team of **educational** specialists to the territory in 1957 to study and report on the impact of European education on the population, the future of children who are successful in elementary school but fail to complete secondary school, and the possible modification of educational measures in order to make educated students better farmers. The final report discusses concerns about the education of **women** and moral education as well. The report also points out, among its suggestions, that education is "but a single element—of capital importance, it is true—of the civilizing action of Europe in Africa."

FONDS REINE ELISABETH POUR L'ASSISTANCE MÉDICALE AUX INDIGÈNES (FOREAMI). The Queen Elisabeth Native Medical Assistance Fund grew out of a study trip made to the **Belgian** Congo by King Albert and Queen Elisabeth in 1928. The purpose of the fund was to promote social and medical services for the benefit of the indigenous populations in the Belgian Congo and Ruanda-Urundi. The project was funded by investments, government subsidies, and charitable contributions.

FORCES NATIONALES DE LIBÉRATION (FNL)/NATIONAL LIBERATION FORCES. One of the strongest, largest, and most violent of the **Hutu** rebel groups, the FNL has remained outside of Burundi's ongoing peace process. It is the armed wing of the **PALIPEHUTU** and has been described by some as a hard-line splinter group; regional leaders designated it a terrorist organization after a particularly violent attack on a **refugee** camp that resulted in the deaths of 160 Congolese **Tutsi** refugees. In answer to this charge, FNL leaders said the group was prepared to face an international court if and when other parties involved in Burundi's violence over the last 40 years also stood trial. The FNL has established a stronghold in the **Bujumbura** Rural Province, a mountainous region surrounding the capital.

There have been several highly visible leaders of this group; Jean Bosco Sindayigaya replaced **Agathon Rwasa** in October 2005 when Rwasa was expelled by the group for his failure to bring the group into the peace process; in a dramatic gesture, about 100 FNL members called upon the **United Nations** and the **African Union** to prevail on Rwasa to put an end to hostilities. They said in a letter that they were "fed up" with the war because they believed the objective of the Hutu-dominated rebel movement to resist the dominance of Tutsi political and military power had been achieved. Also in October 2005, the FNL was threatened by Burundi's government as well as the UN to join the peace process or suffer consequences. That deadline was extended to December 2005, and the group, under Sindayigaya, appears ready to put down its arms. There had been other, earlier signs that the FNL was ready to participate in peace talks; in each case, however, the agreed-upon cease-fires were broken.

FORCES POUR LA DÉFENSE DE LA DÉMOCRATIE (FDD)/ FORCES FOR THE DEFENSE OF DEMOCRACY. One of several **Hutu** militia groups (and one of the more visible and active ones) that emerged in the 1990s, formed to fight the national **army** of Burundi, which at that time was estimated to be approximately 95 percent **Tutsi**. The FDD was the armed wing of the **Conseil National pour la Défense de la Démocratie (CNDD) political party**. The FDD has been implicated in many **human rights** abuses, including attacks and executions of civilians. In April 1997, for example, an FDD offensive in southern Burundi ended with the massacre of both Hutu and Tutsi civilians. However, this group underwent an enormous change that led to a change in Burundi politics.

In late 2003, the FDD began peace talks with Burundi's transitional government. There were several false starts, however, beginning with one faction of the FDD under the leadership of **Pierre Nkurunziza** suspending the cease-fire talks with Burundi's government in February 2004, citing hostilities, blockage of humanitarian aid, and lack of consultation over national issues. By March 2004, Nkurunziza and the government recommitted to implementing their past agreements. In November, then president **Domitien Ndayizeye** reshuffled his cabinet to incorporate the CNDD; he named Nkurunziza minister of state for good governance, making him the third most senior state figure, after the president and vice president. Within the next two months, two more FDD members arrived in **Bujumbura** after years in exile to take up ministerial positions, and more than 6,000 FDD fighters assembled in camps. By early 2005, more than 18,000 FDD members had voluntarily given up their arms to the **United Nations**. In spite of the many hardships that these people underwent in camps (e.g., near-starvation, disease, lack of shelter), they maintained their peaceful stance.

In early 2005, the FDD also formally transformed itself into a political party, combining its political and armed wings into the CNDD-FDD. The CNDD-FDD won the 2005 democratic **elections**—the first that Burundi had held since the beginning of the civil war in 1993—by a large margin (58 percent) and named Nkurunziza as the first president. In spite of their origins as a Hutu rebel group fighting the Tutsi army, the government says its first priority is to bring reconciliation to the war-torn country. Since becoming a political party, it has recruited many Tutsi to its ranks. The CNDD-FDD's primary emphasis is on the need for democracy over ethnic rights and privileges.

FOYERS SOCIAUX. In 1948, the first of these homemaking centers opened in **Bujumbura**. Because the **women** of Burundi and **Rwanda** were traditionally closely tied to farming, the colonial government sought ways to **educate** them in their new roles as urban women. Social workers taught women "household arts" because it was assumed that the women arriving in the city did not know how to organize their households or even how to spend their leisure time. Among the skills taught in the centers were sewing, knitting, darning, fabric cutting, washing, and ironing; when these basic skills were achieved, the women learned principles of hygiene, thrift, and child care. After completing the courses, women were encouraged to return to the centers often for advice as domestic problems arose. These centers grew rapidly and spread to other towns and the rural areas; eventually, the need for more teachers led to a school for homemaking monitors. The Union des Femmes du Congo Belge et du Ruanda-Urundi also opened a home in Bujumbura where women could complete their homemaking and social training.

FRODEBU (FRONT DÉMOCRATIQUE BURUNDI/BURUNDI DEMOCRATIC FRONT). Since even before Burundi's 1962 independence, **UPRONA**, dominated by **Tutsi**, was the only legal **political party**; power within the party was synonymous with power in the country at large. However, in 1986, **Melchior Ndadaye** formed FRODEBU, a party dominated by moderate **Hutu**. The party included many Hutu intellectuals, many of whom had been in exile in **Rwanda** since the massacres of 1972. For a brief time, it was reported that FRODEBU enjoyed what Catherine Watson called "rapturous support" in the country, and in 1993, the party, with Ndadaye at its head, won by a two-to-one margin over UPRONA in Burundi's first multiparty **election**. Ndadaye accomplished several firsts in Burundi's history: the first elected president, first civilian president, and first Hutu president.

After Ndadaye's assassination, *Le Citoyen*, previously considered one of Burundi's most balanced newspapers, reported without adequate support that FRODEBU members had been the killers in many ensuing massacres throughout the country. In fact, following Ndadaye's assassination, some FRODEBU officials who fled into exile organized a new armed movement that committed itself to fighting the national armed forces in order to make stable democratic government possible. The group that emerged from this later became the **Conseil National pour la Défense de la Démocratie-Forces pour la Défense de la Démocratie (CNDD-FDD)**, but FRODEBU remained a viable political party. Throughout the 1990s and into the period from 2000 to 2005 when Burundi was trying to emerge from civil strife, FRODEBU remained the largest primarily Hutu party, and **Domitien Ndayizeye**, representing FRODEBU, became the Hutu president under the power-sharing agreement. In 2004, when the FDD surpassed FRODEBU in numbers and political power, FRODEBU said that it was ready to peacefully accept defeat in a democratic election that occurred in August 2005. Their spokesman declared, "We are democratic. If we are beaten, we are prepared for the next elections; we are not preparing for war."

FRONT COMMUN. At the time of Burundi's 1962 independence, this group was the only opposition to **UPRONA** in the National Assembly. Founded in September 1960, it was a loose electoral coalition (sometimes described as a cartel), which included the **Parti Démocratique Chrétien**, the **Parti du Peuple**, the **Parti Démocratique et Rural**, the Parti de l'Emancipation Populaire, the Voix du Peuple Murundi, and several other minor **political parties**.

FRONT DÉMOCRATIQUE BURUNDI/BURUNDI DEMOCRATIC FRONT. *See* FRODEBU (FRONT DÉMOCRATIQUE BURUNDI/ BURUNDI DEMOCRATIC FRONT).

FUMU (MU-, BA-). In the traditional **religious** beliefs, these medical practitioners have the power to ward off misfortunes caused by malevolent spirits. The symbols of the position are a leopard skin, a headdress made from a cow's tail, and a gourd rattle. These, as well as various healing techniques, are either passed from father to son or learned by apprenticeship to a practicing *umufumu*. In addition to these powers and duties, *abafumu* predict the future, call together spirits during seances, and interpret dreams. Some perform rainmaking ceremonies. The abafumu were highly respected members of society and often became wealthy and politically powerful.

– G –

GABEKAZI (IN-, IN-). Traditionally, this royal bull and his cows always accompanied the *mwami* wherever he went.

GABIRE (BU-, MU-, BA-). When the nomadic, pastoral **Tutsi** migrated into the lake region, they gradually achieved economic, social, and political dominance over the **Hutu**. The Hutu, in a sense, mortgaged themselves to the Tutsi minority in exchange for cattle and protection through a contract called *ubugabire*. This patron-client system was similar to a feudal relationship in that the Tutsi *shebuja* (lord) entrusted his Hutu *mugabire* (serf) with cattle (*inka*). This was not ownership, but symbolized a contract between the parties. The relationship allowed the shebuja to expect services and produce; it allowed the mugabire to expect protection and favors. If the mugabire neglected his duties, the shebuja had the option of demanding the return of the cattle; in fact, the shebuja could break the contract at the slightest provocation.

The stipulations imposed on the mugabire were extensive; for example, although the milk and calves of the cattle entrusted to them generally were considered the property of the mugabire, he could not kill or dispose of cattle, nor could he leave the territory of the shebuju. The shebuju also had the right to set aside a specific cow and all of her calves as his own. But if the mugabire was a good manager of his own property, he could eventually become a manager of a larger area by contracting cattle to others. The contract usually passed from father to son for both patron and client.

The land tenure system, considered feudal by many, was theoretically abolished in 1955. In 1956, the **Conseil Supérieur du Pays** presented a program that suggested that grazing land be owned communally and that independent agriculturists be allowed to consider their cultivated land as private property. This proposal was never actually made into law, and some analysts believed at least as late as 1969 that unless it did become law and the ubugabire system were officially eliminated, the people of Burundi could not achieve a significant improvement in their standard of living. See also AGRICULTURE; *KA*; SLAVERY.

GABIRO (KI-, BI-). These historical sites in Burundi are unusual in that they are neither stone nor metal, but vegetation. Trees planted on tombs are testimony to the ancient presence of people—kings, grand chiefs, ceremonial leaders—invested with great powers.

GABO (BU-, KU-). While the same root with a different set of prefixes is used to mean "husband" (*umugabo*), this word represents many things traditionally masculine. It can mean courage, virility, strength, and ability. It can also mean male genitals. With yet another prefix (*intwarangabo*), it means the chief of the **army**. An *urugabo* is a strong, growing **youth**.

GACOREKE. In the traditional courts of the *mwami* or the *ganwa*, these young girls were charged with the maintenance of the royal palace or residence and the care of and attending to the princes. Variations of the name include *gicoreke*, *mucoreke*, and *nyancoreke*. See also COREKE.

GAHIGI. The person in the traditional royal court responsible for hunting. This was an important post because, according to some legends, **Kiranga** was killed during the course of a hunt. This position was usually held by a **Twa**; variations on the name were *Inagahigi* and *Semuhigi*.

GAKIZA, ATHANASE. A member of **Michel Micombero's "Family Corporation"**—Micombero's wife's uncle—Gakiza was the director of the president's personal spy network.

GANURO (MU-, no plural). During the traditional harvest ceremonies, **women** were honored in the fertility ceremony called the *umuganuro*. Traditionally, women were believed to be symbolically one with the earth; as such, traditional beliefs had women act accordingly. For example, a woman could not jump, climb ladders, or step over brooks. It was thought that every woman held inside all the potential of life. She fulfilled her role in society by bearing children, and it was also thought that if she performed her duties well, fertility would be transmitted to the seeds she planted, thus bringing prosperity to her entire kin group. It is this belief that was demonstrated in the umuganuro ceremony. There is record of the umuganuro being held as recently as 1964, with the format somewhat modified from the traditional. The program included members of the National Assembly, military leaders, international diplomatic personnel, and religious representatives. The royal drummers performed, and various **youth** groups marched in a parade. *See also* KARYENDA; MUSIC AND DANCE.

GANUZA (MU-, BA-). Generally, a master of ceremonies during traditional **religious** rituals and festivals; originally, however, the ganuza was specifically the guardian of the sacred **Karyenda**.

GANWA (MU-, BA-). When a *mwami* (king) came to power in traditional Urundi (but not Ruanda), he received one of four dynastic names: Ntare, Mwezi, Mutaga, or Mwambutsa. Their descendants were named Batare, Bezi, Bataga, and Bambutsa, respectively, and these were the princes of the royal blood, or *ganwa*, until the accession of a king who received the same name as his ancestor; then they became *bafasoni*, a less important honorary title. Rank and privilege played an important role in allocating power and authority, but these were primarily the prerogatives of the ganwa; since the *ganwa* were regarded as a group separate from the ethnic divisions, political competition was traditionally rare between the **Hutu** and **Tutsi**. This changed along with the traditional opportunity structure as democratic ideas and practices began to spread. In the early years of independence in the 1960s, Burundi politics reflected conflicts among ganwa clans and between the monarchy and its opponents, ganwa and antiroyalist Tutsi, regional Tutsi and **Hima**, and Tutsi and Hutu. By the 1970s, the monarchy had disappeared, and the ganwa as hegemonic elites had lost their role. *See also* BATARE AND BEZI; BAMBUTSA AND BATAGA; MUTAGA I (SEENYAMWIIZA); MUTAGA II (1893–1915); MWAMBUTSA I; MWAMBUTSA IV (BANGIRICENGE) (1913–1977); MWEZI I; MWEZI IV (1845–1908);

NTARE I (RUSHATSI); NTARE II (RUGAAMBA); NTARE V (CHARLES NDIZEYE) (1947–1972).

GARAMA (KI-, no plural). The winter solstice, during which the sorghum festival occurs. During this time, the *mwami* presents the dynastic drum, the **Karyenda**, and cattle are said to be made more fertile.

GENDANYI (BU-, BA-). Under the system of *ubugabire*, the court contained many levels of patronage. The gendanyi were young attendants who would eventually gain positions of authority and prestige. They were trusted members of the court and followers of the *mwami* whose activities and responsibilities varied considerably but included being escorts, warriors, dancers, messengers, and police. The English word *courtier* is probably the closest translation. *See also GABIRE.*

GENGE (BU-, MA-). **Ethel Albert** translates this as "successful cleverness," which seems to trivialize both its range of meaning and range of importance in Burundi society. A better translation might be "verbal sophistication." It is a key concept to the norms and values associated with the uses of language. *Ubugenge* primarily applies to the verbal intellectual management of important situations. The specific manifestations of ubugenge are diverse. According to Albert,

> The cleverness of a rogue; the industriousness of a virtuous man whose overlord gives him a cow as a reward for virtue; the skill of a good psychologist-rhetorician in persuading a generous, impulsive, or inebriated superior to give him a cow although he has done nothing to earn it; the skill of a medical healer; the success of a practical joker who has victimized a simple-minded peasant or feeble-minded boy; the wise and just judgments of the *umubashingantahe*; and the technological accomplishments of Europeans are equally good examples of *ubugenge*—for they all succeed in bringing something good to their designers.

See also SHIGANTAHE.

GENI (BU-). As with any society, there are many traditional regulations and taboos around the institution of marriage or *ubugeni*. The Barundi had the expected incest taboos between people and their parents or grandparents, between people and their uncles or aunts, between siblings, and between first cousins; they also had regulations against marriage with one's father- or mother-in-law, but not against other in-law relationships. Marriages could also be forbidden if the two people were from very different social or economic classes, if the two families were feuding, if one of the families had developed a bad reputation, or if the bride was pregnant before the wedding. Many taboos against marriage were also based on physical reasons. Marriage was forbidden if either member of the couple had syphilis (*mburugu*), tuberculosis (*igituntu*), mental disorders (*ubusazi*), or leprosy (*imibembe*), among other things. Marriages were also forbidden or dissolved if the young man had chronic impotence (*umwange*). Traditionally, Barundi married around the age of puberty, usually between the ages of 13 and 15. In fact, marriage was forbidden before the young **woman** developed breasts suitable for child-bearing, had a regular menstrual cycle, and had pubic hair. The majority of Barundi remained monogamous, but polygamy was accepted as part of the culture as well, usually among the upper classes.

GERMANY, RELATIONS WITH. The Conference of Berlin designated Ruanda-Urundi as a German sphere of interest in 1885, but it was not until the 1890s that the government of German East Africa extended its authority to the territory. In 1886, a military post was established in Usumbura (present-day **Bujumbura**), which remained the administrative center for both kingdoms until two separate German residencies were established in 1906 and 1907.

After the death of Mwami **Mwezi IV** Gisabo in 1908, as well as due to the lack of a replacement for the successful *Resident* Von Grawert, the German administration was able to firmly control only Usumbura and the immediate area; German authority diminished in proportion to the distance from the military post. This led to the moving of the residency to the more central **Gitega** in 1912.

German colonial policy provided for missionary **education** of the sons of chiefs in order to equip these boys to later be part of the administration. There were, in fact, only about 190 Germans in both **Rwanda** and Burundi by 1914, about 130 of whom were missionaries; there were just 40 soldiers and six civilian officers.

Although some senior German officers saw World War I as an opportunity to create a great German empire in Central Africa, this was not to be because of the vastly inferior numbers of German forces and weapons. By January 1916, Germany offered only token resistance to the **Belgian** occupation of the region, and by June of that year, Burundi was under Belgian control.

Germany remains involved in Burundi's affairs. It has been a regular donor to reconstruction and social programs as Burundi emerges from civil war. *See also INDER FRAGE.*

GIHANGA. Some myths that are part of Burundi's oral tradition trace the origins of **Rwanda** and Burundi to a common ancestor, Gihanga. In these myths, Gihanga's two sons Kanyaburundi and Kanyaruanda, founded the two kingdoms. There are other myths as well that deal with the origins of the country; some say that Kanyaburundi, who ruled as **Ntare I** Rushatsi, was the great-grandson of Kanyaruanda. Yet another myth traces the origin of Ntare I to the small **Tutsi** kingdom of Buha, located at what is now the southeastern border of Burundi. All of these myths and popular traditions are important in understanding the history of Burundi. Burundi did not have official court historians as did Rwanda, so many details about several of the earlier monarchs are missing. In fact, some information about Burundi has been gathered from the oral traditions of Rwanda.

GISABO (KISABO/KISSABO/GISSABO). *See* MWEZI IV (1845–1908).

GITEGA. Gitega (formerly Kitega) is not a large city (the population is approximately 23,000), but it has been important to Burundi's history. Located to the east of **Bujumbura** in the center of the country near the Ruvuvu River, Gitega was, for centuries before the **Belgian** administration, the capital of Burundi. It was here that the *mwami* held royal court and the *ganwa* received their training. It remains popular with tourists because it has the Burundi National Museum that houses the nation's traditional gold and jewels that belonged to the royal court; several royal drum (**Karyenda**) sanctuaries are located in the area, as well as the *ibwami*, the former residence of the mwami. Gitega is located in the highlands, 1,800 meters (about 6,000 feet) above sea level. The climate is well suited to coffee and banana trees; therefore, Gitega is the site of one of the country's main coffee processing factories and a banana beer brewery. *See also* ARTS AND CRAFTS; GITEGA SCHEME.

GITEGA SCHEME. An integrated rural development project in the late 1970s and early 1980s, sponsored by the **United Nations** Development Program. A special component of the project financed by the United Nations Children's Fund (UNICEF) was entirely devoted to the training of **women** as farmers. Excellent results were achieved in better yields when the women used improved farming techniques and selected seeds and fertilizers in the cooperative. The World Bank was so impressed that a major loan was approved for a much larger national program based on the model of the Gitega Scheme.

GOMA (IN-, IN-). The royal drummers of the Burundi dynasties.

GORORE (IN-, IN-). Generally, a tribute or fee, perhaps for rent or a license of some sort. In terms of Burundi royalty, however, *gorore* is the word for the tribute that was given to the *mwami*. All who visited the court were under an obligation (considered part of a person's moral duty) to bring a gift of cattle to the mwami as well as to his mother.

GOVERNMENT SYSTEM. The current system of government in Burundi is based on the constitution approved on 28 February 2005 in the first democratic **elections** in 12 years. There are three branches of government.

The executive branch consists of the president, who, according to the constitution, is elected by universal suffrage, is head of the government, and is commander in chief of the armed forces. However, the first president under this system, **Pierre Nkurunziza**, was elected by a two-thirds majority in both houses of the legislature. The president is supposed to serve a maximum of two five-year terms. The president appoints a 20-member cabinet, of which 60 percent must be **Hutu** and 40 percent **Tutsi**, and 30 percent must be **women**. The president also selects two vice presidents, one Hutu and one Tutsi, both of whom are to be already-elected members of the legislature; the two vice presidents must also come from two different **political parties**.

The legislative branch consists of the National Assembly and the Senate. The National Assembly comprises at least 100 members, again 60 percent Hutu and 40 percent Tutsi with at least 30 percent of this total women. In addition, three members are to be **Twa**. Members are directly elected for five-year terms. Legislation in the National Assembly passes by a two-thirds majority. The Senate comprises two representatives from each of Burundi's provinces; senatorial representatives are chosen by an Electoral College. In addition, the Twa again have three seats, and (although still controversial), Burundi's living past presidents each have seats. At least 30 percent of the Senate must be women, and legislation is also passed by a two-thirds majority.

The judicial system is headed by a Supreme Court and is based on **German** and **Belgian** codified law as well as Burundi customary law. The 2005 constitution created a Constitutional Court, which is designed to rule on the constitutionality of lower court rulings and government actions. The Supreme Court is the final court of appeal. The **United Nations** Security Council adopted a resolution in June 2005 to create a **National Truth and Reconciliation Commission (NTRC)** and a special court to prosecute war crimes and **human rights** violations committed during decades of civil war; once operational, this commission will fall under Burundi's judicial system and consist of three international and two Burundi commissioners. The commission will investigate killings that have taken place in the country since its independence in 1962 through 2000, when the Burundi parties signed the **Arusha Accord**.

On the local level, Burundi is divided into 17 provinces, each further subdivided into districts (called by the French term *arrondissements*) and communes.

GROUPE DE TRAVAIL. In the late 1950s, the **Belgian** government appointed this parliamentary study group to investigate the conditions under which a transfer of authority to Ruanda-Urundi could be accomplished peacefully. It was probably in anticipation of a visit from this group that Prince **Louis Rwagasore** virtually took control of **UPRONA**.

GURU (IN-, IN-). These smooth, round stones and their purpose are apparently unique among traditional charms and amulets that have been studied in the region. They are symbolically regarded as **Imana**, although there is a distinction between them and the actual Creator, and they have the power to hurt as well as to bless. It seems that only **Hutu** keep *inguru* just outside the entrance to the *rugo* (compound). They are usually a hereditary symbol, but anyone might be told to keep them (by the *mupfumu*) if his wife or crops were not fruitful. A small, circular patch is smoothed out on the ground outside of the entrance, and it is spread with cut grass; occasionally, a tiny hut is built over the inguru. At first only two or three are put in this area, but later more can be added; when this happens, the inguru are said to have given birth. Over the course of many years, the number of inguru may increase to 20 or 30.

Before sowing or planting, a few grains of seed were traditionally scattered over the inguru or else the fields would not bear crops. After harvesting millet, a basket of the early fruits was placed on top of the inguru and left for several days; the millet was then dried, and beer (*terekera*) was made from it. The family's closest friends were called to sit in a circle around the inguru with their feet pointed toward them; the head of the house then sprinkled the inguru and the feet of the participants with the beer. *See also PFUMU.*

GUTHRIE, MALCOLM. The first linguist to classify Kirundi and Kinyarwanda as separate from the **languages** of Uganda and **Tanzania**, but connected with those of the **Democratic Republic of the Congo**.

– H –

HANZA (BA-, rarely used in singular). The Abahanza were a noble **Hutu** clan who were often charged with guarding the property within the *mwami*'s enclosure. Court singers and soldiers were also chosen from among this lineage.

HEALTH. Because of long years of civil strife, the health situation in Burundi has deteriorated since the early 1990s, a time when Burundi was making achievements in modern preventative health care, medical practices, vaccinations, and health **education**. Life expectancy is already low at approximately 48 years for males and 52 years for females; however, with the rapidly increasing **HIV/AIDS** epidemic, it is estimated that this could decline even further to below 40 years by 2010. Vaccination coverage against childhood diseases has decreased from about 83 percent in 1993 to little more than 50 percent in 2005.

Health care is very unevenly spread throughout Burundi, with more than 70 percent of the country's doctors located in **Bujumbura**. Many rural health centers have been destroyed in the fighting since 1993. In 2005, it was estimated that there is one health center per 25,000 people. Mass displacements during the long civil war that began in 1993 have caused large increases in incidents of malaria, cholera, typhoid, and HIV/AIDS. Additionally, Burundi has the highest rate of tuberculosis in the world. The Burundi government and the **United Nations** Children's Fund (UNICEF) are working together to greatly lessen the incidence of malaria; the **international aid** group Doctors without Borders has reopened its cholera treatment center in Bujumbura following a new outbreak of the disease in the capital. In addition to the fighting, the climate has caused an increase in malnutrition. In early 2005, the Burundi government introduced a temporary tax to help victims of famine; ministers and lawmakers are to pay 8 percent of their salaries, civil servants 2 percent, and unemployed households a one-time contribution of the equivalent of $0.09. *See also* KWASHIORKOR.

HEKO (KI-/GI-, BI-/VI-). According to the traditional **religious** beliefs, *iviheko* (charms and amulets) made of sticks and the hair of animals are used both to ward off evil and to generate power for the one who wears them. Special practitioners transfer supernatural energy to the material object through magical formulas; of course, the more powerful the diviner, the more potent the charms. Even after the majority of Barundi were converted to Christianity, most still used charms for a variety of purposes, such as luck in hunting, finding a wife, and curing sick cows. Special amulets are still often made for infants to protect them against such things as intestinal worms, diarrhea, skin irritations, and snakebites. A positive talisman, one bringing good luck and long life, is *ikimazi* (plural: *ibimazi*).

HIGH COUNCIL OF BURUNDI. A decree of 1952 that included administrative reforms was looked upon as a cautious first step in representative government. A 1943 decree had established a system of councils, whose members were appointed, to advise the *mwami* and chiefs, particularly on matters of budget and taxation. The later decree broadened the functions of these councils and established a limited degree of elected representation. Councils existed for each administrative level: subchiefdoms, chiefdoms, districts, and the High

Council of Burundi. This last was presided over by the mwami himself. Part of the membership of each council was chosen by the members of the council immediately below it. In 1956, the governor of Ruanda-Urundi decided to interpret the 1952 decree so as to allow the subchiefdom electoral colleges to be chosen by universal male suffrage. There were 3,904 seats to be filled, and the balloting resulted in the election of 1,664 **Tutsi** electors. Observers believed that these results indicated that there was rapport between the **Hutu** and the ordinary (non-*ganwa*) Tutsi.

HIMA. Another pastoral people, ethnically related to the **Tutsi**, the Hima are often considered to be Tutsi. But the group's original home is not agreed upon. Names given to groups do not always define the limits of a tribe in the accepted sense. They can link a number of peoples that are located far apart and sometimes considered to be separate tribes, or else link only special categories of population among several different peoples; the Hima of Uganda are the more widely written about Hima. Some Western historians and anthropologists say that both the Tutsi and the Hima have ethnic affinities with the Galla tribes of southern Ethiopia; in Burundi, both groups were believed to have migrated from a different direction. Perhaps as a result of this second opinion, the Hima were traditionally set apart from the Tutsi socially. They, for example, did not have the privileges associated with forming alliances with the *mwami* such as marriage to a family member of the mwami or the receiving of cattle. They also did not participate in the traditional structures of Tutsi hegemony over **Hutu**. Some political analysts say that it was the Hima who planned the arrest of **Ntare V** in 1972, one of the events that set in motion a series of massacres within the country. Hima officers have controlled the **army** since 1972.

HINDURE (GI-, BI-). Evil spirits that have changed themselves into some kind of wolf or hyena.

HINZA (MU-, BA-). Knowledge of the **Hutu** before the arrival of the **Tutsi** is limited, but oral traditions indicate that the early Hutu social system was based on the clan and kings ruling over very limited domains, all centered around small-scale **agriculture**. The kings were known as *bahinza*, "those who cause things to grow," and, according to the stories, their strength was based on the popular belief that they were endowed with supernatural powers that allowed them to control the fertility of the earth, domestic animals, and people, as well as to cause rain, protect crops from insects, and protect cattle from disease.

HIV/AIDS. HIV (human immunodeficiency virus) and AIDS (acquired immune deficiency syndrome) are currently the leading cause of death in Burundi. Evidence suggests that HIV/AIDS was present in Burundi at the beginning of the 1980s, even before Western countries recognized its existence and the danger it posed. Since then, the number of people infected has grown; the estimate for infection rates was about 1 percent in 1989, and that number grew to nearly 20 percent infection in urban areas and 8 percent in rural areas by 2003. In 2005, the infection rate lowered slightly and began to stabilize at about 18.6 percent in the urban areas because there has been an increase in the acceptance and availability of condoms. However, Burundi Minister for HIV/AIDS Issues Geneviève Sindabizera has expressed the opinion that, at this rate, the country's average life expectancy could fall below 40 years by 2010.

While the number of infected people has lessened somewhat in the urban areas, the infection rate is increasing in the rural areas. This is largely due to the long civil unrest in the country that has caused hundreds of thousands of people to become internally displaced persons in camps that have very poor conditions. When these people, as well as **refugees** who fled to neighboring countries, return to their homes, the infection rate in rural areas is expected to grow even more. The National Programme for the Fight against AIDS and Sexually Transmitted Diseases and the National Association for HIV-Positive and AIDS Patients are trying to decentralize their activities in order to better reach the rural population.

Burundi's first lady, Aude Ndayize, has joined other African first ladies in African Synergy Against HIV/AIDS and Suffering, an initiative originated in Yaounde, Cameroon. In Burundi, the initiative has focused on training programs for doctors, nurses, and social workers on the prevention of mother-to-child HIV infection.

A focus of HIV/AIDS programs has been **women**. In 2003, 220,000 adults were estimated to carry the HIV infection; of these, 130,000 were women. In 2005, it was estimated that women were twice as likely as men to become infected, in part due to an increased number of rapes during the civil war. A group that has one of the largest increases in infection rates is girls between the ages of 16 and 20. In 2003, the Society of Women against AIDS (SWAA) began promoting the use of female condoms, and the use of this device is growing in popularity among women living with HIV. Of the women who used the device in its initial trial, more than 85 percent felt it was useful, and 76 percent said they felt it empowered them to prevent infection.

HIV and AIDS have affected children as well. In 2003, 27,000 children were estimated to have the HIV infection. As many as 200,000 children have been orphaned because of AIDS.

The spread of HIV and AIDS in Burundi began before the outbreak of the civil war in 1993, but has increased greatly since then, partly because of the war. Already a poor country, Burundi has become impoverished; only a very small percentage of infected individuals have been able to afford necessary treatment. In 2004, Dr. Jean Kamana, Burundi's **health** minister, authorized the civil service insurance company (Mutuelle) to pay 80 percent of the cost of antiretroviral drugs (ARVs), which is what they had been typically paying for other necessary drugs; this, however, will serve only the country's civil servants. At the end of 2004, Silvain Ndayikengurukiye, the person in charge of public relations and communications with the National Council for AIDS Control, said that only about 1,200 out of 25,000 people in the country had access to ARVs. In February 2005, **Germany** gave the country $9.5 million for various projects, including HIV/AIDS control.

HOZA UMWANA (GU-). Burundi lullabies that are a very important part of the country's oral tradition. Sometimes they are filled with historical allusions, and very often they contain stories about the baby's parents or grandparents. They then serve as a source of information within a family about that family's history. Lullabies are used to comfort babies, but never to put them to sleep; in fact, it is traditionally taboo to sing to a baby at night for fear that it could cause nightmares. *See also* MUSIC AND DANCE.

HUMAN RIGHTS. The human rights chief for the **United Nations** Operation in Burundi (ONUB) reported in February 2005: "The human rights situation in Burundi is catastrophic. . . . In the reports that I have received, not a day goes by without cases of murder, rape, or abuse. . . . What is worse is that it is armed men who perpetrate these acts on defenseless civilians." Human Rights Watch has documented hundreds of violations (including rape, looting, theft, torture, forced labor, and restrictions to movement), again perpetrated by armed men—both members of the national **army** and members of rebel groups. In many reports, people were not even certain as to which side had attacked them; observers noted that often some members of attacking groups wore military uniforms while others did not. One Barundi, when asked by Human Rights Watch to explain why it was the civilians who were being abused by the fighting groups, quoted a proverb: "When two elephants fight, it is the grass that gets trampled."

Burundi's human rights group, Iteka, collects statistics and issues a report on violence in Burundi every year. In 2004 alone, it recorded 667 murders and 1,657 rapes despite a dramatic decrease in violence throughout the country. Many rapes and other sexual assaults are not even reported because of the fear of repercussions toward the victims. In fact the number of rapes from 2004 was a substantial increase from 2001, indicating that the human rights abuses in Burundi continue and must be stopped.

The atmosphere of human rights abuses is bleak in Burundi; however, there have been some positive developments. For one, the **international aid** organizations, international human rights organizations, and individuals within **religious** communities have begun to attack the stigma of rape, helping **women** to find support and to be reintegrated into families that had rejected them. Husbands receive counseling on rape as well. Amnesty International believes support in four areas would begin to curb the rise in violence, especially against women:

> developing and expanding community-based activities designed to reduce stigma and ignorance around violence against women; strengthening the judiciary and law enforcement structures so they are able to investigate and prosecute the crime of rape; increasing access to health care for women who have been victims of rape or other gender-based violence and addressing underlying discrimination against women.

The newly elected government of Burundi has taken steps to eliminate some of this gender discrimination; as well, the United Nations has called for the formation of a judiciary body to examine and punish human rights abuses that have come from ethnic conflicts since

Burundi's 1962 independence. *See also* NATIONAL TRUTH AND RECONCILIATION COMMISSION (NTRC).

HUME (GI-, BI-). The souls of people who died violent deaths. In traditional Burundi culture, the *bihume* played a major role; they were said to be malevolent and to wander around seeking humans to disturb. Many people still wear charms for protection against their curses.

HUTU. The Hutu comprise the majority of Burundi's population but have historically been subservient to the minority **Tutsi** population; they are usually numbered at about 85 percent of the total population. They arrived in the region perhaps as early as the 11th century and were traditionally subsistence-level farmers. The Hutu also engaged in food production, ironwork, weaving, woodcarving, and basketry, but in modern days, most of these skills have been lost to the Hutu and are primarily done by the **Twa**.

The Hutu subservience to the Tutsi has created centuries of discord in the country, continuing into the postindependence years. Although in the majority, Hutu had fewer opportunities for **education**; as a result of this, and in addition to it, the Hutu were less likely to be found in civil service, government, and the **army**. They were almost totally dominated in these areas and maintained very little political power. In 1993, Burundi held its first democratic, multiparty **elections**, and **Melchior Ndadaye**, a Hutu civilian, was elected. Unfortunately, because the Hutu were still virtually unrepresented in the national army, Ndadaye was soon ousted from office and assassinated by members of the army; this sent the country into 12 years of civil war, causing the deaths of approximately 300,000 people. Many Hutu organized into rebel militia groups, who fought the Burundi government forces from their countries of exile as well as from within Burundi. Eventually, most of these rebel groups disarmed and joined the transitional government that resulted from the **Arusha Accord**. This peace agreement ensured that the Hutu majority would have a majority representation in the government and at least an equal representation in the armed forces and the national police force. *See also* HUTU AND TUTSI, RELATIONS BETWEEN.

HUTU AND TUTSI, RELATIONS BETWEEN. Historically, at least in the view of many Western scholars and readers, the relationship between these two major ethnic groups is a primary factor in the culture of Burundi, as well as in the neighboring countries of **Rwanda** and the **Democratic Republic of the Congo** (DRC). They have a complex relationship, and numerous conflicts have occurred between the two groups. Conflicts between the **Hutu** and **Tutsi** are estimated to have caused five million deaths (in all three countries) just since the early 1990s; in the 30 years before that, there were many more.

It is important to note that the groups are not so simply defined as any description might imply; there are many factions and belief systems within each group, as well as those that span both, or parts of both, groups. Formally, each group name would carry the prefixes attached to classes 1 and 2 for humans (*see* the reader's note earlier in this volume). Therefore, they would be, in the plural, Bahutu and Batutsi, but the simple forms will be used here.

The relative populations of Hutu and Tutsi have been a source of controversy; the usual figures given are that the Hutu number about 85 percent of the population and the Tutsi about 14 percent. Formal census statistics are hard to find; some modern politicians say that those figures were never true, but were the mistaken estimates of Europeans who assumed that anyone who owned cattle was a Tutsi. It should also be noted that Hutu and Tutsi have intermarried for many generations, thus blurring ethnic distinctions. In any case, whatever census numbers do exist are certainly quite old and probably too outdated to any longer be relevant.

The European occupation of Burundi did not change the apparent unequal division of wealth. Many modern politicians and scholars say that ruling through the Tutsi was natural for the Europeans because of the Europeans' racist beliefs that the Tutsi, who were, on average, taller and lighter skinned, were also more intelligent. But the *ganwa* held most of the political and all of the royal power; the **Germans** and later the **Belgians** ruled through those already in power.

How much of this perpetuation of the ethnic division was conscious on the part of the Europeans is not completely clear. Early documents and books do, in fact, make a point of mentioning the physical differences between the groups. In one of the most cited, *Die Barundi*, Hans Meyer spends several pages on it, as well as many pages on the mental characteristics of the two groups. He describes the Hutu as "like all Bantu . . . by nature intelligent and [with] a lively and sanguine temperament. . . . In spite of their impulsive behavior, the Bahutu are incapable of any strong exertion of will. They are conservative out of inertia and indifference." Later, he says of the Tutsi, "Gradually one discovers the secret of the tremendous superiority of the relatively few Batussi [sic] over the one and a half million Bahutu: they are greatly superior to them in intelligence, calmness, composure, cruelty, cunning, racial pride, solidarity, and political talent" (English translation by Helmut Handzik). One fact of the colonial period was that, in the later years of outside rule, as nationalism began to emerge, fearing unity between Hutu and Tutsi, Belgian rulers banned any **political party** that crossed ethnic lines and encouraged the political parties primarily based on ethnicity.

At the current stage of history, however, these old outside opinions of the two groups are not as relevant as how the two groups view each other. That view, unfortunately, is very negative and has been very negative since the country's independence in 1962. There has been a series of brutal civil wars and massacres, usually springing from the ethnic inequality and mutual dislike and fear. The facts are that from independence until 1993 there was only one Hutu head of state (briefly); all of the political leaders came from the minority population, as did most members of the national **army**. It is also true that the first Hutu president (**Melchior Ndadaye**, elected in 1993 in the first democratic **election**) was assassinated—just a few months after taking office—in a coup attempt by the army. Serious ethnic civil wars, each killing many hundreds of thousands of people, occurred in 1965, 1972, 1988, and 1993, with the last one continuing for 12 years as a series of attacks by the army on villages and Hutu militia groups and by Hutu militia on the army and on civilians.

The world took more notice of the small country following the 1972 massacre, which is said to have eliminated the vast majority of Hutu intellectuals and emerging political leaders. It was also the massacre that saw the death of Burundi's last monarch, **Ntare V**. The world again began to pay heed to the country during the latest extended period of unrest, which corresponded to an ethnic civil war in neighboring **Rwanda** as well. The **Organization of African Unity** continues to examine the ethnic concerns in the region, but also continues to recommend preparation for the worst.

One of the most respected and prolific of all Burundi scholars, René Lemarchand, says, "Nowhere in Africa has so much violence killed so many people on so many occasions in so small a space as in Burundi during the years following independence" (*Burundi*, 1994, xi). Even before the most recent series of massacres, another important Burundi scholar, Catharine Watson, said: "The Hutu burn with the idea that they have always been oppressed. The Tutsi are haunted by the idea that they are the Palestinians of East Africa, about to be hounded from Burundi, already driven from Rwanda" ("After the Massacre," 1989, 51).

The ethnic conflicts of Burundi and Rwanda remain intertwined even today. Some scholars have, over the years, suggested many possible solutions to the problem, some even suggesting that the region should designate one country for Hutu and the other one for Tutsi. While this radical solution was never seriously considered, Burundi's newfound peace has come because of an intricate power-sharing agreement, the **Arusha Accord**, that guarantees both groups a say in the government and in the national army and police force.

HUTURA (KU–)KWI-)). Because of the many years of **Tutsi** domination and, some say, the resulting **Hutu** self-hatred in Burundi, a phenomenon has been observed whereby Hutu undergo this "shedding" of their ethnicity. *Kwihutura* literally means "to de-utuize oneself."

– I –

IBARE (ICI-, IVY-). If the *mwami* had a residence in the territory of a chief or subchief, this residence was immune from local jurisdiction. Literally, *icibare* means an area reserved for a child, and *icibare c'umwami* means a royal privilege.

ICA (KW-). The act of murder. There were a great many possible punishments for murder in the traditional society, some of which remain viable today. The assassination of a *mwami*, a prince, or a chief carried the death penalty, not only for the murderer but for all members of his immediate family. The murderer himself would be crucified and then castrated. Most murders of ordinary Barundi (regardless of ethnicity) were avenged by individual families, but the punishment was symbolically pronounced by the mwami. The death penalty was the usual pronouncement; the family or the clan usually decided on the method.

IGITSHUTSU. Traditional beliefs of Burundi are that all people and animals possess the same principal life force, which is projected into physical existence. This universal soul, *igitshutsu*, disappears when an animal dies, but is transformed into a spirit of the dead when a human dies.

IJENDA. Shortly before the aborted **Hutu** revolt in 1972, the southern **Tutsi**, known as the **Bururi** group, who had been traditionally kept out of the political system, were on the verge of a violent clash with Tutsi from central and northern Burundi. The group in this conflict that had the northern location was the Ijenda.

IKIZA. Literally meaning "catastrophe," *ikiza* is sometimes used to describe the residual fear and mutual ethnic suspicion that remain in Burundi even today and that prevent a peaceful coexistence of the citizens.

IMANA. Probably at least 65 to 70 percent of Barundi have been converted to Christianity, but those (both **Hutu** and **Tutsi**) who have not still share traditional animistic **religious** beliefs in which Imana, a powerful spirit, is the Creator. In fact, even many of the country's Christians still practice some of these traditional rituals. When he took corporeal form, Imana was always a white lamb with no markings; he was said to skip and gambol about. The term *imana* also refers to the force of good that causes such things as prosperity, joy, peace, and fertility and is the intangible life force of all things both organic and inorganic. Human beings, animals, plants, stones, fire, and rivers all have *imana*, a soul.

There are no institutionalized public cults, idols, or priests dedicated to Imana (he is honored but not feared because he has no power to harm), but individuals perform informal ceremonies. For example, a woman might leave a pitcher of water for Imana before going to sleep at night with the hope that he will make her fertile. In fact, traditionally, no married woman who still had expectations of child bearing would ever go to bed without seeing that there was water (*amazi y'Imana*) in the house because Imana was supposed to create during the night. Creation was not thought to occur at the moment of conception only, but to continue for several nights; if Imana found no water, he might not be able to create correctly. A ritual performed usually by Hutu centers around the belief that the smooth stones in brooks and rivers carry the power of Imana. Several stones (*inguru*) are collected and placed in a small hut built outside the *rugo*; the stones are given offerings of meat, milk, broken pots, pumpkin shells, and beer (*terekera*). The belief is that eventually they give birth to 20 or 30 additional stones, demonstrating spiritual fertility.

There are few if any creation myths or legends concerning Imana's relationship with humans, but within the oral tradition, stories tell of Imana's travels through the country. One story tells of Imana's becoming visible in order to chase death. There is a saying in Kirundi that indicates the country's strong belief in a superior being: *Imana Y'I Burundi* ("Burundi is Imana's country"). Both the Barundi and the Banyarwanda have many praise names for Imana; some of the more common ones are Rurema, the Creator (*-rema*, "create"); Rugaba, the Giver (*-gaba*, "give, rule"); Rugiravyose, the Doer of All (*-gira*, "do"; *-vyose*, "all"); and Inchanyi, the Fire Lighter (*-chana*, "light a fire" or "blow up a fire").

An oral tradition explains why Imana no longer lives among humans as he once did. He used to talk to humans, causing the development of children, until one day he created a disabled child. The parents were very angry and began looking for an opportunity to kill Imana with a knife. Of course, Imana saw all of this and said, "If they are going to behave like that, I will depart to my own place and not show myself any more. Then I can create as I please, and if they are not satisfied, they can just grumble!" As a result, the tradition tells us, he never shows himself any more, but some are lucky enough to see him in his occasional unguarded moments.

There are many Kirundi words that have derived from the name Imana. For example, *ivyamana* means divine attributes or the attributes of a soothsayer; *igihamana* (plural: *ibihamana*) means a godsend or good luck; *indoramana* means theology or theological; *ikimana* is a false god or idol; *ikiremamana* (plural: *ibiremamana*) is a congenital defect or malformation; *ubuyobokamana* is faith and service to Imana; and *bumana* is a natural state. *See also GURU*; *IGITSHUTSU*; *KA*; KIRANGA; *PFUMU*; RWUBA.

IMANA KAMINUZA. During the early days of independence, **UPRONA** (Parti de l'Union et du Progrès National) divided into two factions, and the breach was never fully healed. In September 1964, this summit conference was held in Kitega (present-day **Gitega**), and the impasse between the two factions was made clear. About 20 **Hutu** and **Tutsi** from each wing of the party came together to, according to a report from the conference, "debate in common the means to achieve national unity . . . and the total reconciliation of the UPRONA leaders." To that end, they gave priority to "the constitution of a single Executive Committee."

IMFURA. According to anthropologist **Ethel Albert**, *imfura* implies "speaking well" and is one of the primary characteristics of good breeding and aristocracy. She states that, among the upper classes, the ideals of oratorical ability are most stressed and that aristocratic boys are given formal **education** in speech making from about the age of 10. This education includes the composition of impromptu speeches appropriate in relations with superiors in status or age, formulas for petitioning a superior for a gift, composition of praise poems (*amazina*), self-defensive rhetoric intended to deflect an accusation or the anger of a superior, and formulas for addressing social inferiors, for funeral orations, for making judgments in disputes, or for serving as an intermediary. *See also ZINA.*

INANJONAKI. The mother of **Ntare I** Rushatsi, the first king of Burundi. According to some oral traditions, Ntare's father is unknown; according to others, his name was Rufuko, but little more is said about him.

INARARIBONYE. By 1961, many of the old **UPRONA** chiefs had severed their ties with the party in order to set up their own political organizations. **Léopold Biha**, who never forgave Prince **Louis Rwagasore** for his political views or his popularity, founded the Inararibonye Party in 1961. In Kirundi, the name refers to the elders and is often associated with a legend about Mwami **Mwezi IV** Gisabo. After killing a lion, the *mwami* removed the skin and wore it as a cape. As the sun became hotter, the skin began to shrink and to choke him. At this time, the Inararibonye arrived and took the mwami to a nearby lake, immersing him in the water and freeing him from the lion skin.

INARYANGOMBE. Kiranga's mother, also given as Inakiranga, Njanja, or Kajumbu. According to Bernard Zuure, to explain the independent and rebellious spirit that Kiranga exhibited, she once lamented: "Tell me, people from here. / I gave birth to an imbecile. / He is a bad subject. / I tell him this: / Rwogamabenge [her name for Kiranga] do not go far away / You will die there. / He does not listen, he goes. / Stop, do not go into the bush alone. / He does not listen, he goes."

INDER FRAGE. In the early part of the 20th century, the **Germans** considered the many non-African, non-European merchants in Ruanda-Urundi to be a problem. They referred to this problem as the *Inder Frage* or "Indian Question" (by "Indian" was meant all Asians). This was controlled through the governor's ordinance of March 1905, declaring that "until further notice entrance to the sultanates of Ruanda and Urundi is permitted only from the military station of Usumbura [**Bujumbura**], and only with written permission from the district officer."

INKINZO. As one of the radical **Tutsi**-based **political parties** that became vocal after the death of President **Melchior Ndadaye** and the ensuing massacres, the Inkinzo Party stated that the **FRODEBU** government should be tried for crimes against humanity. Among these crimes, it listed the spread of killings on the hillsides and the refusal of government officials to leave foreign embassies, an act that was described as caring more for their own safety than that of the population at large.

INTAGOHEKAS. Following the death of President **Cyprien Ntaryamira** and the subsequent shakiness of the coalition government, Intagohekas ("those who never sleep"), an extremist **Hutu** militia group, were known to chase **Tutsi** from the hills in the countryside (where mostly Hutu lived) and to attack **refugee** camps where tens of thousands of displaced Tutsi lived.

INTERNATIONAL AID. Burundi is a very poor country, and its long periods of civil unrest have further slowed its development. As a result, the country is very dependent on foreign aid, which has been sporadic throughout the country's history. In 1996, following **Pierre Buyoya**'s coup to regain the presidency, other countries in the region placed economic sanctions on the country, curtailing all but the most basic humanitarian aid and trade. This further devastated an already weak **economy**. Since 2000, however, and the beginning of a real peace process in Burundi, other countries in the region, as well as the rest of the international community, have pledged large sums to help the country rebuild.

Burundi remains heavily dependent upon foreign financial aid and technical assistance, with Belgium as the main donor in the period following independence. The **United States**, France, **Germany**, and the **United Nations** have also granted financial and technical assistance. In early 2005, for example, Germany pledged $9.5 million specifically for a water supply project, rehabilitation of **refugees**, and **HIV/AIDS** prevention and control. In addition, the Belgian government granted Burundi two million euros ($2.4 million) to pay civil servants' salaries and help boost the country's social stability. For long-term aid plans, a joint Belgium-Burundi commission will determine priorities for international aid.

Also in 2005, United Nations Development Program donors from several countries and institutions pledged more than $1 billion over a three-year period to strengthen peace and security, promote reconciliation, and spur development; the countries involved include the United States ($135 million), Great Britain ($50 million), Germany ($46.2 million), and Belgium ($44.6 million), along with the European Union ($279 million) and the World Bank ($140 million). Unfortunately, not all of the money that was pledged actually came through; a shortage of funds caused the United Nations World Food Program to slash its food aid to more than two million Barundi.

In addition to these pledges of aid, the International Monetary Fund and the World Bank in August 2005 offered Burundi debt relief under the Enhanced Heavily Indebted Poor Countries (HIPC) Initiative, which, over time, will lower Burundi's debt payments by approximately $1.5 billion in debt. Furthermore, various agencies of the United Nations have contributed funds for specific **educational**, **agricultural**, and social programs, all aimed at the eventual economic independence and sustainability of the country.

After the democratic elections of 2005, the Burundi government offered free primary education; they then appealed to the international community for $35 million to expand its educational sector.

INYENZI. Literally "cockroaches," Inyenzi is a secret terrorist organization comprised of **Tutsi** exiles from **Rwanda**. They made three attempts to invade Rwanda in November and December 1963; the second (on 20 December) coincided with the breakup of a conference between the Rwanda and Burundi governments on the dissolution of their customs and monetary union. This conference had been acrimonious at times, and the Rwanda government suspected that the Burundi government gave the Inyenzi free rein to invade at the end of the conference. The Burundi authorities denied this.

IYEREZI (MU-, BA-). There were traditionally many types of ceremonial dances, the most highly admired dancers being the **Twa**. Men and women never danced together; rather, dancing was primarily for entertaining in the court. At the courts of kings and chiefs, there was always a carefully selected troupe of dancers, the *abiyerezi*, chosen from the young warriors. *See also* MUSIC AND DANCE.

– J –

JAMBO (I-, MA-). Verbal ability has long been highly regarded in Burundi society, making the oral tradition a strong one. In Kirundi, this general term refers to speech or eloquence (in Swahili, it is a greeting). Because the kingdom of Burundi was historically less centralized than **Rwanda**, fewer poems, songs, and stories chronicle the history of the country; nevertheless, the richness of the oral arts exists. Criteria for classification of such arts vary depending on whether one is primarily concerned with content or form, but many historians have distinguished four large categories, each containing several smaller groups (plural forms are given below, followed by the singular prefix in parentheses, if relevant).

The first is the narrative genre. Included in this group are the *imigani (mu-)*, which include fairy tales, fables, legends, and myths; the *ibitito* or *ibitiko (gi-)*, dramatic stories interspersed with song; and the *ibiganiro* or *ibiyago (ki-)*, dialogue stories and chronicles.

The second large category contains the puzzles and proverbs. These include *ibisokozo* or *ibisokoranyo (gi-)*, riddles; *imigani (mu)*, proverbs; and *imyigovyoro (mu-)*, truisms or adages.

The third category comprises musical and lyrical stories. Among them are *uguhoza umwana*, lullabies; *ugucura intimba*, laments; *imvyino*, wedding songs; and *ibimpwiri* (*ki-*), rounds sung by men and accompanied by hand clapping. Within this third category are two smaller groupings: *ugukeza umuvyeyi*, songs praising motherhood; and songs that are specialized according to the musical instrument that accompanies them. Examples of the latter are the *inanga*, songs accompanied by the zither.

The fourth, and perhaps largest, category comprises the *amazina*, which are discussed at length under their own entry (*zina*), and the *ibicuba* (*gi-*) or praises of pastoralism. *See also HOZA UMWANA*; MUSIC AND DANCE.

JEUNESSE NATIONALISTE RWAGASORE (JNR)/RWAGASORE NATIONALIST YOUTH. The origins of the JNR (initially known as the Union Culturelle de la Jeunesse Africaine du Burundi) go back to 1959. The statutes of the original organization said,

> Our movement aims at leading humanity towards a greater fraternity, a greater mutual understanding, a greater peace and happiness. . . . Its goals are to orient our **youth** towards a more mature form of nationalism, through appropriate civic training; to inculcate in our future generations of leaders a sense of mutual understanding . . . and to affirm the ideal of equality among all citizens.

Shortly before independence, the government wanted to use the JNR as a "parallel structure" for maintaining peace and order in the African quarters of **Bujumbura**. It became the youth division of the **UPRONA** Party around the time of independence.

Under the leadership of **Prime Nyongabo** and **François Bangemu**, the JNR took on an activist role, which remained its primary characteristic. In January 1962, the JNR launched a series of armed raids against some trade union leaders belonging to the **Parti du Peuple (PP)**. Included in these raids was arson against four houses in the **Kamenge** neighborhood of Bujumbura, during the course of which four prominent **Hutu** leaders were killed, including Severin Ndinzurwaha, permanent secretary of the Christian trade union organization Mouvement Populaire Chrétien, and Jean Nduwabika, president of the union and secretary-general of the PP.

This prompted the *mwami* to dissolve the association and incarcerate its leaders. In 1966, the JNR reformed, still in open defiance of the mwami's instructions.

JEUNESSE RWAGASORE RÉVOLUTIONNAIRE (JRR)/ REVOLUTIONARY RWAGASORE YOUTH. On 10 February 1967, Radio Bujumbura reported that all of the country's **youth** organizations had merged into this one large group.

JIJI (MU-, BA-). A very high-level **Hutu** family that had ties with *ganwa* and the court of the *mwami*. Their alternate name was Abarangaranga, "people of **Kiranga**," and they came from Nkoma in southeastern Burundi. Their roles in the court were many and varied; for example, they served as singers at the weddings of princes. Additionally, it was from this clan that guardians of the royal drum (**Karyenda**) and the wives of Kiranga (**Mukakiranga**) were chosen, and it was also often from this group that subchiefs in the countryside were chosen.

JUDICIAL SYSTEM. *See* GOVERNMENT SYSTEM.

– K –

KA (IN-, IN-). *Inka* (cattle) have been central to many aspects of Burundi society for almost as long as the society has existed. Cows were the basis of the patron–client relationships that dominated the precolonial social and economic structure of the country. An exchange of cattle usually confirmed important agreements. For example, they were traditionally the preferred form of *kwano*, bride wealth. Cows were not generally a source of food, but were regarded almost as living gold, the most highly prized form of wealth and a symbol of prestige; in fact, they were traditionally used for almost anything people in the modern world would use money, for example, payment of a loan or salary. There is a popular saying in Burundi that is translated as "Down with the franc, long live the cow, source of all life."

Because cows are dedicated to **Imana**, they are afforded respect through prayer, attentive care, and taboos. For example, Barundi never boil or even heat milk, because doing so could cause the cow to have a sore udder and stop giving milk; milk may not be drunk on the same day that peas or peanuts are eaten; if a person has an open wound, he or she cannot watch a cow give birth because this would cause the wound to become worse. Myths, legends, and epics abound that illustrate the ways in which cattle and people share their lives. Even in postcolonial days, traditional greetings such as *"Amashyo"* ("May you have herds") and the response *"Amashongore"* ("I wish you herds of females") can sometimes still be heard. "Darling, your eyes are like those of a cow" is considered a profound compliment. *See also KUTSI.*

KABURA, CELESTIN. Before the days of the power-sharing government in the late 1990s, Kabura was one of the approximately 5 percent of Burundi **army** soldiers who were **Hutu**; he has been quoted speaking out against the military. In 1995, he said that the Hutu politicians do not trust the army and, as a result, they insist on keeping some of the very few Hutu soldiers as bodyguards. "When someone kills a Hutu, soldiers go laughing. They don't bother catching them." Kabura also claimed that some **Tutsi** soldiers supply Tutsi militias with grenades and bayonets.

KAGEORGIS, JEAN. An unemployed Greek mercenary, Kageorgis was the assassin who killed Prince **Louis Rwagasore**. Although his role in the assassination was not questioned and he was sentenced to death for it, it was also clear from the beginning that it was a much bigger conspiracy and that he was nothing but a hired killer; the murder was masterminded by **Joseph Biroli** and **Jean Ntitendereza**, the leaders of the **Parti Démocratique Chrétien** and the sons of Chief **Baranyanka**.

KAMAKARE (MU-, BA-). These female counselors to the royal court were aides in charge of milking, among other duties, during the reign of **Mwezi IV** Gisabo.

KAMANA, JEAN PAUL. Imprisoned in Uganda since November 1994, Kamana is accused of directing the assassination of President **Melchior Ndadaye**, which he has denied. He claims that he only told the soldiers to negotiate with the president and that mutinous soldiers held their guns on him as he tried to reach the room where the president was being held. He has not been charged with any crime in Uganda, and Burundi and Uganda do not have an extradition treaty. Several **human rights** organizations, including Human Rights Watch/Africa, submitted a report in July 1994 stating bluntly that the direct commander of the assassination of the president was Lt. Kamana. As a prisoner, Kamana has complained about inaction by the **United Nations High Commissioner for Refugees (UNHCR)**. An officer in that organization has said that these alleged putschists are a dilemma for them because many want to be resettled in a third country, but the UNHCR does not want to get involved with the protection of criminals.

Kamana has continued to maintain that he was framed. In an article by Catharine Watson and Alan Zarembo, he was quoted as saying, "The mutinous soldiers came to my residence and put me into a jeep and took me to the palace. But I told them to stop firing. That created an atmosphere of mistrust between me and them, so they locked me up in a room in the tank barracks. I was in that room when Ndadaye was killed." An international inquiry of the events of October 1993 reported that Kamana addressed a large group of excited troops on a barracks basketball court and announced that Ndadaye would be killed. In 1999, Burundi's Supreme Court sentenced Kamana, who was still in Uganda, along with four other former **army** officers, to death for their participation in Ndadaye's assassination.

KAMATARI. The brother of **Mwambutsa IV** and a descendent of the Bataga. *See also* BAMBUTSA AND BATAGA.

KAMATARI, ESTHER. In October 2004, Kamatari announced her candidacy for president of Burundi in the anticipated 2005 **elections**. Kamatari is a niece of the last *mwami* of Burundi; as a member of the *ganwa* (royal clan), she said that she came from a group with "no blood on its hands." Her plan was to "reconcile Burundians with themselves" by electing her and also restoring the monarchy in the country. She led the Abahuza ("Rally") Party while living in France, where she has lived since the early 1970s. In 1970, after many members of the royal family were killed, Kamatari fled Burundi. Since then, she has lived in Paris and has had a successful career as a model, the first black supermodel in France.

KAMENGE. A suburb of **Bujumbura** that has a history of violence in the ongoing struggle between **Hutu** and **Tutsi**. The people of the area (primarily Hutu) have more than once been the victims of attacks by Tutsi political groups and **army** personnel. In January 1962, the president of the **Jeunesse Nationaliste Rwagasore (JNR), Prime Nyongabo**, held a meeting in Kamenge and shortly afterward launched a series of armed attacks against some Hutu. In this suburb, four houses were set on fire, and during what later became called the "Kamenge incidents," four prominent Hutu were killed. The riots that followed understandably created an even more explosive atmosphere in the country, which helped to strengthen ethnic division within **UPRONA**. In the following two years, a group of Hutu students began to plot against the government in retaliation for these incidents. After the 1992 events, many sanctions were set against the JNR, which was eventually dissolved by the *mwami*. The organization resurfaced in 1966.

Following the attempted coup and the assassination of President **Melchior Ndadaye** in 1993, Kamenge, called by some the "last Hutu stronghold," once again emerged as a location of violence. Several incidents occurred, involving the mostly Tutsi army and Hutu militia groups in the area; the one involving the highest death toll as well as the most concern from the **Organization of African Unity** and the **United Nations** occurred in June 1995. During a three-day period, army personnel surrounded the suburb where Hutu militia were alleged to be hiding; at a time reported to be 13 hours before the time given to civilians as a deadline to evacuate, the army entered the neighborhood, leaving between 25 and 40 people (mostly children and elderly) dead. Another series of repercussions resulted from this attack, one of which left nine dead in Musaga, a Tutsi neighborhood. Throughout Burundi's 12-year civil war, Kamenge remained a dangerous neighborhood; it was often the location of raids by both the national **army** and rebel groups. *See also* NDINZURWAHA, SEVERIN; NDUWABIKE, JEAN; NDUWAYO, ANTOINE; NTAWUMENYAKARIZI, BASILE.

KAMYI (MU-, BA-). There are two different historical roles attributed to these people of honor in the court of the *mwami*. Some sources say they were tutors to the royal children as well as something similar to court protocol officers. The more common description of their role was that of royal milkers. These were young **Tutsi** males, chosen from very noble families, usually of the Banyakarana clan. A young milker spent a lot of time being initiated into the rites of the court; he did not have direct contact with the royal cows until he reached the age of 15. The milkers were required to remain celibate; any sexual contact rendered them ineligible for royal service. Many considered these young men to posess supernatural powers.

KANDEKE, JEAN. In late 1962, when the **Jeunesse Nationaliste Rwagasore (JNR)** made threats of violence against **Hutu** trade unionists and politicians, Kandeke was among the victims. At that time, he was a supporter of the **Parti du Peuple (PP)** and was in charge of a local cooperative. The threats were sometimes only that, but Kandeke was bludgeoned almost to death by a group of JNR militants.

KANUGUNU. Considered by many to be the most powerful and energetic of **Ntare I**'s descendants (he was his great-grandson), this chief was also the most influential of all the **Batare** during the reign of **Mwezi IV** Gisabo. In his attempt to follow Ntare's policy, Gisabo waged long wars against his opponents in all areas of the country. During these wars, Kanugunu was killed, apparently with the assistance of the **German** troops, thus deepening the long hatred between the Bezi and the Batare.

KANYENKIKO, ANATOLE. In early 1995, a coalition government comprising at least 13 **political parties** and led by President **Sylvestre Ntibantunganya** was in office, apparently struggling to keep peace following the deaths of presidents **Melchior Ndadaye** and **Cyprien Ntaryamira**. The leader of the strongest opposition party, **Charles Mukasi**, threatened to topple the fragile government, but said he did not want to use violence to achieve his ends. In February, his party, **UPRONA**, virtually shut down **Bujumbura** in a general strike to press for the resignation of Prime Minister Kanyenkiko; some hardliners in UPRONA considered him to be too sympathetic to Ntibantunganya's government. Kanyenkiko said that he would not resign until the two major parties agreed on his successor, but Mukasi said the strike would continue until Kanyenkiko's government collapsed. Kanyenkiko finally did resign, about a week after the beginning of the strike, and was replaced by Prime Minister **Antoine Nduwayo**. Kanyenkiko said in a statement read on state radio that he had quit in the interest of the country and "to avoid problems such as steering Burundi in the same path as **Rwanda**."

KARANI (MU-, BA-). A general term referring to assistants, secretaries, or scribes, who were traditionally those responsible for the historical record keeping of the chiefdoms and the court. The secretary of a chiefdom was called *umukarani w'igihugu c'umuganwa*, and the secretary to the *mwami* was called *yare umukarani w'umwami*.

KARIBWAMI, PONTIEN. The president of Parliament during the brief tenure of President **Melchior Ndadaye** in 1993. Like the president and other members of the government at that time, Karibwami had also been a **refugee** following the 1972 massacres. He was killed during the 1993 coup attempt during which President Ndadaye was also killed.

KARYENDA. The royal or sacred drum, a symbol of the office of kingship and, in turn, a symbol of social and political unity. Traditionally, when the *mwami* killed the enemies of the kingdom, the victims' genitals were hung from the drum. The traditional royal court had many rituals and ceremonies that included and even centered around the Karyenda. The symbolic wife of Karyenda is **Mukakaryenda**. Karyenda is one of the three main pillars of the monarchy, along with **Kiranga** and cattle (*inka*). *See also KA*; MPOTSA; MUSIC AND DANCE.

KASHIRAHAMWE, PASCAL. A brother-in-law of **Michel Micombero** and a member of the "**Family Corporation**," Kashirahamwe was president of the Banque Commerciale. As such, he dominated the economics of Burundi during his tenure.

KEBA (MU-, BA-). Personal rivals or competitors. In the oral tradition of the society, stories and proverbs were invented and repeated about these people.

KEVVI (MU-, BA-). Under the *ubugabire* system of patronage, these were the very important court cooks, who had the complete trust of the *mwami*. They also were responsible for carving and serving meat in royal households. *See also GABIRE.*

KILIMA. Although Chief Kilima's real identity is obscure, it is clear that he was one of **Mwezi IV** Gisabo's most formidable rivals. According to legend (some begun by Kilima himself), he was the descendant of one of **Ntare II**'s sons, Nyanumusango, who had lived with the Bafulero in the Congo for a time. One of Nyanamusango's sons, Njitshi, married a Bafulero girl named Naabakile, who bore Kilima. In later years, Kilima allied himself with a group of chiefs of the Ruzizi Valley and established his claims over the northwestern region of Burundi by finding followers among the **Hutu** and murdering all existing **Tutsi** there; he became known as "Batutsi-killer." Note that, if these legends are to be believed, Kilima and Gisabo were closely related by blood; this rivalry would then show clearly the long-standing hatred between **Batare and Bezi**, including fratricidal strife between Gisabo and his elder brothers.

Kilima's territory continued to grow during the **German** occupation and with the coming of the **Belgians**. Later, Kilima's four sons, Ruhabira, Rusimbi, Kalibwami, and Rwasha, were each given extensive tracts of land by the Belgian administration. One oral tradition states that Kilima, who had been a rival claimant to the throne, was killed by Gisabo; Kilima's head was then displayed in the royal *kraal*. However, Gisabo died in 1908, and Kilima probably died later.

KINIGI, SILVIE (1953–). After the first democratic **election** in June 1993, which voted in the first **Hutu** president, Kinigi (a **Tutsi** married to a Hutu) was appointed prime minister. She lived through the original violence in October of that year, being granted asylum at the French embassy. At that time, she said, "It's very difficult to say who has power now. The **army** does not seem to want to lose it. I have no military, no police force, and no control of the media. I have nothing." She said she believed that the coup leaders panicked when they realized they were faced with a popular uprising by Burundians who had overwhelmingly voted for President **Melchior Ndadaye**. Kinigi reported that 60 percent of the army was still loyal to her and that the coup had been organized by officers mainly from Burure Province. She also appealed for international military intervention, saying that there was no guarantee of the security of civilian governments at that stage and that she could not "approve of my government entering into negotiations with people who assassinated our leaders." Several days after the attempted coup, Kinigi took control of the country again and ordered troops back to the barracks, promising to punish those taking part in the coup.

Several months later, in April 1994, following the death of Burundi's next president along with the president of **Rwanda**, Kinigi declared, "There is now an open war between the army and these Hutu mercenaries [Hutu militants were arming peasants in the countryside]." She reported that the only hope was that Burundians would become exhausted by the fighting. She, like many moderate residents of the country, also saw the problems of 1993 and 1994 as resulting from democracy being thrust on the country too abruptly: "We entered into democracy without having the means of dealing with it. The process was too rapid. There was no time to form political leaders. So parties formed on the simple criteria of ethnicity. With Rwanda, we have in common inexperience in democracy and ineptness in managing power."

KIRANGA. An early Kirundi–English dictionary written for a missionary group defines *Kiranga* as an "evil spirit worshipped by Barundi; similar to Satan." This definition, while often repeated in later descriptions, does not do justice to the spirit of Kiranga. Also known as Rikiranga or Ryangombe, he is, in the traditional **religion**, the powerful leader of all ancestral spirits and the hero spirit. Barundi traditionally believed that Kiranga could prevent **Imana** from helping people, so they had to placate him in order to leave a clear channel for Imana's blessings to flow through. There is little or no prayer directly to Imana; most of the worship is to Kiranga. Oral traditions say that he came from **Rwanda** during the time of the clan state. It is believed that he was killed by a buffalo while hunting, and then all of his friends committed suicide near his body; Imana gave them a special place to lead lives of pleasure.

Young men perform rituals, chants, and dances to honor Kiranga. During the *kubandwa*, a grain harvest festival, these young men paint themselves and decorate small spirit huts. One of the groups personifies Kiranga, who appears carrying a sacred spear.

There are priests who are the human abodes of Kiranga's spirit and who act as mediators between spirits and people. The priests' positions are usually attained through heredity and inherited talent, but occasionally a man may be seized by the spirit and given the power of mediation. When an offering is made, the priests may speak to the spirits, delivering prophesies. Although the sect has some features of a cult (members traditionally believed that nonmembers would burn in an eternal fire), it is one area that has abolished ethnic differences as a consideration. Kiranga's initiates of varying degrees of rank call themselves *abana b'Imana*, "the children of Imana."

The worship of Kiranga is thought to have originated in the long-disputed area around the current border between Rwanda and Burundi some time before the early 17th century. In Burundi, based on oral tradition as well as historical probability, Kiranga almost certainly predated the reign of **Ntare I**, although some legends have the two arriving simultaneously and establishing a mutually dependent relationship. Indeed, there was an ambivalent relationship between Kiranga's followers and the court, influenced by two factors: that the religious system was in place before the beginning of the dynasty and that there simply were now two royal figures. A Burundi proverb even proclaimed "Kiranga is the king of all beings, living or not." F. M. Rodegem, through the recording of Burundi texts, suggested that Kiranga respected the *mwami* and that the mwami feared Kiranga and was wary of opposing his decisions. Over time, kings devised myths proclaiming their superiority over Kiranga. *See also* *BANDWA*; *GAHIGI*; INARYANGOMBE; *JIJI*; MUKAKIRANGA; *PFUMU*; *ROZI*; *SHEGU*; *SIGO* AND *KANGE*.

KIRUNDI. *See* LANGUAGE.

KORO (MU-, MI-). This was a tribute owed to the *mwami* or chief. It was paid in either labor or cash.

KORORA (GU-). Traditionally, there appear to be no formal laws against abortion, but it was often treated as a criminal offense. The practice (*gukorora*) was seldom mentioned publicly, but apparently, if an unmarried **woman** was pregnant, on rare occasions she might induce abortion by intense massage and herbal treatments.

KURA (GU-). In traditional Burundi society, there were few rituals associated with maturation. There were, for example, no rites associated with circumcision or clitoridectomy. Additionally, sexual taboos were not considered significant before *gukura*, the transition from childhood to puberty between the ages of 12 and 15.

KURU (BU-, IM-). This is translated as "senior person," "seniority," or "superiority" and is a guiding principle of all behavior. Caste order is known to all interlocutors in a context; thus, the order in which individuals speak in a group depends on their seniority. According to **Ethel Albert,**

> The senior person will speak first; the next in order of rank opens his speech with a statement to the effect of "Yes, I agree with the previous speaker; he is correct, he is older and knows best, etc." Then, depending on circumstances and issues, the second speaker will by degrees or at once express his own views, and these may well be diametrically opposed to those previously expressed. No umbrage is taken, the required formula of acknowledgment of the superior having been used.

KUTSI (MU-, BA-). In traditional society, cows (*inka*) were so important to the culture that these people were special servants whose only job was to collect cow dung from the enclosures. *See also KA.*

KUVAMUKIRIRI. The traditional Burundi naming ceremony. When a child has grown hair, is learning to walk, and is in decreasing danger of infant death, the kuvamukiriri takes place. Generally, names relate to attributes of **Imana**, familiar incidents, or events occurring around the time of birth. The Barundi are creative with names; some examples might be Kaimana ("Little Imana"), Mbonimana ("Gift of Imana"), or Keschimana ("Ornament of Imana"). A couple's 11th child is often named Misage ("To go too far"), the 12th Ijana ("Hundredth" or "Many"), and the 13th with a prayer to Imana to stop the overabundance of gifts: Niboyo ("Cease"). If a couple has lost several children during infancy or before, they sometimes guard a new child with names that mean such things as "mouse excrement" or "prostitute" in the hope that the name will be unattractive to malevolent spirits.

KWAHUKANA (Verb form: AHUKANA). Divorce was not very common in traditional society, and it almost always involved the denouncement of the woman or her abandonment of the home. If this happened, the parents of the couple would try to bring about a reconciliation. There were, however, a number of situations where the two partners mutually agreed to a divorce. There were also specific laws governing those faults of either partner that were grounds for the other demanding a divorce. The faults attributed to the wife included sterility (although the husband often simply chose polygamy as an alternative to divorce; polyandry was less often an option for **women**, but it was not unheard of); laziness or dirtiness; incurable illness; use of witchcraft against the husband, his parents, or his cattle; repeated adultery; incompatible personality; and refusal of conjugal relations. Faults attributed to the husband as possible grounds for divorce included insufficiency of the bride price (determined by the wife's father), insufficient feeding of the wife, grave public insult of the wife (although this would not include adultery, as the traditional society was, if not always practically, polygamous), incurable or contagious disease, and sexual impotence. In cases of legal divorce, children below the age of puberty stayed with their mother with an allowance from their father; then they became part of the paternal clan. *See also BUDUDIRA; GENI; KWANO; KWIRUKANA; TABWA; ZIRO.*

KWANO (IN-, IN-). The bride price or matrimonial price. Generally, in traditional Burundi society, cows (*inka*) served as gifts in the marriage contract (from the groom to the bride's family). There was no true marriage unless the matrimonial pledge was given; this exchange of gifts represented fertility in the coming marriage. The matrimonial price, of course, varied according to the class of the parties involved. The price for a princess could be as many as 15 cows. For a wealthy, non-*ganwa* **Tutsi** woman, the price was usually a pregnant cow and a heifer or, if that was not possible, a healthy cow and a heifer. Poorer Tutsi women brought, at least in principle, one pregnant cow. Among the **Hutu**, the traditional price was one cow or two bulls, if possible. *See also KA.*

KWASHIORKOR. This malnutrition condition was quite prevalent in young children because of the traditional Burundi diet, which included little protein. When the children were weaned, they changed to a predominantly carbohydrate diet. Kwashiorkor resulted in the deaths of many children, as well as a high rate of liver disorders among the survivors of the disease. Protein is now a larger part of the diet of the Barundi.

KWIRUKANA **(Verb form:** *IRUKANA***).** This condition of marital separation was usually the step before an official divorce was pronounced and was quite different from the situation of *intabwa*. The wife was free to either return to her family or search for better fortune elsewhere. The husband could always ask for his wife to return to their compound, and in some situations, he could demand it. *See also KWAHUKANA*; *TABWA*.

KWISHONGORA **(Verb form:** *ISHONGORA***).** Supposedly strictly to be performed by men, these traditional songs are long, lyrical, rhythmic declamations, full of trills and requiring a clear, fairly high-pitched voice. *See also* MUSIC AND DANCE.

– L –

LABOR UNIONS. According to the Confédération des Syndicats Libres du Burundi (Confederation of Free Unions of Burundi), an umbrella trade union, at least 60 percent of the 80,000 formal private-sector employees are unionized in Burundi. The **army**, police force, and foreigners are prohibited from participating in unions. The Labor Code of Burundi protects the rights of workers to form unions; however, there has been a fragile relationship between unions and the government for a long time. As recently as 2003, the president and treasurer of the Confédération des Syndicats du Burundi (Confederation of Burundi Labor Unions) were detained for several days and their organization's computer placed under police custody when the two men criticized the transitional government at a labor meeting. This was strongly protested by the International Confederation of Free Trade Unions in a letter stating that the detention "contravened

human rights and trade union rights, including the right to free speech, and was a curtailment of the union's freedom to analyze national political developments when workers' interests were at stake."

LAKES AND RIVERS. Lake Tanganyika is the most important body of water for Burundi, as well as being a border for three other countries (Zambia, **Tanzania**, and the **Democratic Republic of the Congo** or DRC). The lake holds 18 percent of the world's liquid fresh water and is a crucial food source for much of East Africa. It is the only port in Burundi. From 1995 to 2000, the Global Environmental Facility through the **United Nations** Development Program set up the Lake Tanganyika Biodiversity Project to ensure that the lake's biological diversity is maintained. Lake Tanganyika is regarded as one of the most biologically important habitats on Earth and serves as a showcase for evolutionary studies because of its great age, stability, and variety of plants and animals. Recently, the fish supplies have diminished, and marine biologists and environmentalists link this to global climate change.

Another lake important to Burundi is Lake Gacamirinda in the northeastern part of the country. Environmentalists fear that it is in danger of disappearing entirely due to a serious drought between 1998 and 2000 and the destruction of forests and water grasses.

There are many rivers in Burundi. The country's small rivers flow into the basins of two of the world's great rivers: the Congo and the Nile. The most important river flowing into the Congo Basin is the Ruzizi, which originates at Lake Kivu and forms part of the border between Burundi and the DRC. Among the tributaries of the Ruzizi are the Lua, the Nyamagana, the Kaburantwa, and the Mpanda. The Ruvubu and Kagera rivers are the southeastern sources of the Nile; along with the Kanyaru and the Lua, the Kagera forms the border between Burundi and **Rwanda**. The Ndahangwa, Dome, Mulembwe, and Nyengwe rivers flow into Lake Tanganyika. Burundi's southeastern region is drained by the Muragarazi River, which, along with the Ruvubu, separates Burundi from Tanzania. None of these rivers is navigable. *See also* ENVIRONMENT.

LANGUAGE. The national language of Burundi, Kirundi, is very closely related to and mutually intelligible with the language of neighboring **Rwanda**, Kinyarwanda. Both are members of the Bantu subgroup of the Niger-Congo linguistic family. Speakers of the two languages comprise the third largest group speaking any African language. The two larger groups speak Swahili and Lingala; Kirundi/Kinyarwanda differs from these two languages in that they are not *lingua francas* throughout large sections of Africa, but instead still function in their original areas.

Kirundi, as is characteristic of the Bantu subgroup, is a complex language from a Romance or Germanic perspective. Typical of Bantu languages is a system of gender categories, numbering between 13 and 19. These, of course, are not genders in the same sense as the common usage of the word; rather, they are general classifications of words that form categories, which in turn determine prefixes on all classes of words. Additionally, Kirundi is a tonal language—another difficulty for speakers of atonal Western languages. All verbs, for example, fall into one of two tone classes, distinguishable by the presence or absence of a high tone.

In 1948, **Malcolm Guthrie** classified Kirundi and Kinyarwanda as group D60, which is significant primarily because it separated the languages from those of Uganda and **Tanzania**, while connecting them with many of the languages of the **Democratic Republic of the Congo**. Guthrie himself said that there was little linguistic significance to this grouping and that it was really a geographic consideration. Nevertheless, little separation of this type had previously been done, and it was a useful exercise. In 1953, a **Belgian** linguist, A. Meeussen, criticized this grouping, and his new studies under the Tervuren School produced a narrower regrouping. Many of the specific characteristics of Kirundi are discussed in the notes beginning this section.

Kirundi and Kinyarwanda are unusual languages in that they are spoken by all Barundi and Banyarwanda. Unlike most other African nations where linguistic divisions reflect ethnic ones, both major ethnic groups (as well as the **Twa**, whose dialect, however, is said to be distinguishable) in both countries speak the national languages. As the language is clearly Bantu in origin, it was most likely the language of the **Hutu** at the time of the **Tutsi** migration into the region. The adoption of the regional language by the dominating group is also an unusual situation; the fact of it might lend credence to the idea that ethnic strife was nonexistent in these earlier times. The universal usage of Kirundi by all Barundi has created two other situations considered unusual in the region. First, although Swahili, the *lingua franca* for much of East Africa, is widely understood in **Bujumbura**, its use of Swahili as a vernacular is largely unnecessary. Additionally, because of the common language among the people, the ethnic groups are far more difficult to distinguish than those of, for example, Tanzania. The groups intermarry, share histories, and share a great many spiritual beliefs and rituals as well.

Although Kirundi is the national language and, with minor regional variations, is spoken and understood throughout the country, French, the language introduced by the Belgian administrators and missionaries, is also widely used in higher **education**, official documents, newspapers, and broadcasting. *See also* MEDIA.

LIGHT ON THE EVENTS OF NTEGA AND MARANGARA. One of a series of ethnic massacres began in August 1988. The origins of the killings are not completely clear, but many **Hutu** said that they had been expecting violence since a coup in September 1987 during which the **army** removed **Jean-Baptiste Bagaza** as president and replaced him with **Pierre Buyoya**. However, many **Tutsi** accused Hutu extremists of having planned an uprising for a long time. Western diplomats said that neither explanation was correct; they claimed that President Buyoya was a sincere moderate and that the uprising had not been planned by the government. Instead, they said that it was a local situation that had gotten out of hand. The government said that Hutu dissidents entered the country from **Rwanda** and incited the Hutu villagers to violence. This version said that the Hutu were "high on hemp" and bloodthirsty. It also said the rebels killed other Hutu who did not want to participate.

It is the official government theory that was circulated by the Ministry of Information in a 43-page booklet called *Light on the Events of Ntega and Marangara*. Some of the things claimed in the book include the following:

> It should be noted that the tactic of the drugged rebels was not only to kill with spears, arrows, stones, and machetes, but also to take a certain number of prisoners, notably girls who they forced to follow them after killing their parents. . . . These girls were used for various tasks before being raped. . . . Many were chained up and they drowned in the Akan-

yaru River. Because the delirious mob was setting fires and carrying out unheard of acts of violence, it was necessary to call the forces of order. . . . The army, therefore, did what it could to stop the carnage. They used their weapons not against civilians, but against the rebels. . . . Some innocent victims of all ethnicities were hurt by bullets. . . . The terrorists killed both ethnicities.

In any case, it is true that the killings centered around the communes of Ntega and Marangara in the already tense northern part of the country. Other nearby provinces were also affected. In Kirundo Province where Marangara is located, there had been unrest the previous year when Hutu found out that the ethnicity of students was being listed in school records; they feared that these records would keep their children from secondary school. When a local Hutu representative to the National Assembly brought the subject up in **Bujumbura**, he disappeared.

By 1988 in Marangara, the Hutu were not happy with four particular Tutsi civil servants in the area, who they said discriminated against them. On 5 August, a small uprising took place during which the villagers demanded that the four be removed and then panicked when three military vehicles arrived. On 6 August, the Hutu felled trees across roads and destroyed bridges in order to block the army. The villagers feared a repeat of the 1972 massacres and began to arm themselves. The Tutsi provincial governor met with the local population and claimed that the Hutu had been very frightened but vague as to why they were frightened. The Hutu claimed that they had been quite specific, asking for the removal of the four civil servants and asking the governor to act against "Tutsi plotters."

About a week later, a wealthy Tutsi coffee merchant (alleged to have been involved in the 1972 massacres) refused to pay money he owed to some Hutu; he killed five of them. The Hutu then mobilized, surrounding the merchant's house for hours and eventually killing him and his family. The events that followed remain unclear. Some church and aid groups said that the army arrived right away to arrest the merchant's killers and immediately began to kill Hutu. A nun said that the Hutu turned on the Tutsi, killing many whole families and that the army did not arrive for two days. All agree, however, that once the army arrived, the Hutu were on the run. The estimated total dead was between 5,000 and 13,000. Some sources claimed there were as many as 24,000 dead and 23,000 unaccounted for. Western diplomats said that the lower number of deaths is closer to correct because most of the people fled the dangerous areas quickly.

After the massacres, the government allowed journalists to enter the area. Catharine Watson reported that the journalists saw no evidence of marijuana use, prisoners, or rebel tracts. They reported evidence of bayonet wounds and other atrocities against Hutu **women** and children.

LITERATURE. As with many traditional cultures, the popular literary forms of Burundi revolve primarily around oral histories of the country. Burundi's oral tradition includes the expected repertoire of stories, legends, fables, riddles, poems, and songs that have been passed from generation to generation by word of mouth. **Jan Vansina**, however, argues that there is very little of historical value in the stories of Burundi, unlike in those of neighboring countries. Nevertheless, there is a body of oral literature, songs, and proverbs that has now been collected and written down. The **Tutsi** are especially known for their epic songs and dynastic poetry (although it is true that this does not occur to the extent of the art forms in **Rwanda**). *See also* MUSIC AND DANCE; *ZINA*.

LITO (KI-, BI-). This is a type of elegy traditionally sung by young **women** and accompanied by very melancholy and sentimental **music**. These songs, it is said, were quite popular as evening entertainment for families having several daughters.

LYANGO (MU-, no plural). This patrilineage was the primary grouping around which competition among the **Hutu** centered during the communal elections of 1960. Although the smallest grouping, it remained the dominant form of political organization in the northern part of the country until independence in 1962.

– M –

MACOONCO. While a fairly minor historical figure, Macoonco's story is one that points to the difficulty of depending upon oral traditions for historical fact. According to **Jan Vansina**, it is culturally permissible in Burundi to alter any tale to make it more entertaining and satisfying for the audience, regardless of other documented facts, should they exist.

Macoonco rebelled against **Mwezi IV** Gisabo and was captured by **German** officials and imprisoned in Usumbura (modern-day **Bujumbura**). He died in prison, but it is here that the facts become obscured. The popular folk tale says that one day he saw from the prison window two messengers from the *mwami* walking down from the hills. He was certain that they had been sent to order his death, so he committed suicide in his cell—when in fact, so the story goes, they had come to ask for a reprieve for him. German records provide a different account: Macoonco had attacked a German officer in an escape attempt and was killed by other guards. There is no evidence of any messengers from Gisabo, nor is this likely, but the original storyteller apparently thought the suicide was a more satisfying story, and so it remains the "truth."

Vansina discusses at length the idea of historical truth and its relativity. He says that Barundi have the idea that as soon as something is accepted as historical truth, they do not think about whether or not it really happened as tradition describes it; analysis is unnecessary, and often historical or logical discrepancies are dismissed by saying such things as "perhaps things could have happened differently in former times."

MALI PROPOSAL. During an emergency meeting of the Council of Ministers of the **Organization of African Unity** in 1964, both Ghana and Mali proposed discussions that included the so-called Congo problem. The Mali Proposal resulted in an ad hoc commission, chaired by President Jomo Kenyatta of Kenya, mandated to help the efforts of the government of the **Democratic Republic of the Congo** (then Zaire) in national reconciliation and to seek all possible means to bring about normal relations between territories formerly attached to the Congo and its neighbors, "especially the Kingdom of Burundi and the People's Republic of the Congo (Brazzaville)."

MANIRAKIZA, MARC. As the minister of foreign affairs, Manirakiza was the representative of the Burundi government who announced at a Nairobi news conference in 1965 that neither the **United States** nor **China** had been implicated in the assassination of Prime Minister **Pierre Ngendandumwe** even though diplomatic relations with China had been temporarily suspended. He said that relations would be resumed "as soon as the confusion is lifted." In fact, relations did not resume until 1971.

MASUMBUKO, PIÉ (1931–). Following the assassination of **Pierre Ngendandumwe**, Masumbuko acted briefly as prime minister. In 1963, three prominent citizens, Masumbuko among them, were arrested and accused of participating in a conspiracy to undermine the security of the state. He also had the distinction at that time of being the only African physician in Burundi.

MATANA TUTSI. Within the **Tutsi** ethnic group were many factions, usually based on location. Often, conflict among these groups was more important to the dynamics of Burundi politics than was conflict between Tutsi and **Hutu**, and the seats of power constantly changed. During one period (from around the end of **Michel Micombero**'s presidency to the mid-1980s), the Matana were one of the primary groups in conflict with the **Rutovu**. Their leader was **Artémon Simbananiye**, who was foreign affairs minister from 1972 to 1974.

MAUS, ALBERT. A **Belgian** settler and formerly *resident* of **Rwanda** as well as a member of the Conseil du Vice-Government Géneral, Maus was one of the key individuals associated with the **Parti du Peuple (PP)**. He was known to give generously of his time and financial resources to the **Hutu** cause, and he acted as an intermediary between the PP and the administration. He was said to be pathologically anti-**Tutsi** and committed suicide upon learning of the **UPRONA** victory in 1961.

MAYUGI, NICOLAS. The first **Hutu** president of **UPRONA**, serving in this capacity from 1991 to 1995. Before that, Mayugi held the position of minister of higher **education** and research (1988–1991), and earlier he had taught at the Institut Pédagogique of **Bujumbura**.

MBANZABUGABO. After the death of his father **Kanugunu**, this chief held his ground against **Mwezi IV** Gisabo during the latter's continuing campaign to control all parts of the country (the policy that was supported by the **German** residents). Mbanzabugabo's role in Burundi politics continued for a very long time; he was the father of André Muhirwa, who was to become Burundi's first prime minister in October 1961. *See also* MIREREKANO, PAUL, AND ANDRÉ MUHIRWA.

"MBWIRE GITO CANJE." Entitled "Listen My Son," this pamphlet was the 1961 product of **Paul Mirerekano**. The title of the booklet comes from the proverb, *Mbwire gito canje gito c'uwundi yumvireho*, which has been more narrowly translated as "I am addressing my good-for-nothing son, but let others also learn a lesson." It was written in the form of a political manifesto and became an important document for **UPRONA** supporters. It gives an indication of what the monarchy meant to the Barundi at the time just before independence in 1962, and it also shows that Mirerekano's views on political issues were closely connected with his conception of the role of the *mwami*. He begins: "Let the Owner of the Drum, the Mwami of Burundi, reign. Let mwami-ship be strong. Let it strengthen public order and the union of all Barundi in peace and justice!"

The pamphlet goes on to discuss such things as avoiding the example of neighboring countries and remembering the importance of devoting one's energies "around the drum" (**Karyenda**). Other points of the pamphlet include: "Remember the beautiful customs of the realm. . . . Too many people have forgotten the customs and traditions of the past, and therefore no longer know the proper behavior to adopt towards others. . . . The Barundi who are mindful of the established order know that to solicit each other's assistance is the basis of love and unity among men." Mirerekano sought, according to René Lemarchand, to justify tradition on the basis of its longevity, "arguing that men must, on principle, obey their habitual social and political impulses." However, Lemarchand also charitably points out that Mirerekano's ideas are not purely reactionary, but, rather, a sign of his own personal commitment to the monarchy in times when the monarchy was not being directly challenged, but when so many changes were occurring.

MEDIA. The primary method of communicating national news has been by radio. There are approximately 440,000 radio sets in the country. The government runs the only radio station with national coverage, La Radiodiffusion et Télévision Nationale de Burundi (RTNB), so it is subject to censorship as well as the constantly and rapidly changing political climate. In **Bujumbura**, there is also access to BBC World Service, Radio France Internationale, and the Voice of America on FM frequencies. In 1996, the European Union–funded Bonesha FM was inaugurated in Burundi, and it set up Radio Umwizero that year. Radio Publique Africaine (RPA) is privately owned, but receives some **United Nations** funding.

All of these stations are subject to government intervention. In 2002, Burundi's defense minister banned all media from interviewing any rebels. The ban came after local news agencies carried an interview with **Agathon Rwasa**, then leader of the **Forces Nationales de Libération**. In the interview, Rwasa denounced an alleged government plot to assassinate him and threatened to take retaliatory actions against the regime in Bujumbura. In April 2005, the Conseil National de la Communication (CNC), the government-appointed regulatory body, suspended RPA for two days for, among other things, "offending public morals" by reporting on the rape of an eight-year-old girl and threatening public security by "deforming" the words of former president **Jean-Baptiste Bagaza**.

Additional stations include Radio CCIB, operated by the Burundi Chamber of Commerce; Radio Culture, partly funded by the Ministry of **Health**; and Radio Isanganiro, which is privately owned and funded. In May 2000, a church-sponsored radio station called Ivyizigiro (Radio Hope) began broadcasting programs focusing on peace initiatives along with **youth** and **women**'s issues.

The government also runs the only regularly broadcasting television station in Burundi, but in 1993, Tele 10 began a cable service in Bujumbura, primarily broadcasting **sports** events; there are fewer than 100,000 televisions in the country. RTNB operates its radio and television stations in Kirundi, Swahili, French, and English.

In spite of the lengthy civil war that began in 1993, people of Burundi are beginning to acquire more access to the Internet.

Several newspapers are regularly published in Burundi. The main agency is Agence Burundaise de Presse (ABP), which is government controlled; smaller press agencies include Azania and Net Press. As the government power has shifted over the years, so has the political stance of its daily newspaper, *Le Renouveau*; additionally, there is *Ndongozi* ("Pacesetter"), funded by the **Catholic Church**; *Arc-en-Ciel* ("Rainbow"), a privately owned French-language weekly; and *Ubamwe* ("Unity"), a government-owned weekly. *See also* VOIX DE LA RÉVOLUTION/VOICE OF THE REVOLUTION.

MEEUSSEN, A. *See* LANGUAGE.

MELADY, THOMAS. The **United States** ambassador to Burundi and Uganda from November 1969 to June 1972 publicly criticized the lack of **United Nations** action over massacres in the two African countries. In a letter published in the *New York Times* in early 1975, Ambassador Melady wrote as follows:

> I now know the clear moral injustices of **South African** apartheid from personal experience and have condemned it in two books. But what about other similar evils? I was present in Burundi in 1972 when most of the at least 90,000 **Hutu** were killed in what was a selective genocide. Why did the UN General Assembly not speak about this horror?

Melady is the author of *Burundi: The Tragic Years*, which describes the 1972 massacre. In it, he expresses surprise, indicating that there had been no signs of impending violence prior to 1970.

MICOMBERO, MICHEL (1940–1983). Micombero was recalled from the Military Academy in Brussels where he had been training from 1960 to 1962 when Burundi attained independence. He was appointed captain and head of the police from 1962 to 1965. From 1965 to 1966, he was chief of the secretaries of state, appointed by Mwami **Mwambutsa IV**. Mwambutsa fled the country following the attempted coup in 1965 and left Micombero in control while Prime Minister **Léopold Biha** was recovering from the wounds he received during the coup. In July of the following year, Mwambutsa was ousted as *mwami* in his absence by his son Charles Ndizeye, who claimed that he was forced to assume power to prevent further deterioration of the situation in the country following his unsuccessful attempts to persuade his father to return.

Micombero denied the allegations that the ousting of Mwambutsa was the first step toward turning Burundi into a republic. He said that the mwami's allegations that the crown prince was a puppet in the hands of extremists were groundless. Micombero further said that his intention was to redefine the role of the crown, returning to the principles in the 1962 constitution, which meant that the mwami would still reign but would not have as much power to actually rule. On 11 July 1966, the new mwami, **Ntare V**, asked Micombero to form a new government. One day after accepting the task, Prime Minister Micombero presented a 14-member cabinet with five posts held by **army** personnel, while he retained the posts of minister of defense and minister of civil administration. In short, the country had undergone a peaceful military coup.

In November 1966, Micombero and other military leaders deposed the monarch and proclaimed Burundi a republic, naming himself the first president and continuing to hold the posts of prime minister and minister of defense. He replaced the eight provincial governors with army officers and established a **Conseil National de la Révolution (CNR)** of 12 military officers, which he said would rule until a new government could be formed and would also draft a new constitution, the old one having been suspended by the last mwami when he assumed power and dismissed Prime Minister Biha.

This, of course, was a major turning point in the history of Burundi in ways that were both obvious and more subtle. Although conflicting factions continued to be central to Burundi politics, their dynamics shifted because Micombero represented a new generation. He was from the **Bururi** region, but was of mixed **Tutsi-Hima** origins and from a family that did not rank high in traditional prestige; he was far removed from the Bezi-**Batare** conflicts that were so prominent before and around the time of independence in 1962. Regional affiliations, however, became increasingly important. Micombero also stated that Burundi's international obligations would be honored and expressed hope for improved relations with **Rwanda**, **Tanzania**, and the **Democratic Republic of the Congo**.

The CNR first announced in December 1966 that Micombero's term as president would be seven years, at the same time promoting him to colonel. Shortly after this announcement, Micombero announced that all governmental directives would be issued as presidential decrees after consultation with the attorney general.

During the following two years, Micombero continued to make many changes in his cabinet, constantly reshuffling, sometimes removing ministers without replacing them, and seldom explaining any of these actions. He did, however, give a reason for dismissing the commander of the army, Albert Shibura, and replacing him with Thomas Ndabemeye: he said there was reason to believe that "a small group of irresponsible men" had tried to "take advantage of the Republic." He also decreed during 1967 that the police should be integrated into the national army.

In November 1970, Micombero delivered a State of the Nation address, in which he spoke of the need to improve the lot of the Burundi peasant. This was thought to be a bid for **Hutu** support, although he did not directly refer to ethnic tensions. Indeed, around that time, he did free many Hutu political prisoners in an attempt to heal the rift between the ethnic groups. In his address, he also promised that there would be a national referendum and a new constitution the following year. In addition, during 1970 and into 1971, tensions between the Bururi Tutsi and other Tutsi came to the fore again when rumors spread of a coup attempt by a group of nonsouthern Tutsi. In 1971, the chief politicians of this group were arrested and brought to trial for treason, and many were sentenced to death. However, in early 1972, the Tutsi were so strongly divided that Micombero feared an intra-Tutsi civil war and commuted the death sentences.

Micombero dismissed his entire government as well as the executive secretary of the ruling **UPRONA** Party in April 1972. This corresponded to the return of Mwami Ntare V (Charles Ndizeye) to Burundi, and within hours, the government radio station announced that "imperialist stooges and traitors who support the monarchy tried to overthrow the Republican rule and its constitution." The radio reported riots in Bujumbura, which included deaths, and fighting in **Gitega**, where Ntare was under house arrest. During the riots, an attempt was made to rescue the mwami, but he was killed. Further fighting in the southern regions was reported. This was the beginning of the largest bloodbath in Burundi's history (up to that time), ending with anywhere from 100,000 to 200,000 dead, most of them

Hutu. Western diplomats and government officials called it genocide. The degree to which Micombero was personally responsible
for the killings remains unclear; however, shortly after the massacres, he descended into depression and heavy drinking, and many
speculate that this could have been the result of deep guilt for his
role in the massacres.

Micombero had promised a new order when he took power, but
under his government, Burundi slipped even further into economic
and political stagnation as well as ethnic strife. The tensions among
Tutsi from different regions continued, and the massacres of 1972
confirmed that discrimination against the Hutu had become endemic,
in spite of the initial attempts by Micombero to resolve the ethnic tensions. In November 1976, two years after Micombero had himself
elected to a second seven-year term as president, he was deposed in
another bloodless military coup led by Col. **Jean-Baptiste Bagaza**, a
member of Micombero's so-called "**Family Corporation.**" Micombero was placed under house arrest, and Burundi's only **political
party**, UPRONA, was dissolved. The armed forces' broadcast announced that no one had been hurt and the country was calm. Micombero sought asylum in Somalia, where he died of a heart attack
in 1983.

MILNER-ORTS AGREEMENT. This agreement of 30 May 1919
partitioned East Africa. It constituted the official proposal of the
British and **Belgian** governments that part of **German** East Africa be
administered by Britain and part—Ruanda-Urundi—by Belgium.

MINANI, JEAN. Shortly after the 1993 coup attempt, **Health** Minister Minani proclaimed a government in exile and accused the **Tutsi**-
dominated Burundi **army** of committing genocide against the **Hutu**
group since the coup. He also claimed that the military was rounding
up villagers, protecting the Tutsi and killing the Hutu. Understandably, the November 1994 **election** of Minani, a Hutu, to the National
Assembly created a great deal of controversy. Members of **UPRONA**
accused him of inciting Hutu against Tutsi after the coup attempt and
President **Melchior Ndadaye**'s murder. UPRONA also claimed that,
while on a visit to **Rwanda** earlier in 1994, Minani had urged the
people of Burundi by broadcast to oppose the coup plotters. Minani

became the president of the **FRODEBU** Party and the Speaker of the National Assembly but was accused by members of the party of corruption and being responsible for the party's loss in the 2005 election. A *Net-Press* editorial, which ran several times in January and February 2005, said that Minani was "lazy and unfit to run for president" of Burundi.

MIREREKANO, PAUL, AND ANDRÉ MUHIRWA. The histories of these two men are so closely intertwined that a fuller picture can be given if they are described together. Upon the death of Prince **Louis Rwagasore**, much of the ethnic harmony that he had engineered was lost. **UPRONA** divided into factions competing for control of the party. Two of the most powerful factions were led by Mirerekano and Muhirwa. Muhirwa was a **Tutsi** *ganwa* of the **Batare** clan and Rwagasore's successor as prime minister; Mirerekano was a **Hutu**. Each had supported Rwagasore, but each also claimed to be his rightful successor, and the political conflict expanded into an ethnic one.

In addition to their ethnic backgrounds, the two men differed in other respects. For example, Mirerekano was said to possess a simplicity of manners and to have retained a sturdy and simple outlook of a Hutu peasant his entire life. He was described as a merchant and a mystic with a sense of moral rectitude. He was a strong supporter of the crown. Muhirwa, politically shrewd as well as aristocratic, treated Mirerekano with contempt, describing Mirerekano's views as tinged with Tutsi chauvinism. Muhirwa was a Murare and the son of Mbanzabugabo, an enemy of Mwami **Mwezi IV**. After the death of his father in 1930, Muhirwa and his brothers were exiled by the **Belgian** residency; they returned to Burundi in 1931 after spending a year and a half in **Tanzania**. Muhirwa attended the Groupe Scolaire at Astrida and graduated in 1942. In 1944, he received a small chiefdom (Buhumuza) many kilometers from his original home, but in 1953, he married the *mwami*'s daughter and was reinstated to the chiefdom of his ancestors.

Even before independence, the trust authorities tried to prevent the two men, as well as Rwagasore, from engaging in political activities. Mirerekano, once the national treasurer of UPRONA, was exiled in 1960 and not permitted back into the country until 1961. What they had in common, therefore, was their conviction; each considered himself the rightful heir to Rwagasore, and neither was willing to concede the UPRONA presidency. Mirerekano pointed out that he had been appointed interim president by Rwagasore upon his return; Muhirwa responded that, since he had taken Rwagasore's place as prime minister, he was also entitled to Rwagasore's seat in the party. Their two factions became known as the **Casablanca Group** (led by Muhirwa) and the Monrovia Group (led by Mirerekano), the former having an anti-Western orientation and the latter a more neutral one.

In late July 1962, less than a month after independence, Mirerekano called a mass meeting of the rank and file of UPRONA at Rwagasore Stadium in **Bujumbura** to renew his bid for the chairmanship of the party. He denounced the attitude of the Muhirwa government during the **Kamenge** incidents, implying that they had been planned by people high in the government. He also reminded the people how Rwagasore's view of the meaning of independence had been betrayed by his successor (Muhirwa's government). As the story is told, the audience seemed to be showing signs of restiveness, and authorities summoned a unit of (mostly Hutu) gendarmes to the stadium to arrest Mirerekano and disperse the crowd. Instead, however, many of the gendarmes rallied around Mirerekano and acted as his personal bodyguard, while others did nothing but watch.

After the stadium incident, the mwami announced that a new executive committee of UPRONA would be elected by the rank and file of the party. The elections, however, were held in **Muramvya** and were mostly attended by Muhirwa's supporters because only a small fraction of Hutu were given the official passes necessary to travel in order to vote. The resulting executive committee consisted of **Joseph Bamina** (a Hutu) as president and Mirerekano and Muhirwa as two out of three vice presidents. However, Mirerekano refused to attend any meetings of the new committee and organized a separate UPRONA wing.

Muhirwa resigned as prime minister in June 1963. This began a new phase of Burundi politics marked by a stronger participation of the court in government affairs. Muhirwa was a suspect in the assassination of Prime Minister **Pierre Ngendandumwe**. In September 1966, a tract circulated in Bujumbura that demanded the execution of Muhirwa and other antimonarchists. The execution did not occur, but he was imprisoned after **Michel Micombero** overthrew the mwami; he was released in November 1967. Muhirwa then received a position with the port authority of Bujumbura, but, even in this seemingly innocuous post, remained feared and hated by Hutu leaders.

In May 1964, Mirerekano was implicated in a plot against the **Albin Nyamoya** government and fled to **Rwanda**. He returned to Burundi in early 1965. During his exile, however, he continued to write to the mwami about the dismissal of the Nyamoya government and the expulsion of the **Chinese** from Burundi. There is evidence that he was also in contact with the **United States** Central Intelligence Agency during this time. Other evidence suggests that Mirerekano did not actually write all of the letters attributed to him, particularly letters conveyed through the **Catholic Church**, because Mirerekano did not write well in **languages** other than Kirundi, and the letters were written mostly in French.

After his exile, still very popular with the Hutu, Mirerekano was elected vice president of the National Assembly. His popularity and his ability to raise the ethnic consciousness of the Hutu had been a concern of Tutsi **army** officers and government officials; they had agreed to sentence him in absentia to 20 years in prison, but changed their minds when he won the majority of the votes in Bujumbura. In October 1965, a group of Hutu army and gendarmerie officers tried to take over the royal palace while another group wounded Prime Minister **Léopold Biha**. After this incident, almost every Hutu leader was arrested. Mirerekano was among those sentenced to death, but the sentence was not carried out.

MISSION POUR LA PROTECTION DES ÉTABLISSEMENTS DÉMOCRATIQUES AU BURUNDI/MISSION FOR THE PROTECTION OF DEMOCRATIC INSTITUTIONS IN BURUNDI (MIPROBU). In early 1994, MIPROBU, which consisted of 47 officers from the **Organization of African Unity**, was sent to Burundi to discuss with the Burundi military how to protect existing democratic institutions. Both the military and the opposition parties agreed to convene.

MONROVIA GROUP. *See* CASABLANCA AND MONROVIA GROUPS.

MPOTSA. Located in the center of Burundi, south of the province of Muramvya, the hills of Mpotsa were the ancient home of both the queen mother (*mugabekazi*) and the sacred royal drums (**Karyenda**).

MUHIRWA, ANDRÉ (1920–2003). *See* MIREREKANO, PAUL, AND ANDRÉ MUHIRWA.

MUKAKARYENDA. Sometimes referred to as Madame Tambour in writings about Burundi, she was the symbolic wife of **Karyenda**, the sacred dynastic drum. The role was occupied by a young girl charged with maintaining the drum; her sacred role required her to be a virgin.

MUKAKIRANGA. Frequently, throughout the Central African area, main divinities had human wives who were dedicated solely to them and not allowed to marry mortal men while they were in the spirit's service. The most important of these women was known as Mukakiranga, the official wife of **Kiranga**. According to **Johannes-Michael Van Der Burgt**, the master, Kiranga, owned two herds of cattle, each guarded by a *ngabe*, or sacred bull. Kiranga also had a sacred mountain administered by a virgin who was designated as his wife. This priestess came from the Abajiji clan, had great authority, and was exempt from paying any dues or taxes to the *mwami*, but she was condemned to permanent virginity and was watched constantly to prevent her from straying. If she did, she was put to death along with all members of her family. She assumed her position at the same time that the mwami did; if he died, she was forced to poison herself, and if she died before the mwami, she was replaced by another young girl. Monseigneur Gorju said that Mukakiranga and the mwami were equals who ruled Burundi together. The mwami was the visible chief, and Kiranga incarnated himself in his wife. Through *kubandwa*, she became Kiranga in person. *See also BANDWA*; *JIJI*.

MUKASI, CHARLES. In 1993, just after **Melchior Ndadaye**'s assassination, Mukasi, the head of **UPRONA**, allegedly broadcast messages from **Rwanda** telling **Hutu** to kill **Tutsi**. After the appointment of **Jean Minani** as Speaker of the National Assembly in November 1994, UPRONA strongly protested. Mukasi was quoted as saying: "We cannot have a person with such a background as a Speaker." Following this appointment and a three-week standoff that virtually shut down the capital, UPRONA withdrew from the assembly. Minani eventually stepped down. In early 1995, when the president dismissed two UPRONA ministers who had skipped a cabinet meeting, Mukasi said in a news conference that the government "should be overthrown at all costs." A two-day strike at this time also shut down **Bujumbura**.

MULELE, PIERRE. *See* MULELISTS.

MULELISTS. A group named for Pierre Mulele, the main organizer of the Kwilu rebellion in the **Democratic Republic of the Congo (DRC)** in 1964–1965, although the Mulelists were never actively involved in this rebellion in the DRC. Their role in Burundi remains unclear, but they are cited as having recruited **Hutu** and organized the initial stages of the 1972 massacres.

MURAMVYA. Located in west central Burundi, Muramvya was the home of the most ancient and the most important royal domains. The descendents of these ancient kings carried on the dynasties of Burundi into the modern age.

MUSAPFU. The Abasapfu clan was an antimonarchical group from **Bururi** that was held responsible for an attempted coup in 1967. The Abasapfu have an interesting origin, related by René Lemarchand from Father M. Rodegem. He says that they are **Tutsi** of high-ranking status, originally from a **Hima** clan. For a reason that history has obliterated, one day Mwami **Ntare II** decided that all Abasapfu should be killed. He gave this task to the Abongera clan, who destroyed their cattle and crops and killed everyone they could find. One of the few survivors was a small boy who had remained hidden; he was taken to the *mwami*, who kept him at his court under his protection and named him Musapfu to commemorate his adventure.

MUSIC AND DANCE. Traditionally, folk tales and fables have been set to music, a practice that has caused little distinction between poetry and music. Burundi, however, does have a history in the musical arts. Traditional songs are in the form of a rhythmic chant accompanied by hand clapping, and these songs were originally intended to praise the king.

Some of the most popular musical instruments include such traditional instruments as the *umuduri*, which is a musical bow with one string; the flute; the zither; various types of horns; the *ikembe*, a thumb piano; the *indonongo*, an instrument similar to a small violin; the *inyagara*, a rattle; and the *inanga*, which is similar to the sitar. Drums have always been important in the cultural history of Burundi and remain so; the unique drumming techniques were passed from father to son. Traditionally, a group of drummers would follow the king on his travels. Still known as the Royal Drummers, this group began performing outside of Burundi in the 1960s and has gained international recognition, often described as one of the greatest percussion ensembles in the world. The group collaborated on a recording in 1975 with the American folk singer Joni Mitchell and is said to have influenced many British rock and roll bands in the 1980s; its unique sound has come to be known as the "Burundi Beat."

Dance has long been central to all major celebrations in Burundi. There are two traditional dance forms: the *abatimbo* is a ritual dance, and the *abanyagasimbo* is a lively, very acrobatic dance. Burundi's world famous Intore dancers still perform traditional warlike dances, wearing leopard skins, elaborate headdresses, and ankle bells.

After the long period of civil strife that began in 1993, various groups in Burundi have been attempting to revive some of the country's traditional arts as a means of community building. For example, in June 2004, the Ruyigi Youth Festival included **women**'s groups singing and dancing about peace and reconciliation, a group including young ex-rebel combatants dancing to show that war is not useful and to encourage collaboration in development programs, and various groups using music and dance to denounce **HIV/AIDS**. This particular festival ended with a dance by three people—one **Hutu**, one **Tutsi**, and one **Twa**—to symbolize the necessity of working together for the good of the country. *See also HOZA UMWANA*; KARYENDA; *IYEREZI*; *JAMBO*.

MUTAGA I (SEENYAMWIIZA). The third monarch of Burundi, reigning from about 1735 to 1765.

MUTAGA II (1893–1915). When **Mwezi IV** died in 1908, the lack of an adequate replacement for him created what the **Germans** considered a period of ongoing chaos in Burundi. His successor was his 15-year-old son, Mutaga. Mutaga was a weak leader, certainly in part because of his extreme youth. The German *resident* in Urundi wrote in 1911, "The Mwami himself has nothing to say except in his own village. . . . In short, his political influence is non-existent; he exists because tradition says he must, but he is not the ruler of the country." Supposedly, the dominant influence on Mutaga was his mother, **Ndirikumutima**, but his mother's strongest rival, **Ntarugera**, another prince of the royal blood, also influenced the *mwami* considerably. The struggle between these two was probably the chaos described by the Germans, because Mutaga took on more of a leadership role as he matured.

The Germans supported Mutaga's authority, assuming that the situation would improve over time. It did not immediately improve, however, because the young mwami died at the end of 1915. The circumstances surrounding his death are somewhat mysterious. According to Pierre Ryckmans, considered a reliable source by many historians, Mutaga died because of a love affair. As Ryckmans told the story, one of Mutaga's wives was having an affair with his brother, Prince Bangura. Mutaga eventually became suspicious and kept a close watch over the two alleged lovers. One day, finding them together, Mutaga stabbed Bangura in the chest with his spear. Bangura, in trying to defend himself, stabbed Mutaga in the abdomen. Both died, Mutaga only a few days after Bangura. According to official German documents, however, Mutaga and his brother were victims of malaria.

MUTWENZI. In the traditional royal court, Mutwenzi ("the dawn") was a sister of the *mwami*, who participated in the *umuganuro* ceremony. She also participated in a ritual sexual union with the mwami at dawn on the day of his enthronement. *See also GANURO.*

MUYENZI, GONZALVE. A **Tutsi** born in **Rwanda** and employed by the **United States** embassy from 1962 to 1965, Muyenzi was the confessed killer of Prime Minister **Pierre Ngendandumwe**. The new prime minister quickly reported that there was no evidence that the United States had been involved, but that "Tutsi extremists" were responsible.

MWAMBUTSA I. The fourth monarch of Burundi, reigning from about 1765 to 1795.

MWAMBUTSA IV (BANGIRICENGE) (1913–1977). That he ascended to the throne at the age of two explains the extremely long reign of **Mwami** Mwambutsa (1915–1966). One of the last acts of the **German** government was Mwambutsa's installation upon the death of his father, **Mutaga II**; because of the new mwami's age, a regency was established to rule on his behalf until he reached the age of majority. The years of his reign spanned and exceeded the **Belgian** occupation of Burundi.

During the Belgian occupation, Mwambutsa was often criticized by his own people as being too attracted to the European people and culture. He was frequently portrayed as a hard-drinking womanizer who was often in serious debt. The Europeans criticized him as being unqualified for his job. Each side, of course, had motives for their criticism other than the behavior and leadership of the mwami. Many Barundi were hoping for more backing of the pro-**Batare** factions from the Belgian *resident*.

Mwambutsa himself was not consistent in his royal leadership, but from 1962 to 1965, following independence, the crown acted as the main stabilizing force in the country against rising criticism from both ethnic groups. The mwami was often a symbol of national unity. At times, he maintained supreme authority over the constitution, often overruling decisions of the elected government. However, he spent part of the postindependence years in Europe, often claiming poor health; history sometimes portrays him as having been uncomfortable with his power and frightened of what he saw happening in Burundi, prompting these many trips out of the country.

An abortive coup in 1965 caused the near-collapse of the entire **governmental system** that was built around the crown, as well as the liquidation of most of the **Hutu** leadership. Following this attempted coup, Mwambutsa again left the country—for the last time, as it happened—conferring substantial powers on his son, Charles Ndizeye. It was unclear at the time whether this was a form of abdication, but he was, in fact, deposed in exile by Ndizeye, who was to rule under the dynastic name of **Ntare V**. Mwambutsa voiced sharp disapproval of the move, but remained where he was. After the ethnic massacres of 1972, during which Ntare V was killed, Mwambutsa offered to return to Burundi as mwami, but his offer was not accepted. *See also* RWA-GASORE, PRINCE LOUIS (1932–1961).

MWAMI. The Kirundi word for king; the plural form is *bami*. Much of the power of the bami and the other native authorities was abolished beginning in 1917. For example, domestic slavery was eliminated in 1923, and the triple hierarchy of the chief of crops, chief of pastures, and chief of armed units was replaced by a single authority. The bami are intriguing in the cultural context as they are closely associated with both political and religious functions. Each mwami was the medium between the people and supernatural forces. The word (actually *mu/bu-uumi*) is related to the verb *ku-aama*, "to be fertile."

The bami are also intriguing because they point out the cyclical nature of Burundi history. There are four dynastic names of bami, and the names themselves form a cycle: Mwambutsa, Ntare, Mwezi, and Mutaga. Traditionally, each king in the cycle has an ideal character, and each ideal type reappears every fourth generation. Ntare is the conqueror who founded the dynasty and is expected to continue to found dynasties; Mwezi is the ruler who must maintain his power in the face of rebels and who lives a long life; Mutaga is traditionally a good king but very unlucky; and Mwambutsa's purpose is to prepare the way for a new Ntare.

Burundi history is static on these points concerning the bami, and the traditional tales reveal some of the historical background of many modern conflicts. For example, under the reign of **Mwezi IV**, a series of uprisings occurred involving members of the family of *abatare*, the collective noun meaning "those who could become Ntare." Traditionally, each uprising is described as a separate incident with no mention of any interconnections. The Bezi-**Batare** conflict was to live on for many generations. The crown was never identified with either of the main ethnic groups, although many of its ritualistic aspects seem to be more closely traced to the **Hutu** than the **Tutsi**.

Following independence in 1962, the importance of the role of the mwami fluctuated, but the court remained generally strong due to the support of **UPRONA** and its nationalist underpinnings. The last mwami, **Ntare V**, was killed during the ethnic fighting in 1972. *See*

also BAMBUTSA AND BATAGA; MUTAGA I (SEENYAMWI-
IZA); MUTAGA II (1893–1915); MWAMBUTSA I; MWAMBUTSA
IV (BANGIRICENGE); MWEZI I; NTARE I (RUSHATSI); NTARE
II (RUGAAMBA).

MWEZI I. The second monarch of Burundi, reigning from about 1705
to 1735.

MWEZI II. *See* MWEZI IV (1845–1908).

MWEZI IV (1845–1908). Born Gisabo (sometimes written as Kisabo,
Kissabo, or Gissabo), he was *mwami* of Burundi from 1860 until his
death. He is sometimes documented as Mwezi II, and that he was indeed the second Mwezi in the cycle of the monarchy is just as possible.

At that time, Urundi was not a centralized state, and Mwezi's reign
was a constant struggle against district chiefs. Although Gisabo tried
to wield absolute power according to the traditions of the Barundi, he
was, in fact, quite limited in his power and regarded the **German** in-
trusion as a threat to his already precarious position. The initial contacts between Captain von Bethe, the head of the German military
station in Usumbura (modern **Bujumbura**), and Gisabo in 1899 were
friendly; Gisabo eagerly assured von Bethe that he and his people
would cooperate and submit to German authority. What Gisabo actually hoped, however, was to defeat his enemies and establish his own
absolute sovereignty with no German interference. Unfortunately,
Gisabo was defeated more often than he was victorious, and his authority diminished rather than increased.

Another German captain (von Beringe) described events in
Urundi in a long political report in July 1902. He was convinced that
Gisabo was an enemy of the Europeans and that most of the chiefs
in Urundi were enemies of Gisabo. Von Beringe requested permission for an "Urundi expedition" of three months, during which time
he wanted to gain Gisabo's submission to German rule once and for
all. He recommended war against Gisabo. G. A. Götzen, the governor of German East Africa, believed in peaceful rather than punitive
actions in Urundi, but was, at first, unable to stop von Beringe, who
executed his campaign against Gisabo. In June 1903, von Beringe

notified his government that the expedition had been a success and that Gisabo had submitted to German rule after losing 200 men in the fighting.

Götzen was furious, believing that the military station had never been seriously threatened by Gisabo, and he set out to try and repair the damage. In April 1904, Götzen ordered Usumbura to regard all chiefs as subordinate to Gisabo, on the condition that Gisabo would continue to recognize German sovereignty. The chiefs to whom von Beringe had granted independence consequently renewed their hostilities against both Gisabo and the Germans. One of the chiefs, Machoncho, to whom von Beringe had granted independence, attempted to kill von Beringe's replacement, Grawert, who shot the chief in self-defense.

By 1906, the German military had achieved a great deal in Ruanda-Urundi. The sovereignty of Gisabo over Urundi had been restored, and von Beringe's "divide-and-rule" policy had been corrected to Götzen's original policy of "indirect rule." By 1908, Gisabo, with Grawert's help, had brought the remaining district chiefs under his control, thus stabilizing the central government of Urundi more than ever before. However, this German control over Urundi, which had taken so many years to achieve, was undone by the 1908 death of Gisabo at the age of 63. His death was followed not by revolution, as the Germans feared, but by what the Germans regarded as chaos. The new king (**Mutaga II**) was quite young and had no influence at all, the Burundi government being dominated by the king's numerous older relatives.

After his explorations in Africa, Sir Richard Burton said that Gisabo was able to assemble a considerable number of warriors who could strike fear in the hearts of his neighbors. Years later, after Gisabo's death, Hans Meyer said that he had been without doubt the most important sovereign in all of East and Central Africa. *See also RIMBA*.

MWUNGERE. Various functions of the traditional court were constant, and those who were in the position took on a new name. The guardian of the royal cattle (*umwungere*) took on Mwungere as his given name.

– N –

NAHAYO, IMMACULÉE (1948–). In the August 2005 series of **elections**, Nahayo was elected Speaker of the National Assembly, Burundi's lower chamber of Parliament. She is the first **woman** to hold this position and attributes "wisdom acquired with age" as the reason for winning the election. Nahayo received a teaching diploma in 1969, and then taught in **Gitega** Province until 1973, when she was forced to flee the country; she went to the **Democratic Republic of the Congo (DRC)**, where she also taught. In 1974, Nahayo enrolled in Bukavu University in the DRC, where she obtained a bachelor's degree in biochemistry. She taught at a Congolese secondary school until 1983, and then at a seminary in **Rwanda** until 1991. In 1991, Nahayo returned to Burundi, where she first became an advisor to the minister of **sports** and culture, and then a laboratory technician at the Centre for Food Technologies. In 1995, she left Burundi again, this time for **Tanzania**, after she joined the **Conseil National pour la Défense de la Démocratie-Forces pour la Défense de la Démocratie (CNDD-FDD)**. While in Tanzania, she worked for several nongovernmental **international aid** organizations, returning to Burundi after the CNDD-FDD signed a cease-fire accord in November 2003. She is the widow of a former minister of the interior and the mother of six.

NAHIMANA, ANTOINE. A member of the conspiracy to kill Prince **Louis Rwagasore**, Nahimana was sentenced to death by the Court of First Instance. That sentence was commuted to 20 years of penal servitude by the Court of Appeal of **Bujumbura**. However, a law enacted in September 1962 established a Supreme Court with retroactive competence, and it changed the decision of the lower courts on the grounds that there had been no jury. At this time, the case was reheard by the Court of First Instance, which this time sentenced Nahimana, along with four coconspirators, to death. In early 1963, the Court of Appeal confirmed the judgment, and on 14 January, all five were publicly hanged in Kitega. A British representative of Amnesty International reported that the three judges at the retrial did not understand the complex legal system inherited from the **Belgians** and that the jurors were "completely in the dark about the whole proceedings."

NANDABUNGA. Mwezi IV's daughter was an unusually famous person in Burundi because she accomplished what few, if any, other **women** had. She received the chiefdom of Buyenzi-Bweru (in Ngozi), which she commanded by herself under the rightful title of Muganwa. She was married twice; little is known of her first husband, but her second husband was a non-*ganwa* **Tutsi** named Munyakarama and did not share in the administration of the chiefdom.

NATIONAL ASSEMBLY. *See* GOVERNMENT SYSTEM.

NATIONAL TRUTH AND RECONCILIATION COMMISSION (NTRC). In early 2005, the **United Nations** Security Council asked Secretary-General Kofi Annan to work with Burundi leaders to create a body to prosecute alleged war crimes from the nearly 45 years of the country's independence. At that time, the council also called for the establishment of a Truth and Reconciliation Commission to determine the cause and nature of the crimes committed during this same period of time. The council said that the people responsible for war crimes and other "crimes against humanity" needed to face justice in order to deter future crimes and end "the climate of impunity" in Burundi and the entire Great Lakes region of Central Africa. The government of Burundi quickly endorsed this plan. While the actual National Truth and Reconciliation Commission, comprising five members—three international and two national—has not begun its work, it has been established under Burundi law and charged with "establishing the truth about acts of violence committed during the cyclical conflicts that have plagued Burundi since July 1, 1962, the day of independence, establish and identify those responsible, and identify the victims." The panel will also propose measures to promote reconciliation and decide on restitution to victims.

NDABEMEYE, CHARLES. The chief of staff under President **Michel Micombero**, Ndabemeye was present at a meeting with members of the government when Rumonge was attacked in the early stages of the massacres of 1972.

NDADAYE, MELCHIOR (1953–1993). After the 1972 massacres, Ndadaye spent 11 years in exile in **Rwanda**. Upon his return to Burundi in

1983, he worked for nine years on underground political activities and spent two months in prison in 1988 after calling for greater democracy at a meeting following the Ntega and Maragara massacres. A new constitution, paving the way for multiparty government, was approved by over 90 percent of the electorate in March 1993. That constitution disallowed political organizations that advocated "tribalism, divisionalism, or violence" and stipulated that **political parties** must represent both the **Hutu** and **Tutsi** ethnic groups. In Burundi's first democratic, multiparty **election** in June 1993, Ndadaye was the clear winner for his **FRODEBU** Party, surpassing the incumbent **Pierre Buyoya** by a two-to-one margin. At the time of election, Ndadaye, a 40-year-old banker, was the first Murundi president to be elected who was a civilian and a Hutu. His opponents tried to portray him as inexperienced with no political ideas except ethnic retribution, but in fact he was an intellectual who had previously formed two political parties: a workers' party (**Umugambwe Wa'bakozi Uburundi**) in Rwanda in 1975 and FRODEBU in 1986.

Some members of Ndadaye's FRODEBU Party compared him to Martin Luther King Jr.; he taught that justice would not occur unless members of his party showed respect for others as well and was said to have preached nonviolence and nonsectarianism. In the week following his election victory, Ndadaye announced an amnesty for about 500 political prisoners that was seen as a conciliatory gesture to both Tutsi and militant Hutu. Under this amnesty, hundreds of Hutu prisoners accused of taking part in ethnic clashes of November 1991 were to be released, as was a group of Tutsi soldiers who took part in a March 1992 coup attempt intended to counter Buyoya's attempts at reforms.

Ndadaye also tried to create a broad-based government, appointing nine Tutsi among his 23 ministers, including **Silvie Kinigi**, the first **woman** prime minister. Additionally, he tried to integrate the Tutsi control in the security forces and find ways to repatriate hundreds of thousands of mostly Hutu refugees living in other countries. In the September–October 1993 issue of *Africa Report*, Catharine Watson wrote that an **army** coup against the new administration was highly unlikely: "An army coup would set the country on fire. FRODEBU enjoys rapturous support. If Ndadaye or his term were harmed, every Tutsi family in Burundi would be in danger." In spite of this prediction, however, on 21 October 1993, 100 days after the election, Nda-daye was killed in a military coup attempt. His last words are re-ported to have been, "Be careful of what you are about to do; it is very, very dangerous."

Four days later, the coup leaders were calling for negotiations to return power to civilians, but once again in the history of independent Burundi, the coup and assassination led to years of further ethnic bloodshed. Hutu radicals began killing Tutsis soon after the assassi-nation; the army responded to these killings with its own widespread killing of Hutu civilians. The death toll from these killings exceeded that of the 1972 ethnic massacres and continued through the 1990s. This part of Watson's prediction proved true. Another article in the same publication implied that if Ndadaye were assassinated, every Tutsi family would lose at least one of its members; although those specific figures are not available, that, too, has apparently happened.

Relief agencies reported that the fighting begun during the coup at-tempt may have forced as many as one million people to flee to neighboring countries. The **United States** suspended its $16 million aid program to Burundi after the coup and later rejected an appeal to send troops there as part of a **United Nations** peacekeeping mission. Instead, the United States joined other members of the Security Council in asking UN secretary-general Boutros Boutros-Ghali to send a fact-finding team, which did arrive in Burundi in March 1994.

In May 1999, the Burundi media reported a judgment in the trial of those implicated in Ndadaye's assassination. The Supreme Court sentenced five members of the army to death and 23 others to prison. Thirty-eight people were acquitted, 10 cases were sent back to the court on appeal, and five cases were dropped because the suspects had died. No high-ranking army officers were convicted.

NDAYIZEYE, DOMITIEN (1953–). As part of the **Arusha Accord**, a transitional government was designed to lead Burundi to peaceful, democratic **elections**. Under this agreement, signed in 2000, **Pierre Buyoya** (a **Tutsi**) would remain president for 18 months with a **Hutu** vice president; after this period, the vice president would become pres-ident and appoint a Tutsi vice president. Ndayizeye was Buyoya's vice president, and then, as a member of **FRODEBU**, he became president. The transition was indeed peaceful, although there were some delays.

Ndayizeye is an electrical engineer by training. Like many educated Hutu, he fled Burundi in 1972 and began his political life in exile, first in **Belgium**, where he went to school, and then in **Rwanda**, where he worked after he graduated. Like Buyoya, Ndayizeye seemed to balk at part of the transitional process, stalling the election (according to some analysts) in order to introduce a controversial debate on changing some articles of the newly drafted constitution. When even his own FRODEBU Party rejected his proposed changes, Ndayizeye finally agreed to the election. His party, to the surprise of many, was not victorious, and Ndayizeye peacefully stepped down in favor of the winner of the popular vote, the **Conseil National pour la Défense de la Démocratie-Forces pour la Défense de la Démocratie (CNDD-FDD)** and its presidential candidate, **Pierre Nkurunziza**. Upon conceding defeat, Ndayizeye urged all parties to accept the "will of the people."

NDENZAKO, LEON. In 1965 when the **United States** ambassador to Burundi, **Donald Dumont**, and two other embassy officials were ordered to leave Burundi under accusations of conspiracy against the government, the United States retaliated and expelled Ndenzako, the Burundian ambassador, from Washington the next day. The ambassador was summoned to the State Department to receive a note containing a strong protest about the expulsions in **Bujumbura**.

NDIKUMWAMI, RICHARD. The head of intelligence under President **Melchior Ndadaye**. Ndikumwami, like the president, had been a refugee following the 1972 massacres.

NDIMANYA, IGNACE. Ndimanya, the former minister of public works, was among three prominent citizens accused of participating in a conspiracy to undermine the security of the state in 1963. The two others were **Thaddée Siryuyumunsi** and **Pié Masumbuko**.

NDINZURWAHA, SEVERIN. During the initial **Kamenge** incidents of 1962, four prominent **Hutu** lost their lives in the violence. Ndinzurwaha, who was then permanent secretary of the Syndicats Chrétiens (Christian Trade Unions) and national secretary of the teachers' association, was among them.

NDIRIKUMUTIMA. When **Mwezi IV** died in 1908, Burundi politics were in confusion and turmoil. His 15-year-old son succeeded him as **Mutaga II**, but the new *mwami*'s youth prevented him from exercising the power necessary to stop some of his father's rivals from reclaiming parts of the territory as their own. Ndirikumutima was the queen mother and fought hard for her son. When Mutaga died very young and was succeeded by his infant son, who ruled as **Mwambutsa IV**, Ndirikumutima remained in charge of his regency.

NDIZEYE, CHARLES. *See* NTARE V (CHARLES NDIZEYE) (1947–1972).

NDUWABIKE, JEAN. In 1962, Nduwabike was among the young **Tutsi** militants affiliated with the **Jeunesse Nationaliste Rwagasore** who made threats against **Hutu** trade unionists and politicians. At the time, he was the president of the Syndicats Chrétians (Christian Trade Unions). Later that year, when he was also national secretary of the **Parti du Peuple (PP)**, he was killed in one of the **Kamenge** incidents.

NDUWAYO, ANTOINE. Following the resignation (caused by a general strike called for by **UPRONA**) of Prime Minister **Anatole Kanyenkiko**, Nduwayo became the prime minister under the coalition government of President **Sylvestre Ntibantunganya** in February 1995. Ntibantunganya is **Hutu**, and Nduwayo is **Tutsi**; this ethnic mix, while theoretically necessary in the volatile atmosphere following the 1993 assassination of President **Melchior Ndadaye**, was potentially explosive in its own right. The president and prime minister, representing the interests of their separate **political parties**, did not agree on many governmental policies.

Upon his appointment, Nduwayo called for the restoration of peace, cautioning that nothing could be achieved before that goal was attained. In March 1995, Nduwayo appointed seven new government ministers. During that same month, Nduwayo and Ntibantunganya worked together to sign an agreement brokered by the French mission to pursue stability, protect lives, and encourage the return of about two million **refugees** living in camps.

However, in June, Nduwayo was a central figure in orchestrating an **army** operation in the **Bujumbura** suburb of **Kamenge** against members of the Hutu militia. He urged civilians to evacuate, but many were killed in this and other violent operations; Nduwayo claimed that these deaths were inevitable because the Hutu guerrillas had been shielding themselves with civilians. At the first Independence Day celebration that occurred during his term of office (1 July 1995), the prime minister and the president celebrated separately— the president in **Gitega**, which has a majority Hutu population, and the prime minister in Bujumbura, which is almost completely Tutsi. This was seen to emphasize the separation of the two ethnic groups. *See also* HUTU AND TUTSI, RELATIONS BETWEEN.

NDUWUMWE. The son of **Mwezi IV** and one of the principal chiefs of Burundi during his father's reign. It was he who gave assurance to the regency of the country during the early part of **Mwambutsa**'s reign, when the *mwami* was still a child. Nduwumwe was also among the leading experts concerning the secrets of the royalty.

NETTOYAGE. Literally "cleaning up" or "mopping up," this French term has been used to describe the actions of the Burundi **army** during **Hutu** uprisings throughout the history of the country. It has come to mean "ethnic cleansing" in Burundi.

NGENDANDUMWE, PIERRE (1930–1965). In March 1963, as tensions between the **Casablanca and Monrovia Groups** were increasing, Prime Minister André Muhirwa ordered the arrest of three Monrovia Group leaders, alleging conspiracy against the state. Mwami **Mwambutsa IV** intervened, releasing the three men, and the Muhirwa government was dissolved three months later. Ngendandumwe, a 31-year-old **Hutu** loyal to the Monrovia Group, was appointed as the new prime minister. The change in government marked a change in the general political workings of Burundi; from this time until the abolition of the monarchy and the forming of a republic, the prime minister and his cabinet were answerable only to the *mwami*, who became the chief initiator as well as the executor of all legislation in the Parliament.

It was somewhat ironic that Ngendandumwe led the government during this time of strong intervention by the court. In 1959, he had written in a report that the "*bami* and the chiefs" were the ones to emerge as "the great beneficiaries of the decree of July 1952," which established the hierarchy of subchieftaincy, chieftaincy, territorial, and national councils. He went on to say that "the recent tragedy in Ruanda-Urundi does not consist only in the fact of white colonization but also in the paradox that in spite of representing a minority, the near totality of chief, subchief and judge are in the hands of the **Tutsi**."

Having a Hutu prime minister and the strong intervention of the court did little to calm the tensions between the two ethnic groups or the factions of **UPRONA**. In what have been described as "Byzantine practices," Tutsi extremists brought about the downfall of the Ngendandumwe government by maneuvering the Monrovia regime into recognizing the People's Republic of **China**; this was contrary to the preferences of the **Belgian** and the **United States** embassies, of course, but it was also contrary to those of the mwami. In March 1964, the mwami dismissed four Hutu ministers who court officials said held views "which did not fit in with the peaceful coexistence of the country's two tribal groups." At this point, Ngendandumwe resigned as prime minister, and **Albin Nyamoya** took over.

In January 1965, the mwami withdrew support from Nyamoya and once again asked Ngendandumwe to form a government. Just three days after doing so, as he was leaving from a hospital visit to his wife, who had just given birth, Ngendandumwe was shot and killed. Tensions between the two groups grew even stronger following this act of violence, and relations became so bad that accommodation was not considered possible. Although China was not implicated in the assassination, diplomatic relations between **Bujumbura** and Beijing were suspended.

In fact, the killers were a group of **Rwandan** Tutsi **refugees**. A week after the assassination, Burundi police announced that a Rwandan employed as an accounting clerk in the U.S. embassy had confessed to the murder. Acting Prime Minister **Pié Masumbuko** stressed that Washington was not involved. In February, another Rwandan named Butera (who also worked for the U.S. embassy) was arrested, and a ballistics expert reported that the bullet that had killed the prime minister came from a revolver found in his possession. Butera was the son of Rukeba, a well-known Rwandan guerrilla. Finally, in December 1967, Burundi's Supreme Court, for lack of evidence, acquitted all the others who had been accused of involvement in the assassination. Among them were the accounting clerk, **Gonzalve Muyenzi**, and the former president of the **Jeunesse Nationaliste Rwagasore**, **Prime Nyongabo**. The death of Ngendandumwe, a moderate Hutu, provoked yet another new crisis in Burundi politics. In May 1965, the first parliamentary **elections** since 1961 were held. UPRONA was challenged by the Hutu-supported **Parti du Peuple**. The result was a Parliament in which Hutu held 80 percent of the seats. *See also* MIREREKANO, PAUL, AND ANDRÉ MUHIRWA.

NGEZE, FRANÇOIS. The minister of interior in **Buyoya**'s government, Ngeze was one of the rare **Hutu** who held any position of power between 1965 and 1993. He is mentioned as a reason for outsiders to look more deeply into the Burundi situation; the general assumption of disadvantaged Hutu pitted against the majority and ruling **Tutsi** becomes somewhat more nuanced when it is known that such powerful Hutu exist, however rarely. After the coup of 1993, which resulted in the death of President **Melchior Ndadaye**, Ngeze was made head of the new ruling **Committee of National Salvation** and claimed that he had been forced to support the coup and assume a leadership role.

NGUNZU, PIERRE. From the time of **Ntare V**'s 1966 overthrow of **Mwambutsa IV**'s rule, many people who were prominent under the old monarchy lost their positions, their reputations, and often their lives. Formerly the minister of **education** in the André Muhirwa government, Ngunzu was placed under arrest in September 1966 along with other prominent citizens, but was released within 48 hours after the court intervened. This was probably an act intended to remind the government of the court's traditionally expected role. *See also* MIREREKANO, PAUL, AND ANDRÉ MUHIRWA.

NICAYENZI, ZÉNON. When the August 1962 "stadium incident" involving the surprising support of **Paul Mirerekano** by a group of gendarmes occurred, Nicayenzi, then commissioner in charge of the armed forces, put the **army** in a state of emergency. Only two months before this incident, Nicayenzi had talked about the union of **Hutu and Tutsi**, who he said were "intimately linked to each other" and free of the problems that plagued the two groups in **Rwanda**.

NKURUNZIZA, PIERRE (1964–). Current president of Burundi, elected in August 2005 for a five-year transition period, following a 12-year civil war. His father, elected to the National Assembly in 1965 and later governor of Ngozi and Kagansi provinces, was killed during Burundi's 1972 ethnic massacres, so Nkurunziza had an introduction to ethnic politics very early in his life. He entered the University of Burundi in 1987, hoping to enroll in the Faculty of Economic Sciences or the High Military Institute, but instead was admitted to the Faculty of Physical Education and Sports. At that time, **Hutu** (Nkurunziza's ethnic group) were rarely admitted to the military institute. After graduating, he taught in secondary schools and later as a lecturer at the University of Burundi; he also lectured at the military institute and coached a soccer team.

In 1995, the primarily **Tutsi** national **army** attacked the campus of the University of Burundi. The soldiers killed about 200 students and tried to kill Nkurunziza, shooting at him and burning his car. After this incident, he fled the country and joined the **Conseil National pour la Défense de la Démocratie (CNDD) political party** in exile and its armed wing, the **Forces pour la Défense de la Démocratie (FDD)** as a soldier. The CNDD-FDD was, for several years, the largest Hutu rebel group fighting against Burundi's government troops. In 1999, Nkurunziza was badly wounded during the fighting and left for dead. He hid for four months with no medical care. Today, Nkurunziza, a born-again Christian, remains certain that God saved him.

In 2001, the CNDD-FDD held its first congress, during which Nkurunziza was elected the party's leader. In 2003, after several negotiating sessions, Nkurunziza signed a cease-fire agreement with Burundi's transitional government. Shortly afterward, the CNDD-FDD disarmed and joined the transitional government. Nkurunziza became the minister for good governance, a position he held until being elected president nearly two years later.

The Burundi people were very much behind the CNDD-FDD, and the party soundly won the parliamentary **elections** of 2005, the first elections held in the country since 1993 when **Melchior Ndadaye** was elected president and assassinated within just a few months, starting the 12-year civil war. As the party leader, Nkurunziza was the clear presidential choice; his party chose him because they believed his policies would promote reconciliation. The party's platform involved the uniting of all Barundi and all political parties. In an interview shortly before the election, Nkurunziza said, "We stand for equality for all. We believe in a strong, united and prosperous Burundi where everybody lives in harmony. . . . We will surprise everybody by incorporating all parties and all tribes into our government."

This is exactly what happened. Many members of **UPRONA** (a traditionally Tutsi political party) and **FRODEBU** (a traditionally Hutu party) have joined the CNDD-FDD, seeking a nonethnically based government. Moreover, upholding the **Arusha Accord**, all three of the country's ethnic groups are guaranteed representation at all levels of government, as are **women**, a previously underrepresented group.

Nkurunziza is married with two children. He did not see his family for eight years during the civil war when he was fighting mostly in the bush and from **Tanzania**. He continues organizing prayer meetings at his home and still enjoys playing soccer.

NTAMAGARA, AUGUSTIN. The leader of the **Fédération des Travailleurs du Burundi**, a vehemently pro-**Tutsi** and anti-Western group. In September 1966, he organized a meeting at a stadium during which he was reported to have said: "Let the people's enemies— **Ndenzako**, Nsengyumva, and Muhirwa—have their heads chopped off, and their bodies thrown to the dogs." In October 1967, Ntamagara was one of many to be demoted to a position of negligible power in the new government. *See also* MIREREKANO, PAUL, AND ANDRÉ MUHIRWA.

NTARE I (RUSHATSI). When the **Tutsi** first arrived in the area that is now **Rwanda** and Burundi, each individual's control was limited to a small area; a chief ruled only one or two hills. It was Rushatsi, the first Burundi monarch, whose dynastic name was Ntare I, who consolidated a number of these smaller realms and established his rule over a larger area centering around what is now **Muramvya**. Oral historians place his reign from about 1675 to 1705. *Intare* is the skin of a lion and was a symbol of royalty. Some legends suggest that the monarch's family name or surname before he adopted Ntare was Rufuko, but others say that this is the name of his father.

NTARE II (RUGAAMBA). Often considered to be the first monarch of what would become modern Burundi, his reign was approximately from 1795 to 1852. During his rule, Rugaamba expanded the established boundaries of the kingdom considerably to include areas that are now part of **Rwanda** and **Tanzania**. These territorial conquests added much to his fame and reputation as one of Burundi's most illustrious kings. Rugaamba, in order to consolidate his territory, spread the wealth from his victories to his sons, some of whom began to assert their independence from the reign of their father. This is considered to be the point in Burundi's history when the *ganwa* began playing an important and decisive role in the political system. From then on, the *mwami* sought to evict relatives and followers of their predecessors and to replace them with their own people. This, of course, included sons evicting their fathers' loyal supporters and was the beginning of the **Batare**-Bezi conflict that affected so much of Burundi's 20th-century politics.

NTARE V (CHARLES NDIZEYE) (1947–1972). The last *mwami* of Burundi, Ntare's dynastic order is sometimes documented as III or IV; III is most likely the correct number, based on the rotation of kings every four generations. Also, nothing of another Ntare III or Ntare IV has been documented.

After an abortive coup in October 1965, Mwami **Mwambutsa IV** left Burundi for Europe, passing many of the powers of the crown over to his son, Ndizeye. In July 1966, Prince Charles announced over the radio that he was taking over the throne of Burundi from his father. Mwambutsa condemned the rebellion against his authority and accused extremist elements of manipulating his son. The 19-year-old prince said in his address that he wanted to bring an end to "four years of chaos and anarchy, of nepotism and corruption." He also said that he wanted to "bring about a revaluation of the Murundi personality in the context of a continuous and harmonious economic development." Ndizeye dismissed Prime Minister **Léopold Biha**, suspended the constitution, and asked **Michel Micombero** to form a new government. In September, he was formally proclaimed mwami of Burundi in coronation ceremonies held in the ancient capital of **Muramvya**. In his coronation speech, the newly installed Ntare V called on all Barundi to heal their ethnic divisions: "I shall reign in the name of all of you, and for you. My reign will seek to bring back understanding in all Burundi."

Initially, there was great enthusiasm over the coronation, but it was very short lived. The new mwami attempted some political maneuvers but was too young to have mastered the arts of palace intrigue. This effort brought him into conflict with **Tutsi** politicians, some of whom abolished the monarchy entirely in November 1966 while Ntare was on a state visit to Léopoldville (Kinshasa) in the **Democratic Republic of the Congo**. This coup that ousted the final king of Burundi and proclaimed Burundi a republic was led by Micombero and two subsequent coup leaders, **Jean-Baptiste Bagaza** and **Pierre Buyoya**.

Ndizeye went first to Europe, settling for a time in **Germany**, and eventually to Uganda, where he convinced President Idi Amin to aid him in his return to Burundi. Amin attempted to do so, extracting from Micombero in March 1972 a written guarantee of Ndizeye's safety. One of Micombero's letters to Amin stated, "Your Excellency can be assured that as soon as Mr. Charles Ndizeye returns to my country he will be considered as an ordinary citizen and that as such his life and his security will be assured." Ndizeye decided to take advantage of the promise of amnesty and was taken to **Bujumbura** on Amin's personal helicopter. When he arrived, he was transferred to a Burundi military helicopter and flown to a destination that was unknown to others at the time. There he was arrested and accused of plotting (or, according to one Burundi radio report the day after his arrival, actually leading) an invasion assisted by West German mercenaries. A radio report the day after his arrival warned the people of Burundi to be on their guard against the threat "to which the republic almost fell victim. . . . Militants, we must not forget that this was not only an attack against our republic; it was Africa and the honor of Africa that was the target of these sworn enemies of the African continent."

The next two months were chaotic in Burundi. The arrest of the former mwami was the first in a chain of events that would become known as the massacre of 1972. Ndizeye died about a month after his return to the country; the details of how or by whose hand are unclear, although it was not a natural death. Some reports say that an attempt was made to rescue him from house arrest, and he was killed during the ensuing struggle. After a **Hutu** revolt that resulted in the deaths of many thousands of Tutsi, the Tutsi retaliated and slaughtered many tens of thousands of Hutu. Micombero retained power through all of this.

NTARUGERA (?–1920). An elder brother of Mwami **Mutaga II.** Ntarugera was one of the chiefs who took advantage of his position as **Mwezi IV**'s son to acquire as much land as was possible. He eventually became known as one of the greatest and richest men in Burundi and was feared in Mutaga's court. Along with his mother, **Ndirikumutima**, he became a regent in the court of his infant nephew, **Mwambutsa IV**, and was highly thought of by the colonial governor. He died in 1920. In 1947, Mwami Mwambutsa was quoted as blaming Ntarugera and his other uncles for his own lack of a European education and his resulting desire to send his own son away to school.

NTARYAMIRA, CYPRIEN (1955–1994). A founding member of **FRODEBU**, Ntaryamira took over as president of Burundi following the assassination of President **Melchior Ndadaye** in the attempted coup of October 1993. He was appointed head of state by the National Assembly, but the appointment was challenged in the Constitutional Court. The National Assembly had, shortly before, amended the constitution, thus allowing the assembly to elect a successor rather than hold general **elections**. Ntaryamira was finally inaugurated in February 1994. His term of office was very short; in April 1994, the plane in which he and **Rwandan** president Juvénal Habyarimana were traveling crashed near Kigali, the capital of Rwanda. The incident initiated months of civil war in Rwanda, where citizens were convinced that the plane had been shot down. In Burundi, a fragile peace was maintained; the majority of the citizens chose to consider it, at least publicly, as an unfortunate accident. During this time, the people of Burundi were already fighting each other in a civil war that was to last 12 years; analysts believe that this latest presidential death was almost buried beneath the already explosive atmosphere of the country. Both of the presidents killed in the crash were **Hutu.**

NTAWUMENYAKARIZI, BASILE. One of the prominent **Hutu** who lost their lives in the earlier of the **Kamenge** incidents in January 1962, he was a **Parti du Peuple (PP)** militant as well as the principal of a secondary school.

NTIBANTUNGANYA, SYLVESTRE (1956–). Like President **Melchior Ndadaye**, Ntibantunganya had been a **refugee** following the massacres of 1972. He was appointed the minister of foreign affairs after the democratic presidential **election** of June 1993. In the attempted coup during which Ndadaye was killed, Ntibantunganya's wife was also killed by soldiers sent to look for the foreign affairs minister. Following the death of Ndadaye's successor, **Cyprien Ntaryamira**, in April 1994, Ntibantunganya was the popular choice for president, but he did not accept the office until late 1994. He remained the head of a weak and often explosive coalition government until the middle of 1996, and he had little power over the **army**, which was almost completely **Tutsi**; he is **Hutu** and appointed a Tutsi prime minister in an attempt to strike a balance among the various **political parties**. He was overthrown in a bloodless coup by former president **Pierre Buyoya** in 1996. Some political analysts have characterized Ntibantunganya's administration as extremely incompetent in spite of his attempts at ethnic coalitions.

NTIRUHAMA, JEAN. The minister of the interior in 1962, Ntiruhama was severely criticized by a group of **Hutu** deputies for his alleged collusion with the **Jeunesse Nationaliste Rwagasore** leaders during the **Kamenge** riots. The accusations brought against him were sometimes vague and the evidence often scanty, but the belief that the government may have been at fault served to strengthen racial solidarities, especially among the Hutu parliamentarians. By the end of 1962, the Hutu parliamentary group, which represented about half of the total membership of the National Assembly, became known as the Monrovia Group. *See also* CASABLANCA AND MONROVIA GROUPS.

NTITENDEREZA, JEAN (?–1962). The son of **Baranyanka** and the brother of **Joseph Biroli**, Ntitendereza became one of the founders of the **Parti Démocratique Chrétien (PDC)**. He was hanged in **Gitega** in 1962 for his involvement in the assassination of Prince **Louis Rwagasore**.

NTU (BU-). The qualities of an ideal male were clearly defined in traditional Burundi society. Above all else, he was *ubuntu*, an exemplar of goodness, as well as polite, refined, and knowledgeable about proper behavior in all circumstances. This root with other prefixes is also important: for example, *muntu* (plural: *bantu*) means "being," "an individual," or "to be human"; *ihwanyabantu* means "nationality"; *muryabantu* means "cannibal."

NYABYUMA (MU-, BA-). In the traditional society, these were the guardians of the relics and charms among the royal treasures.

NYAMOYA, ALBIN (1924–2001). A **Tutsi** (but not *ganwa*) loyal to the **Casablanca** faction of **UPRONA** and a relative through marriage of Mwami **Mwambutsa IV**, Nyamoya became prime minister upon the resignation of **Pierre Ngendandumwe** in April 1964. In his first address to the National Assembly, Nyamoya reaffirmed Burundi's "traditional policy of non-alignment and neutrality" and the government's desire to have friendly relations with all countries. He also assured the assembly that he would make inquiries into charges of corruption among some civil servants. Very quickly he had reason to repeat these promises. His term of office coincided with rebellions in the **Democratic Republic of the Congo (DRC)**, then Zaire, so the factor of **Chinese** intervention in the area was a major focus at the time. During his short time in office, Nyamoya tried to maintain good relations with neighboring countries. For example, he affirmed that **Bujumbura** University would continue to admit students from the DRC even though the DRC had expelled Barundi students that year.

By June 1964, a great many **refugees** from the DRC were in Burundi. In fact, the government specified the number at 5,052: 5,000 civilians, 41 soldiers, and 11 politicians. Nyamoya denied accusations that the acceptance of the refugees was motivated by any considerations other than humanitarian ones. The Nyamoya government prohibited public meetings among the refugees as well as the formation of armed groups, the possession of weapons, and the circulation of what it called political propaganda. In spite of these precautions, Nyamoya contacted the chairman of the **Organization of African Unity (OAU)** ad hoc commission on DRC as well as the secretaries-general of the OAU and the **United Nations**, charging that Zairian military aircraft had bombed communities in Burundi twice.

In December 1964, a large cache of arms and ammunition was discovered near **Gitega**, and rumors of an impending coup sponsored by China quickly circulated. Very shortly after that, alleging errors and misjudgment on the part of Nyamoya, the *mwami* withdrew his support from Nyamoya's government and again asked Ngendandumwe to form a cabinet.

NYANGOMA, GERVAIS. Following the legislative elections of May 1965, Nyangoma became the director general in the prime minister's office. He was believed to have participated in the planning and execution of the coup that occurred in October 1965. In fact, although there is no conclusive evidence, Nyangoma was said to be the most actively involved and is generally assumed to have been the one who originated the idea of the coup against the monarchy.

NYANGOMA, LEONARD. *See* CONSEIL NATIONAL POUR LA DÉFENSE DE LA DÉMOCRATIE (CNDD)/NATIONAL COUNCIL FOR THE DEFENSE OF DEMOCRACY; FORCES POUR LA DÉFENSE DE LA DÉMOCRATIE (FDD)/FORCES FOR THE DEFENSE OF DEMOCRACY; POPULAR DEMOCRATIC HUTU ARMY.

NYARURIMBI (MU-, BA-). The supreme court judges in the *mwami*'s traditional court tribunal. Related words include *abarimbi*, descendants of the original Karimbi clan, an important **Hutu** family, and *Umurimbi*, which is synonymous with *Umuhutu* in the country's historical poetry.

NYENUMAGAMBA. In traditional Burundi society, the queen mother (*mugabekazi*) held a very important political and ceremonial role. If she died before or during the reign of the *mwami*, he could name an adoptive mother, usually a young woman, to fill the role; this was similar to the tradition of replacing **Mukakiranga** if she died before the mwami did. The ceremonial name for the substitute was Nyenumugamba. One had to be chosen because a mwami could not ascend the throne without a queen mother; as the saying went, *"Ubwami barabusangiye"* (The royal power must be shared).

NYONGABO, PRIME. While a student at the Université Officielle in Lubumbashi, Zaire (the **Democratic Republic of the Congo**), Nyongabo was one of the founders of the **Jeunesse Nationaliste Rwagasore**, later becoming the organization's national president. He was also known to have launched the 1962 **Kamenge** incidents, which prompted the *mwami* to dissolve the organization. The leaders were imprisoned, but the organization was revived in 1966. Nyongabo later became the foreign minister in **Michel Micombero**'s cabinet.

NYOVU (I-, I-). Collectively used uncultivated pastures for cattle found outside a group of family enclosures (*rugo*).

NYWANA (KU-). In traditional Burundi society, members of different clans would occasionally develop strong friendships that led to the sharing of clan identities. This, the *ukunywana* or blood brotherhood, was accomplished in a formal ceremony. The two individuals involved formalized the relationship by mixing and drinking the blood from skin incisions on their chests. As part of the ritual, they pledged eternal loyalty and mutual assistance, particularly in the accumulation of cattle (*inka*).

NZAMBIMANA, EDOUARD. One of the earliest appointments of **Jean-Baptiste Bagaza** after the 1976 coup was that of Nzambimana as prime minister. In early 1978, Prime Minister Nzambimana announced that the country's military rulers were planning to hand over power to civilians in 1981, which would have been five years after the overthrow of **Michel Micombero** and his government. Nzambimana eventually lost his place on the **Central Committee** of **UPRONA** in 1984.

NZIKORURIHO, DIDACE. Following **Pierre Buyoya**'s complete and unhesitating acceptance of his defeat in the **elections** of June 1993, the **army** also upheld the election results. When a group of officers tried to move against the elected government in July, just a week before its swearing in, Lieutenant Colonel Nzikoruriho, the deputy chief of staff, dismissed it as "just some small boys gone astray."

NZOHABONAYO, SYLVÈRE. A member of **Michel Micombero**'s "**Family Corporation**" (he was the brother of **Athanase Gakiza**, who was Micombero's wife's uncle), Nzohabonayo was appointed director-general for judicial, administrative, and political affairs in the office of the presidency. In March 1974, he became the attorney general.

– O –

OKO (BU(W)-, AM-). In the traditional lineages, the *ubwoko* was the largest grouping—the clan or **patriclan**.

ORGANIZATION OF AFRICAN UNITY (OAU). The OAU was established in 1963 by 32 independent member states. The organization's objectives were to promote unity and solidarity among African countries, to eradicate all forms of colonialism from Africa, to defend sovereignty and independence, and to promote international interdependence. By 2000, the OAU comprised 53 African countries, including Burundi. In 1996, the OAU strongly condemned **Pierre Buyoya**'s coup, some members calling for Buyoya's removal; the organization discussed the possibility of a multinational military intervention (with Chad, Malawi, Uganda, **Tanzania**, and Zambia agreeing to contribute troops and the **United States** offering to provide transportation). The military intervention did not occur, but shortly after this discussion, Tanzania and Kenya declared an economic embargo on Burundi; because Burundi is landlocked, the vast majority of its imports and exports are processed through ports in these two countries. The OAU did send a 46-member military observer mission.

In 1995, the Carter Center in Atlanta, Georgia (founded by former U.S. president Jimmy Carter), working with the OAU, organized a summit of African heads of state in Cairo, during which the subject of the fundamental problems of ethnic conflict in Burundi was discussed. It is from this summit that the eventual **Arusha Accord** emerged. *See also* AFRICAN UNION (AU); MISSION POUR LA PROTECTION DES ÉTABLISSEMENTS DÉMOCRATIQUES AU BURUNDI/MISSION FOR THE PROTECTION OF DEMOCRATIC INSTITUTIONS IN BURUNDI (MIPROBU).

ORO (BU-). This word means "poverty" or "misery"; many names in Kirundi replace their subject or object morpheme with the *-bu-* from *ubworo*. For example, Burahenda is a woman who causes intoxication.

– P –

PALIPEHUTU (PARTI POUR LA LIBÉRATION DU PEUPLE HUTU/PARTY FOR THE LIBERATION OF THE HUTU PEO-

PLE). This **political party** had its roots outside of Burundi; in 1980 it was begun in Mishamo, a **refugee** camp in **Tanzania**, by Rémi Gahutu, who died in 1990. It has since become known as the most radical and uncompromising of all **Hutu** opposition movements. In 1989, a PALIPEHUTU document stated, "The myth of ethnic superiority was the source of a feudal ideology intended to maintain and protect the interests of the feudal monarchy. The feudal lords in turn used this ideology to humiliate and dehumanize the Hutu serfs." Since the fighting in 1990 and 1991 and the attempted coup in 1993, the PALIPEHUTU has become quite active in Burundi. It is often accused of initiating attacks even if no proof exists; it is also accused of attempting to sabotage the reconciliation process. Very few points of agreement exist between the extremists in PALIPEHUTU and the moderates in **FRODEBU**.

PARTI DE LA RÉCONCILIATION DES PERSONNES (PRP)/ PEOPLE'S RECONCILIATION PARTY. In 1992, prior to the first democratic **election** since Burundi's independence, this seemingly anachronistic **political party** emerged. It was a royalist party, advocating a parliamentary monarchy with a prime minister and a council of both **Hutu** and **Tutsi**. Its leader in **Bujumbura**, Jean Bosco Yamuremye, did not see this as anachronistic: "The King, who will act as an arbitrator, remains above ethnic categorization—a constitutional monarchy is the only way to ensure national unity in Burundi."

PARTI DE L'UNION ET DU PROGRÈS NATIONAL (PARTY OF NATIONAL UNION AND PROGRESS). *See* UPRONA (PARTI DE L'UNION ET DU PROGRÈS NATIONAL/PARTY OF NATIONAL UNION AND PROGRESS).

PARTI DÉMOCRATIQUE CHRÉTIEN (PDC)/DEMOCRATIC CHRISTIAN PARTY. The elder sons of Chief **Baranyanka**, **Joseph Biroli** and **Jean Ntitendereza**, launched this **political party** just prior to Burundi's 1962 independence when they severed ties with **UPRONA**. The party's leaders were directly involved in the chain of events that led up to Prince **Louis Rwagasore**'s death and were convicted of the conspiracy.

PARTI DÉMOCRATIQUE ET RURAL (PDR)/DEMOCRATIC AND RURAL PARTY. Founded by a famous *ganwa* of Bezi origins, **Pierre Bigayimpunzi**, this was one of the **political parties** that emerged just prior to Burundi's 1962 independence when many of the old **UPRONA** chiefs severed their ties with the party and set up their own political organizations. *See also* BATARE AND BEZI.

PARTI DES JEUNES TRAVAILLEURS DU BURUNDI (PDJTB)/ YOUNG WORKERS OF BURUNDI PARTY. During the time just before Burundi's 1962 independence, 23 **political parties** were registered. Among them were some based on ethnic interests and solidarity. This party was among those based on particular social class.

PARTI DU MOUVEMENT DE L'EMANCIPATION D'HUTU (PARMEHUTU)/PARTY OF THE HUTU EMANCIPATION MOVEMENT. This was a movement in **Rwanda** begun in 1959 and committed to the **Hutu** cause. It would eventually have an effect on Burundi politics as the country approached independence, causing an identification of the Burundi Hutu with those in Rwanda. This was perhaps not an accurate identification at the time, but one that would have much to do with emerging **political parties** and ethnic strife.

PARTI DU PEUPLE (PP)/PARTY OF THE PEOPLE. Founded in 1959, influenced by events in **Rwanda**, this **political party** became the most known and outspoken of the **Hutu** parties by 1961. In 1965, Hutu candidates won the national **elections** with a total of 23 out of 33 seats in the National Assembly. Official reports, however, obscured the victory for the Hutu and the PP, stating only that **UPRONA** was victorious and the PP won 10 of the seats, not that UPRONA was in disarray and not the cohesive party they wished to present to the country and the world.

PARTI POUR LA LIBÉRATION DU PEUPLE HUTU/PARTY FOR THE LIBERATION OF THE HUTU PEOPLE. *See* PALIPEHUTU.

PARTI POUR LA REDRESSEMENT NATIONAL (PARENA)/ PARTY FOR NATIONAL RECOVERY. This is described as a radical **Tutsi** party, partly because it is the only recognized **political party** in Burundi that was not a part of the coalition government initiated by a power-sharing agreement signed in late 1994. It is led by former president **Jean-Baptiste Bagaza**.

PATRICLAN. This is the largest of the levels of kinship groups in traditional Burundi society. People in such a group recognize a common paternal descent line, but often are unable to identify a specific ancestor. Interestingly, in spite of their original ancestral differences, both **Tutsi** and **Hutu** may belong to the same patriclan. *See also OKO.*

PFUMU (MU-, BA-). These people were soothsayers, healers, magicians, clairvoyants, or oracles and were central to Burundi's ancient traditional society. In the tradition of **Imana**, clairvoyant individuals were considered benefactors to humanity; however, these people acted quite apart from Imana and were, instead, in close league with **Kiranga**. Besides being able to divine the future, the *abapfumu* could give charms and medicines as well as detect thieves and murderers.

POLITICAL PARTIES. Because there have been few **elections** in Burundi's history, there have also been, until recently, few viable political parties. Upon its independence in 1962 and for more than 25 years after, the country's dominant party was **UPRONA**, the Parti de l'Union et du Progrès National; in fact, except for competition from the **Parti Démocratique Chrétien (PDC)** in the very earliest years after independence, UPRONA was the only party that consistently dominated the country and produced heads of state. UPRONA disbanded in 1987 and reformed in 1990.

Following Burundi's 12-year civil war, and in anticipation of the **Arusha Accord** and attempts at a power-sharing peace, many other political parties emerged between the early 1990s and 2004. The largest one is **FRODEBU**, the Front pour la Démocratie au Burundi, which is the party of the assassinated president **Melchior Ndadaye** and the last president before the election, **Domitien Ndayizeye**. Its members are mainly **Hutu**, and the party is considered to be moderate. Other important parties (both primarily Hutu) are the **Conseil National pour la Défense de la Démocratie (CNDD)** and **PALIPEHUTU** (Parti pour la Libération du Peuple Hutu/Party for the Liberation of the Hutu People); both of these parties were originated by exiled Hutu and both had armed militia wings, the **Forces pour la Défense de la Démocratie (FDD)** and the **Forces Nationales de Libération (FNL)**, respectively. The disastrous 1993 election was dominated by UPRONA and FRODEBU; at that time, PALIPEHUTU was an outlawed group, and Ndadaye was able to mobilize them behind his candidacy. In the 2005 elections, the CNDD-FDD, which had joined the government in 2004, became the winning party, taking 58 percent of the popular vote; UPRONA received only 7 percent of the vote. In addition to these large, dominant parties, there are at least 20 others that have made claims for leadership. Among the better known are the primarily Tutsi **Parti pour le Redressement National (PARENA)**, led by former president **Jean-Baptiste Bagaza** and primarily Hutu Front pour la Libération National (FROLINA). *See also* FRONT COMMUN; INKINZO; PARTI DE LA RÉCONCILIATION DES PERSONNES (PRP)/PEOPLE'S RECONCILIATION PARTY; PARTI DÉMOCRATIQUE ET RURAL (PDR)/DEMOCRATIC AND RURAL PARTY; PARTI DES JEUNES TRAVAILLEURS DU BURUNDI (PDJTB)/YOUTH WORKERS OF BURUNDI PARTY; PARTI DU MOUVEMENT DE L'EMANCIPATION D'HUTU (PARMEHUTU)/PARTY OF THE HUTU EMANCIPATION MOVEMENT; PARTI DU PEUPLE (PP)/PARTY OF THE PEOPLE; UNION NATIONALE DU BURUNDI (UNB)/NATIONAL UNION OF BURUNDI.

POPULAR DEMOCRATIC HUTU ARMY. Officials reported that after President **Melchior Ndadaye**'s assassination in 1993, armed groups left the districts of Kinama and **Kamenge** and reorganized into the self-declared Popular Democratic Hutu Army led by the former minister of interior and public security, **Leonard Nyangoma**. In September 1994, they reemerged in Kamenge.

– Q –

QUINCUNX. Although the word is English, one finds it often as a description of the pattern common to the basketwork of Burundi. It is an arrangement having five points or components, one at each corner and one in the center of a square or rectangle. Many baskets were decorated with strips of black or mauve fibers, dyed with mud from marshes, and arranged in these geometric patterns. Combinations of narrow fiber strips subtly represented the natural latticework of banana leaves, a common artistic theme because of the importance of the banana plant as a main source of beer, considered a necessity in many social relations. *See also* ARTS AND CRAFTS.

– R –

REFUGEES. The refugee situation in Burundi is complex, with at least three different aspects to consider. The first is that hundreds of thousands of Barundi have fled their homes since the beginning of Burundi's 12-year civil war in 1993. These refugees, however, are in addition to the estimated 100,000 refugees that had already been displaced from ethnic conflicts in 1972 and 1988. Many have found refuge in **Tanzania**, **Rwanda**, and the **Democratic Republic of the Congo (DRC)**; the majority have gone to Tanzania. Since voluntary repatriation programs began in 2002, many of these refugees have returned to their homes in Burundi, but it is not a simple process. For many, the homes and fields that they left have been either destroyed or inhabited by others. Nevertheless, approximately 160,000 refugees have returned from Tanzania between March 2002 and April 2005 with the assistance of the **United Nations High Commissioner for Refugees (UNHCR)**, whose office provides shelter, medical care, instruction in nutrition and crop production, and primary **education**; the UNHCR hopes and expects all refugees from Tanzanian camps to be repatriated by the end of 2006. Tanzania is gradually closing camps as their populations decrease. An estimated 4,000 Barundi remain as refugees in Rwanda, but that situation is even more complicated.

Second, in addition to the Burundi refugees in Rwanda, there are also Rwandan refugees in Burundi. Since the two countries have such a close relationship historically and share many of the same ethnic conflicts, they have also had parallel refugee situations. Since the early 1960s when both countries became independent of colonial powers and of each other, the Burundi-Rwanda border has known a great deal of refugee activity: when the **Hutu** in Rwanda acquired power in 1960, many **Tutsi** fled to Burundi, and many have remained. As conflicts arise, more Rwandans flee to Burundi; it is estimated that there are approximately 8,000 Rwandan refugees in Burundi. As well, during the rising tensions in the DRC, Congolese refugees have fled to both Burundi and Rwanda; estimates vary, but approximately 30,000 Congolese were in camps in the two countries in the summer of 2005, and that number was expected to increase.

The third aspect of the complex refugee situation in Burundi and the entire region is the vast numbers of internally displaced persons (IDPs), those people who fled their homes but remained within the borders of their own countries. In Burundi, this internal displacement has been happening for decades; however, the latest and largest displacement has occurred since 1993. After the assassination of **Melchior Ndadaye**, many abandoned their homes in anticipation of fighting or to avoid fighting, and this pattern continued over the next eight or nine years. Each time a new conflict would arise, groups of frightened citizens would leave their regions. The Burundi government also ordered the relocation of hundreds of thousands of mostly Hutu civilians into special camps between 1996 and 2000. The number of IDPs peaked in 1999 with over 800,000 displaced (approximately 12 percent of the population). The camps were dismantled in 2000 under international pressure, but little assistance has been given to IDPs to resettle.

Although the civil war ended with democratic **elections** in August 2005, displacement continues because fighting continues between the new government and remaining rebels from the **Forces Nationales de Libération**. The fighting has centered primarily in **Bujumbura Rural Province** since 2004, and an estimated 30,000 individuals have fled the fighting and remain displaced.

Some international groups (for example, Amnesty International and Refugees International) have expressed concern that, while the UNHCR is doing a lot for the repatriation of both refugees and IDPs, the repatriation might be too fast, causing other **human rights** problems. Because of the problems of land appropriation mentioned earlier, these organizations recommend that the Burundi government enforce a "fair and transparent resolution to all land and property disputes."

RELIGION. Burundi has one of the highest percentages of Christians in the world. It is estimated that about 65 percent of the population is **Catholic** and about 20–25 percent Protestant. A small portion (about 5 percent) follows Islam.

The arrival of the **Belgians** and the quick departure of the **Germans** had different impacts on the Catholic and Protestant populations and missions. The **White Fathers** spoke French, as did the Belgians, and Catholicism was the dominant religion in Belgium.

The Belgians not only permitted the White Fathers to continue their work but also provided funding for mission schools and **health** facilities. This government sponsorship and funding were restricted to the Catholic Church for most of the time the Belgians colonized Burundi.

Many believe that the primary role of the missionary was to destroy traditional beliefs among the people. However, many, if not most, Barundi (**Hutu** and **Tutsi** alike) maintain many of the traditional animistic beliefs. These beliefs include a creator, **Imana**, and a number of other spirits; the most important among these is **Kiranga**. The traditional religion includes two important components in addition to the recognition of Imana: the presence of the spirits of one's ancestors and the existence of a life force that is in all beings. The ancestral spirits can be malicious and must be placated. These departed ancestors are called *ubuzima*, *mizimu*, *imizimu*, or *abasimu*, and they are among the causes of cattle epidemics, crop failure, and sickness because they are supposed to envy the things they had to leave behind. Their influence extends only over their own clan, and the descendents must consult a diviner to discover the reason for the ancestor's anger. These ancestors can often be placated if the family builds a *kararo*, a "little sleeping house" supplied with food and beer (*terekera*) beside the grave.

While the Catholic Church has often been implicated as having involvement with atrocities in **Rwanda**, this did not seem to be the case in Burundi; in fact, the Burundi Catholic Church appears to have tried to make peace throughout the years of civil war. Pope Benedict XVI personally encouraged the bishops of Burundi to work for peace and reconciliation and to counteract "the work of sects."

The Transitional Constitutional Act provides for freedom of religion in Burundi, and the government respects this right in practice. The government requires religious groups to register with the Ministry of Internal Affairs, which keeps track of their leadership and activities.

RENCHARD, GEORGE W. On 7 June 1968, **United States** president Lyndon Johnson appointed Renchard as U.S. ambassador to Burundi. The post had been vacant since January 1966, when Burundi expelled the U.S. ambassador, **Donald Dumont**, on suspicion of involvement with opposition conspirators.

RIMBA (KI-, BI-). This term refers to the court of **Mwezi IV**, which consisted of three principal parts. The *intangaro* was an enclosure divided into two sections, one for the queen's cattle and the other for the *mwami*'s cattle. The *inyubakwa* was the main palace, and the *ikigo* was the grazing pasture.

RUTOVU (TUTSI). *See* MATANA TUTSI.

ROZI (MU-, BA-). In the traditional cults of **Kiranga**, these were the negative sorcerers, casters of bad spells, and general doers of evil. They were thought to cause death, sterility, and other ills. While magic and sorcery were an important aspect of traditional Burundi society, practitioners convicted of this form of black magic (*burozi*) were often sentenced to death by impalement or crucifixion.

RUFUKO. *See* INANJONAKI; NTARE I (RUSHATSI).

RUGAAMBA. *See* NTARE II (RUGAAMBA).

RUGO. Literally, these are fences or fenced circles scattered on the many hillsides (*collines*) in Burundi. Each houses a family unit. *See also CHANYO; SOZI.*

RUKINZU. The *mwami*'s entourage traditionally included the royal drum (**Karyenda**), accompanied by six smaller drums; Rukinzu, the drummer guard; and five *amashakwe* (singular: *ishakwe*), the drummers who keep the cadence of the march.

RUSHATSI. *See* NTARE I (RUSHATSI).

RWAGASORE, PRINCE LOUIS (1932–1961). Often cited as the person who brought Burundi politics toward independence, Prince Louis Rwagasore remains one of the most revered historical figures of Burundi. As the son of Mwami **Mwambutsa IV**, he had many advantages in his life, but it was neither his princely nor even his *ganwa* status for which he is most remembered. The foundations of **UPRONA** coincided with Rwagasore's return to Burundi after he completed his studies at the Institut Universitaire des Territoires d'Outre-Mer in Antwerp, **Belgium**. At this time, he was given the chiefdom of **Butanyerera** to administer, but this apparently did not satisfy his political ambitions; between 1958 and 1959, Rwagasore virtually took control of UPRONA, both anticipating the visit from the **Groupe de Travail** and helping to change the party into a clearly anti-Belgium, pro-independence party.

Many causes explain Rwagasore's popularity and ability to unite the growing elite among both of the major ethnic groups in Burundi. For one, as the son of Mwambutsa, he belonged to the **Bambutsa** clan of the **Tutsi**; thus, he was able to be the acknowledged representative of the Bezi but stand outside of the Bezi-**Batare** conflict as a true national figure, while still having obvious ties to the still popular crown. It is said that this royal tie added some legitimacy to the UPRONA Party, giving it a necessary edge over its opponents. He also had the advantage of a university **education**; although he was not known to be very intellectually sophisticated, his education did seem to give him a more progressive outlook, setting him off quite dramatically from many of the other chiefs. Additionally, he married a **Hutu** woman, which made him more sympathetic to the Hutu cause as well as more popular among the Hutu. Finally, he was simply a very energetic and charismatic figure and an inspiring public speaker.

Rwagasore was not popular among the Belgian administrators. The Belgians referred to the UPRONA leadership as "crypto-communists" and openly sided with their opposition in the **Parti Démocratique Chrétien (PDC)**. In fact, in 1956, the *resident* of Burundi wrote in his annual report that Rwagasore's attitude was typical of "progressive tendencies," which he said reflected those of the former students of the Group Scolaire of Astrida and the former seminarians. This administrator stated that these young men "do not always enjoy the sympathy of the administration, because they lack moderation." While thrown together in this category of young upstarts, Rwagasore actually enjoyed even less popularity from the Belgians than most of the others because of his uncompromising commitment to immediate independence. At one point, he declared, "The Belgians accuse us of being Communists. At the same time, they accuse us of being monarchists and feudal. They must make up their minds as to what we really are." While his populist views were seen as communist by the administration, his antiadministration views enhanced his status as a nationalist leader among the Barundi.

With this prevailing atmosphere, in August 1960, a meeting was held in Brussels to discuss arrangements for the communal elections and plans for administrative reorganization. During this meeting, an addition to an earlier decree was made that stated that relatives of the *mwami* within two degrees of relationship could not receive an electoral mandate, hold political office, or take official part in any political activity. As a result, Rwagasore's role in UPRONA remained strictly an advisory one through many internal changes of party leaders. He remained popular with the public in spite of these restrictions as well as the administration's efforts to discredit him, and he was finally placed under house arrest in late 1960, but in September 1961, after his release, under **United States** supervision, general **elections** to elect a government to lead the country after independence were held. UPRONA won overwhelmingly, and Rwagasore was elected the prime minister of the country.

From the beginning, Rwagasore had understood the need to make UPRONA into a party for the masses. To this end, he tried to incorporate into the formal leadership of the party an even proportion of Hutu and Tutsi. In 1961, the **Central Committee** of the party comprised three Tutsi and four Hutu, this imbalance compensating for the fact that the president and vice president of the party were both Tutsi. In spite of the feelings that much of Rwagasore's political success sprang from his relationship to Mwami Mwambutsa, the relationship between the two was not one of unconditional support; Rwagasore made these conditions clear from the start in the party's second manifest, which stated that the party was prepared to endorse a monarchic regime "only insofar as this regime and its dynasty favored the genuine emancipation of the Murundi people." Rwagasore also made clear that the mwami would stay in office only by surrendering power to the government. For his own part, the mwami never showed a great deal of affection for UPRONA even to the extent of not helping in the political success of his son. Rwagasore was not a member of the "inner circle" of the king's men, many of whom went their separate ways by forming their own preindependence **political parties**.

The most powerful of these opposition parties was the PDC (of the **Front Commun**), which was led by **Jean Ntitendereza** and **Joseph Biroli**. According to testimony, the Belgian *resident* held a meeting in September 1961 that was attended by the European secretary of the

PDC. During this meeting, *Resident* Régnier reportedly stated, "Rwagasore must be killed! . . . The Front Commun lost the elections, but nothing is lost if one gets rid of Rwagasore in time. . . . Once the deed is accomplished, the lake is not too far away." This feeling fed into the Bezi-Batare conflict nicely. On 13 October 1961, less than a year before independence, Rwagasore was assassinated by a hired Greek gunman named **Jean Kageorgis**. The assassination was found to be a conspiracy organized by the rival political faction; Ntitendereza, Biroli, and several other members of the Batare clan were implicated by the assassin, and all were eventually found guilty and executed in January 1963 before approximately 20,000 observers.

It is said by many that Rwagasore's death created a political vacuum that was to influence decades of Burundi politics to follow. Whether this can be verified or not is irrelevant; it is the belief of so many that it is an opinion deserving credence. Very soon after his death, UPRONA fell prey again to fundamental ethnic and ideological divisions, with all measures of ethnic cohesion seeming to disappear. Although André Muhirwa succeeded Rwagasore as prime minister, he and his followers did not enjoy the support of the Barundi as Rwagasore had. Even as much as four years later, when another prime minister, **Pierre Ngendandumwe,** was assassinated, many political analysts attributed the death to the crisis developed in the political void left by Rwagasore's death. Even more than 30 years later, in 1994 and during another crisis in Burundi, some Barundi expressed their belief that the country would have developed completely differently had Rwagasore lived. A Burundi ambassador to the United States, **Jacques Bacamurwanko**, when asked if one man could really have made so much difference, said, "Yes, definitely, if he had been allowed to live longer. . . . Our fathers and grandfathers do tell us that Rwagasore was something else—that had he lived longer, he would have brought about universal changes. I think [Burundi] would have been politically stable, or as politically stable as **Tanzania** next door." *See also* MIREREKANO, PAUL, AND ANDRÉ MUHIRWA.

RWANDA, RELATIONS WITH. Of almost equal size and separated by the Akanyaru River, the two countries of Rwanda and Burundi compose the region that was known to many early explorers as the

"Switzerland of Africa." But in spite of the joint administration of the two countries (as Ruanda-Urundi) under the **Germans** and **Belgians**, Rwanda and Burundi have always been separate entities with separate royal and political structures. In Rwanda, the historical rift was between **Hutu** and **Tutsi**; in Burundi, the conflict was historically more the *ganwa* against the **Hutu and Tutsi** together. In modern days, however, the two nations have had a much more parallel ethnic situation. Since just before independence, the two have been intertwined, with events in one country affecting events in the other.

Hans Meyer said of the two countries,

In Burundi the Tutsi are neither so pleasure-seeking, lazy, mendacious, violent and opportunist as in Rwanda; nor are the Hutu so servile and hypocritical toward the mighty and so impertinent toward the weak; nor is [*sic*] the king and his court so addicted to idleness, wastefulness, intrigue, and so eager to satisfy their depraved and cruel instincts. (*Die Barundi*, 1916, 14–15)

He also said that "despite great differences in status [in Burundi], Tutsi and Hutu conduct friendly social intercourse" and "the Hutu who is better off considers himself socially on the same level as the ordinary Tutsi who has no property."

A great many current news articles about Burundi end by stating that the ethnic makeup of the country is the same as that in Rwanda, implying that the history and development of the two countries have been similar. As stated above, this is not strictly the case, although one cannot deny the similar populations and the influence the countries have had on each other. In Rwanda, the Belgian administration changed some of its practices in the mid-1950s and began permitting Hutu to assume a larger role in public life and assuring them more places in institutions of higher education. In the late 1950s, just before independence, Rwandan Hutu rose up against Tutsi rule, eliminated the monarchy, and killed or drove into exile thousands of Tutsi. Between 1959 and 1962, nearly all administrative positions were transferred from Tutsi to Hutu, so at independence, Rwanda's government was controlled by Hutu. This led the Tutsi in Burundi to find ways to avoid the same transfer of power. The ethnic violence in Burundi in 1972 inspired a new outbreak of ethnic violence in Rwanda in 1973, which led to the fall of the Rwandan government in a coup that year. The assassination of **Melchior Ndadaye** in Burundi convinced many Hutu in Rwanda that compromise with the Tutsi was dangerous, and some of the Hutu who had fled the 1993 violence in Burundi played an active part in the Rwandan genocide of 1994.

René Lemarchand writes: "The **refugee** problem in Burundi cannot be dissociated from its broader regional context. . . . For every outburst of anti-Tutsi violence in Rwanda, one can expect a similar explosion of anti-Hutu sentiment in Burundi, and vice versa" (*Burundi*, 1994, 175). When outside observers discuss the future of either country, the name of the other always comes up. Regardless of the precolonial and colonial histories of the two countries, it has become increasingly clear over the last three decades that they are connected, even if it is in what some call an unholy union. In 1962, they became (at least theoretically) independent not only from their Belgian colonizers but also from each other. Since that time, in ethnic conflict after ethnic conflict, the conflicting ethnic groups of the two countries have drawn together, not only in the eyes of the outside world. Today, both Burundi and Rwanda are relatively peaceful, but they came to peace in different ways. Rwanda has tried to eliminate the specter of ethnicity; the population no longer carries ethnic identity cards, and laws are gradually being passed that deny any importance to ethnicity. Many analysts believe that this is not the way to achieve permanent peace, recommending that Rwanda follow the example of Burundi in facing ethnic differences head-on and making laws to protect the interests of both groups. *See also* HUTU AND TUTSI, RELATIONS BETWEEN; RWANDAN SYNDROME.

RWANDAN SYNDROME. Although many **Tutsi** did not feel that **Melchior Ndadaye** should have been killed, they did feel that the attempted coup of October 1993 was justified. According to Catherine Watson, many said that Ndadaye's government made serious errors by replacing too many Tutsi in the government with **Hutu** in a short time, bringing back Hutu **refugees** too quickly, and trying to bring Hutu, who they said were underqualified, into the military. This, they said, seemed like the "Rwandan Syndrome," a situation dreaded by Burundi Tutsi since the Hutu uprising in Rwanda in the 1950s. At that time, the Hutu overthrew the Tutsi monarchy, killed and exiled hundreds of thousands of Tutsi, and marginalized those who remained. The Hutu maintained power in Rwanda until 1994.

RWASA, AGATHON. Rwasa became the leader of the rebel group **Forces Nationales de Libération (FNL)** in the spring of 2001, when he deposed Cossan Kabura, the group's previous leader. Prior to that, he had been the FNL's chief of operations. Under Rwasa's command, the FNL has been implicated in a multitude of attacks against **Tutsi** civilians; **Hutu** civilians who were suspected of moderate political leanings have also been killed by Rwasa's forces. One of the best-known attacks was against a bus carrying civilians, including **women**, children, and an aid worker from Great Britain. The Hutu passengers were released and given the following message for the Burundi government: "We're going to kill them all and there's nothing you can do." This bus has become known as the *Titanic Express*. In addition, Rwasa was responsible for a massacre of 160 Congolese **refugees** in a camp in Burundi.

In April 2005, Rwasa participated in talks with the **Tanzanian** president, Benjamin Mkapa; this was a hopeful sign to regional leaders and the **United Nations**, who felt this gesture showed Rwasa and the FNL were serious about joining the country's peace process. Shortly after the talks, however, the FNL resumed attacks on civilians. In October 2005, members of the FNL publicly announced their rejection of Rwasa as their leader, accusing him of "gross **human rights** violations." In a statement, a spokesman for the group said, "Rwasa is killing innocent people. He cuts the heads off people, accusing them of collaborating with the **army**." Rwasa is reported to have fled to Tanzania, where he had found refuge in the past. He has been labeled a terrorist by regional governments and remains at large.

RWUBA. The "Miscreator" is thought to be the adversary of **Imana**. His form is not specified; linguistically, he is sometimes referred to with Class 3/4 agreements (as is Imana) and sometimes with Class 1/2 agreements (as with human beings). Rwuba is the most evil of spirits. He watches for his chance to do harm, and his primary goal is to spoil whatever Imana has made. The name, Rwuba, is connected to the verb *ubagura*, which means "spoil" or "ruin."

RYANGO (MU-, MI-). The **Tutsi** and **Hutu** traditionally had essentially the same kinship system, in which the smallest social unit was the local kin group of the male descent line, the *umuryango*, which included all married male members of a family and their wives, as well as unmarried children, both male and female. Each family subdivision had a designated chief, usually the eldest male or *umukuru*. *Umukuru w'umuryango* was the chief of the clan, and *umukuru w'inzu* was the chief of a household or nuclear family. In addition to these family heads, there are many terms in Kirundi for family relationships. Often—and in this case it was clearly true—kinship terms reveal a great deal about a traditional society and the relationships of importance within it.

Following are some Kirundi terms, some quite remote by Western standards, showing the vast intricacies of the clan system. A husband is *umugabo* and a wife is *umugore*, but the husband of two wives is *umugabo w'ihari*; the wives address each other as *umukeba wanje*. A son is *umuhungu*; his mother calls him *umuhungu wanje*, and his father's other wife calls him *umuhungu wa mukeba wanje*. A daughter is *umukobwa*; her mother calls her *umukobwa wanje*, and her father's other wife calls her *umukobwa w'wanje*. The **language** for siblings in a polygamous society is potentially vast, with all of the necessary permutations of relationship. For example, a male calls his brother from the same mother and father *mukuru wanje* if the brother is older and *uwo dusangiye data na mama* if the brother is younger; he calls his full sister *mushiki wanje mukuru* if she is older and *mushiki wanje* if she is younger. A female calls her older full brother *musaza wanje mukuru* and her younger brother *musaza wanje*; she calls her sisters *mukuru wanje* and *butoyi*. If the father is the same but the children have different mothers, the forms of address are different. For example, a male calls his older half-brother *mwene data mukuru* and his younger half-brother *mwene data mutoya*; a female calls her older half-sister *mukuru wanje wo kwa data* and her younger half-sister *murumuna wanje wo kwa data*. If the children have the same mother and different fathers, the incidents of the ward *data* change to *mama*. For example, a male would call his older half-brother *mwene mama mukuru*.

These intricacies extend beyond the nuclear family as well. Each aunt, uncle, cousin, grandparent, and in-law has his or her own form of address. For example, a female would call her older male and female cousins on her father's side *mwena datawacu mukuru* and her younger male and female cousins on her mother's side *mwene mamawacu mutoya*. Paternal and maternal uncles are *sewabo* and *inarume*, respectively; paternal and maternal aunts are *senge* and *mama wacu*, respectively. The son of a man's brother is his *umuhungwacu*, and the son of a man's sister is his *umwishwa*; a paternal aunt refers to her nephews as *umusengezana wanje* and a maternal aunt refers to her nephews as *umuhungu wanje*. There is even a word for the second wife of a sister's husband: *mukebacu*. *See also GABO*; *KURU*.

– S –

SABA (KU-). Literally, this verb means "to solicit aid from someone," and it was used often in **Paul Mirerekano**'s booklet, "**Mbwire Gito Canje**," apparently to impress on the reader the importance of traditional hierarchical relationships.

SAKU (RU-, IN-). The word itself means "curiosity" or "to be very curious," but its root is important in the oral tradition of Burundi. *Amazina y'insaku* is the name of the form that presents and stresses clan rivalries; *izina ry'urusaku* is the name of the form that expresses hatred, animosity, and ill will. *See also ZINA*.

SEMASAKA. Literally, the "father [or master] of sorghum"; in traditional society, the chief of the royal herds. The last Semasaka, under the reign of **Mwambutsa IV**, died in 1935; when **Ntare V** became *mwami* in 1966, another Semasaka was sought, but his reign ended before the office was filled.

SENDEGEYA, PIERRE CLAVER. A third candidate in Burundi's first democratic presidential **election** in June 1993, Sendegeya was a member of the **Parti de la Réconciliation des Personnes**. He received 1.44 percent of the vote, a distant third behind **Melchior Ndadaye**'s 64.7 percent and **Pierre Buyoya**'s 32.47 percent.

SENTARE. A tribunal of the *mwami* that functioned to arbitrate services and activities on a *chanyo* where there were no local regulations to cover the matter. The name is attributed to **Ntare I**, during whose reign the Sentare were the governmental administrators.

SHEBUJA (MU-, BA-). The general term designating one's patron or protector. It was of crucial importance during the period of Burundi's history that relied on a system of patronage (until the 1950s). *See also GABIRE.*

SHEGU (GI-, BI-). At the core of the initiation rite into the cult of **Kiranga**, infants receive the name of an ancient companion of the spirit. These companions are *bishegu*; this is also the word for the politically connected mediums of the court; they were considered extremely powerful and were often sent to exact payment from one against whom the *mwami* held a grudge. **Jan Vansina** relates a story revealing the power of the *ibishegu*: Ndivyariye, a regent of **Mwezi IV**, was ousted after many years in office. The mwami had him strangled, wrapped in mats, and transported to the countryside. However, the porters transporting his body met with thieves along the way and were forced to abandon the body. The regent, who was not yet dead, dressed as a medium and assumed the name of Baruubahuka. Under this disguise, he returned to the court and was accepted as a medium dressed as Ndivyariye, rather than the other way around. The story concludes by saying that people "did not touch him and he left to live in Bweru."

Kiranga was considered the king of bishegu in some traditions. He had a large entourage, including members of his family and other trusted individuals. Among them were, of course, **Inaryangombe** and **Mukakiranga**. In addition, there were Serutwa, Kiranga's son and the carrier of his lance; Kagoro, Kiranga's daughter; Nabirungu, the leader of the pages and hunters; Sakitema (also known as Inamukozi and Inamurimyi), the woman in charge of the cultivation of the land; Kisiga, head of the lance carriers other than Kiranga's; Rubamba, Kiranga's chief sorcerer; and Zura, the one who prepares the dead for burial and attempts to rid them of evil spirits and bad destinies. There are many other lesser bishegu as well.

SHIGANTAHE (MU-, BA-). In traditional society, the advisors at every level of the political hierarchy. They were also recognized elders and judges with whom the highest ideal of public speaking was associated. According to **Ethel Albert**, a shigantahe was expected to be

intelligent, in complete command of the arts of logic, a fine speaker—
i.e., he speaks slowly and with dignity, in well-chosen words and figures

of speech; he is attentive to all that is said; and he is an able analyst of logic and the vagaries of the human psyche. Initiation as *umushigantahe* comes late—usually not before age 45. It is restricted to men of means who can pay for the costly initiation party and who have demonstrated their ability, usually in a long apprenticeship.

Although their function was essentially judicial, the *bashigantahe* wielded considerable political influence and enjoyed considerable esteem in the society.

There were three categories of bashigantahe. At the lowest level were the *bashigantahe bo ku mugina*, entrusted with the task of settling disputes among families or individuals on a *chanyo*. At the *ganwa* level, disputes were handled by the *bashigantahe bo ku nama*. Highest up in the hierarchy and attached to the royal court were the *bashigantahe bo mu rulimbi*. The bashigantahe of the ganwa were held in higher esteem than ordinary chiefs, and those attached to the court were more influential than the ganwa. Because the bashigantahe were selected on their own merits and skills, a **Hutu** could qualify for the office and thus achieve higher status than many ordinary **Tutsi**.

Later, when the government became more centralized, the bashigantahe were the deputies to the National Assembly. Around the end of the monarchy, they were still considered to be the elders whose support was politically necessary.

SHITSI (MU-, BA-). These traditional spiritual mediums could contact a living person, however distant, and make him or her answer, often with the intent of forcing a confession of some offense. In **Rwanda**, the *bashitsi* were even more powerful, also able to invoke the dead.

SHOREKE (IN-). Under the *ubugabire* system of patronage, these were female attendants and servants who were in the constant company of the *mwami*. See also GABIRE.

SIBOMANA, ADRIEN (1953–). Attempts at mending ethnic divisions continued throughout President **Pierre Buyoya**'s administration. In October 1988, the president created a consultative commission on national unity, with 12 **Hutu** and 12 **Tutsi** members, to investigate the massacres earlier that year. Also in October, and more importantly, he re-created the position of prime minister and filled it with Sibomana, a Hutu and former provincial governor. More Hutu were brought into the ruling council so that they eventually became the majority. Sibomana became a member of the legislature in 1994 under the administration of President **Sylvestre Ntibantunganya.**

SIGO **AND** *KANGE (GI-, BI-).* Nature spirits that were once human forms and now inhabit the incorporeal world. They are said to keep to themselves in desolate places such as rock outcroppings, steep valleys, and large expanses of water. Traditionally, anyone refusing to be initiated into **Kiranga**'s cult was threatened with the alternative of becoming one of these spirits, a terrifying prospect. The spirits are malicious and have been said to seize people who intrude on their domains; the results are thought to be seizures, severe stomach pain, and even strokes.

SIMBANANIYE, ARTÉMON. In 1965, as minister of justice, Simbananiye organized a selective genocide of **Hutu** intellectuals after the aborted coup. He was one of the leaders of the repression again in 1972 and was a chief architect of the strategy of promoting southern **Tutsi** into positions of power. In 1974, influenced by the "**Family Corporation**" and others, President **Michel Micombero** removed Simbananiye from the important post of foreign minister he then held. He was appointed minister of **education**, but the national university was withheld from his jurisdiction. During the following year, there was a struggle for power between the Family Corporation and the **Matana** group of Tutsi led by Simbananiye. Simbananiye's power began to rise again in 1976, and he enjoyed renewed access to Micombero. In May of that year, Simbananiye won a major victory when Micombero placed the university under the Matana leader's jurisdiction. The members of the Family Corporation, as well as many development-minded Tutsi considered this a major setback.

SIRYUYUMUNSI, THADDÉE. In 1963, under the leadership of National Assembly president Siryuyumunsi, the Monrovia Group delivered a series of attacks against the policy of the government during the **Kamenge** incidents. It managed to apply enough pressure on the *mwami* to have the minister of interior removed from office, but the effect of this was short lived. Apparently in an attempt to ward off any further trouble, André Muhirwa accused Siryuyumunsi and two other prominent citizens of conspiring against the security of the state and ordered their arrest. Mwami **Mwambutsa IV**, who was in Switzerland at the time for medical treatment, instructed the government to put the men under house arrest rather than in prison. At one time, Siryuyumunsi had been a member of the Crown Council. The men were later released, and in February 1964, the National Assembly (almost all **Hutu**, but still under his presidency; he was a **Hima**) began to protest the interventions of the court. In April 1964, Siryuyumunsi led a National Assembly delegation on an official visit to **China**. *See also* CASABLANCA AND MONROVIA GROUPS; MIREREKANO, PAUL, AND ANDRÉ MUHIRWA.

SIZI (MU-, BA-). Many people were traditionally employed in the entourage of the *mwami*. These were the court poets and songwriters.

SLAVERY. Burundi has a long history of servitude, but not such a long history of actual slavery. When the **Tutsi** arrived in the region between 1500 and 1600, they quickly became the masters of the **Hutu**, who had already been in the area. The Tutsi were cattle herders and preferred not to do farming; the Hutu were excellent farmers and only came to appreciate and respect cattle when the Tutsi introduced the animals to the region. Historically, the two groups established a serfdom or clientage (called *ubugabire* in Kirundi): the Hutu farmed the Tutsi's land and took care of their cattle; in return, the Hutu were allowed to live on the land. In these early days, the Hutu never really owned the cattle; the cattle were a part of the land and the land belonged to the Tutsi, but the cattle represented the bond between the two groups. In 1923, all forms of domestic servitude were officially abolished.

In modern days, however, Burundi has become a country rife with **human rights** abuses. Among these is slavery, which comes in several forms. The most obvious form is that of trafficking children for the purpose of forced child soldiering; during Burundi's 12-year civil war that began in 1993, as many as 16,000 children fought with either the government or opposition forces. In addition to the trafficking of child soldiers, members of the national **army** forced males in camps for internally displaced people to accompany them on military operations to shield them from ambush by rebels; men, **women**, and children in these camps were also forced by the army and rebel groups to cook, fetch water, chop wood, and perform other daily chores without compensation. Those who refused to work or whose work was judged insufficient were reportedly beaten or denied access to their land. Young girls are also used for labor and trafficked to other countries; sometimes, the ostensible reason for this trafficking is for adoption or domestic work, but these girls are most often being sold into prostitution. In 2001 alone, the Global Market against Child Labour and the Panafrican News Agency reported that at least 600 Burundi girls were illegally trafficked under the guise of adoption to various European cities for prostitution.

Burundi ratified the International Labor Minimum Age Convention in 1973, which specifies a minimum work age of 16; however, it has not ratified the Convention on the Elimination of the Worst Forms of Child Labor. In addition, Burundi has not signed any of the following international human rights treaties: the Optional Protocol on the Sale of Children, Child Prostitution, and Child Pornography; the International Slavery Convention and supplementary Conventions on the Abolition of Slavery, the Slave Trade, and Institutions and Practices Similar to Slavery; and the Convention for the Suppression of the Traffic in Persons and of the Exploitation of the Prostitution of Others.

The current government does not fully comply with the minimum standards for the elimination of these forms of slavery; however, it is making significant efforts to do so. Large numbers of child soldiers have been demobilized, and the government has launched extensive public awareness campaigns to ease the children's reintegration into local communities. *See also GABIRE*.

SMBIYARA, CYPRIEN. Former secretary-general of **UPRONA**. **Michel Micombero** replaced him in 1968 with **Gilles Bimazubute**, who also was named secretary of the interior and secretary of civil service.

SOUTH AFRICA, RELATIONS WITH. Burundi has learned a great deal about emerging from a long history of internal ethnic strife from South Africa. Since its own peace process in the early 1990s when the country abolished apartheid, South Africa has also become a recognized leader on the African continent in the area of peaceful reconciliation. Of central importance to Burundi's newfound peace is South African leader Nelson Mandela; because of South Africa's own successful struggle, many from other countries have looked to him personally to help bridge differences between governments and communities. Mandela played an important role in bringing factions in Burundi to the peace agreement that, in 2005, created Burundi's democratic **election** and power-sharing agreement. On one of his visits to a Burundi prison, Mandela is quoted as saying that after seeing conditions in the prison, he wondered whether there were any people of God in the country.

Later in Burundi's peace process, South Africa's deputy president Jacob Zuma took on a leadership role to complete what Mandela had begun, and other regional leaders and elder statesmen also intervened. In addition to these two leaders, South Africa's nongovernmental organizations have played a major part in Burundi's peace and plans for development. The African Centre for Constructive Resolution of Disputes (ACCORD) has been extensively involved, as has been the Action Support Centre, a conflict resolution organization. The government and people of South Africa see peace in Central African countries as necessary to the development of the African continent as a whole.

SOZI (MU-, MI-). This is another word for "hill," important in the culture of Burundi because of the terrain of the country. *See also* CHANYO.

SPORTS. Burundi people have long had an interest in sports, particularly soccer and track, and have participated in international tournaments and games. Since 1993, however, when their civil war began, sports have played a very minor role in the lives of Barundi. As the country emerges from those years of violence and displacement, sports are once again becoming important. Many see sports as a way to resume a normal existence and overcome some suspicions. The National Council of Churches in 2003 began to organize soccer matches between members of the national **army**, civilians, and former rebels. One teenage Burundi player said, "Through sport we can achieve many things, even peace. Sport ignores differences of **religion**, class, culture, and ethnicity."

– T –

TABISHI (I-, MA-). In some situations, divorce settlements were paid to estranged wives from 1940 to 1952. Often, these payments were made out of the returned bride wealth, but alternative arrangements could also be made. The practice ended when the local **Belgian** official ruled that payment of *matabishi* "smacked of concubinage and prostitution." *See also KWANO*; *KWAHUKANA*; *KWIRUKANA*.

TABWA (IN-, IN-). In cases of abandonment (physical or emotional) in traditional marriages, there were specific guidelines for either member of the couple to separate. If the wife was left in this condition of *intabwa*, she was able to live until her death in her husband's home. If the wife committed adultery, she was not strongly renounced if she had children, but her husband could then separate from her. Both members could remain in the compound, but the husband would not spend the night with her again. All cattle came under the jurisdiction of the husband, including all milk and butter. She might, if the husband consented, continue to cultivate small parcels of farmland. *See also KWAHUKANA*; *KWIRUKANA*.

TANZANIA, RELATIONS WITH. In spite of their proximity, Tanzania and Burundi have not historically had a lot of contact. There were a few border skirmishes in the 1960s, but these never came to much beyond mutual protests and subsequent apologies. The apologies were made by the Burundi government; Tanzania remained important to overland trade and imports for Burundi.

When ethnic unrest and massacres began in Burundi, Tanzania became a safe haven for many **Hutu**. In fact, the **PALIPEHUTU** is a product of the **refugee** diaspora; its founder, Rémi Gahutu, was a spokesman for Hutu interests and in 1980 began the party in a Tanzanian refugee camp. The **Forces Nationales de Libération** and the **Forces pour la Défense de la Démocratie** were also mostly formed by Hutu living in exile in Tanzania.

Tanzania has been instrumental in the Burundi peace process since the late 1990s. The late Julius Nyerere, former Tanzanian president, was one of the originators of what would become the **Arusha Accord**, the power-sharing agreement that stopped most of the ethnic fighting in Burundi. After Nyerere's death, other Tanzanian politicians joined the regional leaders to help guide Burundi into a peaceful resolution.

TEGATEGA (MU-, BA-). One who rids others of evil spirits and malevolent spells in the **religion** of the traditional society.

TEKA (I-, MA-). One of the qualities of the ideal male in traditional Burundi society is *iteka*, a respect for all human life.

TEN-YEAR ECONOMIC PLAN. In response to the conclusion of the visiting missions of 1948 and 1951, **Belgium** instituted a series of economic and administrative reforms embodied in a comprehensive Ten-Year Economic Plan for Ruanda-Urundi. Proposals for administrative reforms involved several significant changes in the organization of the indigenous political structure and began a limited degree of representative government. The ten-year plan was based on extensive research into the existing economic situation and an analysis of the immediate and long-range needs of the territory. Proposals included in the plan were economic development projects, the expansion of **education** and **health** programs, and a consideration of the problems of population. Before this plan, Ruanda-Urundi had few, if any, professional schools; within the framework of the plan, the government added two large professional schools for crafts, one in Usumbura (**Bujumbura**) and one in Kigali, and promoted and encouraged the organization of about 30 handicraft schools and sections in the missions of the more rural parts of the countries.

TEREKERA (GU-). Beer (usually made from banana, sorghum, millet, or honey) is a necessity for all socially significant communal gatherings, and this word means to offer a gift to the spirits. The use of beer is not restricted to special ceremonies where large quantities would be consumed. It is an everyday adjunct to social interaction and is involved in large part with friendships, marriages, funerals, and contracts. Sometimes, in addition to being a gift, beer has been used as a medium of exchange. It is offered as an expression of homage as well as for amusement and simple refreshment. It is usually drunk through a straw from a large drinking pot. The type of pot used indicates the status of the drinker. All adults (especially males) are beer drinkers; to refuse beer when it is offered is an insult, and traditionally drunkenness was often considered the mark of a prosperous person.

TEREKEREZI (MU-, BA-). Also known as *baheza*, these priests of pythons were charged with keeping the royal pythons healthy and fertile. The priests were protected by the *mwami* because some oral traditions said that the python carries the spirit of dead kings.

TEREREZI (MU-, BA-). The general term for the family, friends, neighbors, and allies with whom relations are maintained through the regular exchange of beer (*terekera*) and other gifts.

TEZI (IN-, IN-). A specific type of illness or malady attributed in traditional society to the influence of bad spirits or evil spells.

TIMA (MU-, MI-). According to the traditional religious belief, the heart or the center of emotion and spirit in each individual. The counterpart of this soul or conscience is the *ubwenge*, intelligence.

TIMBO (MU-, BA-). A specialist of the royal drum (**Karyenda**), covering both the making and playing of it. A related and similar term is *munyuka* (plural: *banyuka*). *See also* MUSIC AND DANCE.

TONGO (I-, MA-). A small family homestead, less than a hectare (2.5 acres) in size, that usually consisted of at least a hut, a corral for livestock, and a farming area for seasonal crops and bananas.

TONI (MU-, BA-). Traditionally the favored confidants of the *mwami* or chief; they were entrusted with the confidential missions initiated by the leader.

TORE (IN-, IN-). Most commonly known today for their internationally famous dancing, these young men, dressed in leopard skins, elaborate headdresses, and bells on their ankles, were at one time part of the royal **army**. *See also* MUSIC AND DANCE.

TRADE UNIONS. *See* LABOR UNIONS.

TRANSPORTATION. Burundi's transportation system has never been extensive. There are approximately 14,480 kilometers (9,000 miles) of highway, but only 1,028 kilometers (640 miles) are paved. While there are eight airports in Burundi, the international airport in **Bujumbura** is the only one with paved runways. There is no national rail system, other than a rail station in Rusumo on the border with Tanzania. Some private buses operate throughout the country.

Bujumbura has the only port facilities in the country; they were built in 1959 and had a capacity of 200,000 tons. The port was expanded in 1989–1992 to a capacity of 500,000 tons, which is more than twice the average import-export traffic ever handled; since 1994, the total tonnage has decreased even more, particularly after the economic embargo placed on Burundi by other African countries in 1996. The M/V *Liemba* is the main ferry operating on the lake; it runs scheduled service from Bujumbura to Kigoma, **Tanzania**, but this service, while scheduled, is sporadic.

Exports leave Burundi in two main ways. Some are sent by ship to Kigoma and then by rail to Dar-es-Salaam on the Indian Ocean; others are sent by road through Uganda to Mombasa, Kenya. The governments of Burundi and Rwanda are seeking an immediate alternative to these methods of transporting exports. Due to increased fuel prices, the two countries hope to extend the rail system to Bujumbura, to the mineral-rich region of Musongati in **Gitega** province which has several nickel mines, and to Kigali (**Rwanda's** capital). This project has not yet been funded.

TUNGANE (BU-). It was considered essential that the traditional ideal male in Burundi possessed *ubutungane*, sincerity in personal relationships. Advantageous uses of rhetorical skill in business negotiations were also acceptable and, some report, even considered proper although insincere.

TUNG CHI-PING. In May 1964, the day after his arrival in Burundi, Tung, a **Chinese** Embassy staff member, asked for political asylum at the **United States** Embassy in **Bujumbura**. Several weeks later, the Chinese *People's Daily* reported the "kidnapping of Tung Chi-ping, staff member of the Chinese embassy in Burundi, by the U.S. embassy" as "another crime U.S. imperialism has perpetrated in its long series of hostile acts toward the Chinese people." In July, the U.S. embassy disclosed that Tung had disappeared. American efforts to arrange for his departure from Bujumbura had been blocked for two months by the Burundi government. Burundi Radio denounced Tung's disappearance as "an unfriendly act which could damage relations between Burundi and the United States." A U.S. embassy spokesman stated that Tung, who had voluntarily entered the embassy, had also left "by his own choice." Tung believed that he had been sent to Bujumbura because French-speaking Chinese were in short supply; he was assigned as the assistant cultural attaché to serve as interpreter to the attaché, who did not speak French. Tung also believed that his political reliability was doubted.

TURIRE (GI-, BI-). Literally, this is a pitcher of beer (*terekera*) or honey. In traditional Burundi society, closely tied to the patron-client relationship probably because of its highly personal character, was the custom of gift-giving, *igiturire*. The Barundi have a saying: "To ask for a gift is to honor; to give a gift is to like."

TUTSI. The Tutsi are believed to have come to Burundi between 1300 and 1600 from the region of the upper Nile. Some believe them to be descendants of Cush, the grandson of Noah from the Bible, but this has not been proven. The Tutsi were known to be cattle herders, and cattle (*inka*) became a very important commodity in the history of Burundi.

Most estimates put the Tutsi population at approximately 14 percent of the total Burundi population. In spite of this minority status, the Tutsi have held most of the power in Burundi, both historically and in modern, postindependence times. In an unusual historical process, the Tutsi (a distinct minority population) adopted the **language** and spiritual practices of the **Hutu**, who were already in the region, while at the same time dominating the Hutu both socially and economically. After independence in 1962, Tutsi controlled the political and military spheres of Burundi, often maintaining that power through violence against the majority Hutu population but also because of lack of Hutu opportunities to improve their positions. Many historians point out that the Tutsi were favored by the **German** and **Belgian** colonial administrations, thus putting them in a good position to maintain that power after independence.

In the country's first democratic **election** in 1993, **Melchior Ndadaye**, a member of the Hutu majority, was elected president. His assassination by members of the largely Tutsi **army** sent the country into 12 years of civil war. By the mid-1990s, Tutsi **youth** gangs began to form; with the assistance of the national army, these groups helped to drive most Hutu out of urban areas and into exile in neighboring countries, and **Bujumbura** remains an overwhelmingly Tutsi city today.

The conflict ended only when, with the help of other countries, a power-sharing government was established. This **government system** was difficult for many Tutsi to accept because, while giving them 40 percent of the seats in the National Assembly and the Senate, it did not maintain their accustomed total dominance. In fact, 10 Tutsi **political parties** rejected the government's draft constitution in 2004 because it did not guarantee the continuance of this complete power. *See also* HUTU AND TUTSI, RELATIONS BETWEEN; *KA*; MATANA TUTSI.

TWA. The third and least discussed ethnic group of Burundi. The Twa proportion of the population has consistently been estimated at about 1 percent. The Twa are a Pygmy group widely believed to be the original inhabitants of the area that is now Burundi and **Rwanda**. In spite of their earliest residency in the area, the Twa generally remain marginalized economically, socially, and politically. Most Twa live in relative isolation without formal **education** and without access to government services, including **health** care. As early as the 19th century, these groups, known as part of the Forest People, were declining in population. Apparently, one of the first aspects of their culture to disappear was their **language**, and by the early 20th century, most of the surviving Pygmy groups spoke the language of their **agricultural** neighbors.

Because they were and are skillful manufacturers, the Twa made various useful household items and defense weapons. The Twa supplemented their incomes by hunting, gathering wild fruits, and entertaining at the royal court. Many of the country's indigenous **arts and crafts**, particularly basketry, are still the jurisdiction of the Twa. Socially, however, they were discriminated against; often, their physical appearance, mannerisms, and dialect were subject to ridicule. In early 2005, two days before the nationwide referendum on a new power-sharing constitution, at least 200 Twa fled to **Rwanda** in fear of political intimidation; they said that the **Hutu** threatened them with "dire consequences" because of their support of the **Tutsi** against approval of the constitution. The current transitional power-sharing government includes Twa representation in the National Assembly and the Senate.

TWARE (MU-, BA-). The general term for a local leader or subchief, an important post prior to a central government. *Umutware w'intara* was a district subchief; *umutware w'umosozi* was a chief of a *chanyo* or hill; *umutware w'umukenke* was the chief of pastureland from whom others secured their land; *umutware w'inka* was the chief of cattle; *umutware w'ingabo* was the military chief; and *umutware n'uwugaba inka* was the charitable chief who gave cattle to others. The word later evolved from a political to more of a military sense.

– U –

UJUSOHOR. Traditionally, most children were born in the family home. When it was about time for a child to be born, the mother called in many of her female neighbors, often including some who were experienced midwives. Immediately after the birth, the child was washed in cold water and rubbed with butter. To protect the infant from harmful spirits, the placenta was buried under the bed, and the mother kept the umbilical cord as an amulet. After six days of seclusion, the child was presented to the family or clan in the ujusohor ceremony; the mother was honored with a crown of maternity, and she and the child were greeted by the family with gifts. Birth begins the cycles of life and is known as *ukusohore* in Kirundi. The other major cycles of life are *kutera imbuto* (marriage) and *igicaniro* (death).

UMUGAMBWE WA'BAKOZI UBURUNDI (UBU)/PARTY OF BURUNDI LABORERS. A **Rwanda**-based **refugee** organization founded in the late 1970s. This underground group, led by **Melchior Ndadaye**, was the beginning of the **FRODEBU** Party.

UNION CULTURELLE DE LA JEUNESSE AFRICAINE DU BURUNDI (UCJAB)/CULTURAL UNION OF AFRICAN YOUTH OF BURUNDI. *See* JEUNESSE NATIONALISTE RWAGASORE (JNR)/RWAGASORE NATIONALIST YOUTH.

UNION DES DÉMOCRATES BARUNDI (UDB)/DEMOCRATIC BARUNDI UNION. Like the **PALIPEHUTU**, this was a **Hutu** movement that came about in the exiled Barundi population following the 1972 massacres. It lacked the wide international scope of the PALIPEHUTU, however.

UNION DES FEMMES BURUNDAISES (UFB)/UNION OF BURUNDI WOMEN. Founded in 1967, this **women**'s organization was in charge of promoting feminine life, or what has been called in Burundi *"animation féminine."*

UNION NATIONALE DES ÉTUDIANTS BURUNDI (UNEBA)/ NATIONAL UNION OF BURUNDI STUDENTS. Established by many young Barundi who were educated in Europe, this **youth** organization was dissolved along with the **Jeunesse Nationaliste Rwagasore** in 1967 and made part of the **Jeunesse Rwagasore Révolutionnaire**. It was considered a radical student organization with a very pro-**Tutsi** orientation and played a large role in gathering support against the monarchy in the mid-1960s. Its leader was **Gilles Bimazubute**.

UNION NATIONALE DU BURUNDI (UNB)/NATIONAL UNION OF BURUNDI. Just before independence in the early 1960s, old princely rivalries were reasserted. At the same time, many new political factions arose, often with new and sometimes revolutionary goals. In the middle of 1961, there were 23 officially registered **political parties**; some, such as the UNB, were confined to specific regions of the country and were very short lived.

UNITED NATIONS (UN). During the years leading up to independence, the United Nations and the **Belgian** authorities were pitted against each other in the growing tensions within Burundi. In the struggle between **UPRONA** and the **Parti Démocratique Chrétien (PDC)**, many of the final decisions were made by the UN Trusteeship Council in New York. UN resolutions called on the Belgian government to dismiss the interim government (with the PDC in superior numbers to UPRONA) and hold legislative elections. Since independence, the United Nations has granted aid and technical assistance to Burundi. Their primary role in the country and the region, however, has been through the office of the **United Nations High Commissioner for Refugees (UNHCR)**.

During and since Burundi's civil war that began in 1993, various branches of the United Nations have participated in the process of peace and rebuilding under the name of UN Operations in Burundi (ONUB). The organization has had a strong presence in Burundi since it assumed peacekeeping duties in the country, relieving troops deployed by the **African Union** in 2004; this mandate was supposed to end in May 2005, but was extended to June 2006. Approximately 5,000 UN peacekeepers have been in the country, supporting the **South African**–brokered peace.

In addition, the United Nations Children's Fund (UNICEF) has developed a project called Batissons la Paix (the Kirundi name is Gira Amahoro) or Let's Build Peace in cooperation with the Ministry of Basic Education and Adult Literacy. This project aims to help children and **youth** learn the skills they need to resolve conflicts peacefully, to cope with the stress that surrounds ongoing violent conflicts, and to prepare for a less violent future. To that end, UNICEF provides psychological counseling in addition to **education**. UNICEF also helped many children to receive a primary school education as the civil war neared its end; the organization helped about 75,000 children in 2000–2001, about 80,000 in 2001–2002, and more than 100,000 in 2002–2003.

The United Nations Educational, Scientific, and Cultural Organization (UNESCO) is also involved in the process of rebuilding Burundi's infrastructure. In 1996, UNESCO instituted the Global Education Action Plan, the main objective of which is to achieve 100 percent enrollment in schools by 2010 and to set up a system of community schools.

In March 2005, UN secretary-general Kofi Annan recommended the establishment of two panels: a nonjudicial **National Truth and**

Reconciliation Commission (NTRC), and a special chamber within Burundi's existing court system to bring to justice those responsible for "genocide, crimes against humanity and war crimes committed in the country" since its 1962 independence.

UNITED NATIONS HIGH COMMISSIONER FOR REFUGEES (UNHCR). The office of the United Nations High Commissioner for Refugees began its involvement in the Burundi region around the time of independence and was first concerned with **Tutsi refugees** following the 1959 uprising in **Rwanda**. Since then, the Tutsi refugees from Rwanda and the **Hutu** refugees from Burundi have continued to make the region a concern to the UNHCR. The refugees from both countries have fled to the **Democratic Republic of the Congo (DRC)**, **Tanzania**, Uganda, and various European countries, as well as Rwandans to Burundi and Barundi to Rwanda. The host countries, particularly the DRC, have had difficulties in both the resettlement and repatriation of the displaced people. There has also been a number of uprisings against the two countries fomented by refugees while in exile.

The UNHCR reported in 1991 that the Burundi Hutu refugee population had reached approximately 240,000. Many are the result of the 1972 massacre, but there are increasing numbers from 1988, 1991, and 1993. A tripartite agreement of the UNHCR, Burundi, and Tanzania led to the repatriation of many refugees in 1991; this group has been named as being responsible for much of the violence in the country later that year. As of the end of 1995, the primary immediate concern was with Rwandan refugees in Burundi and the DRC, but there is no denying the effect this has on Burundi, Burundi refugees, and Burundi's relations with its neighbors.

As Burundi emerged from 12 years of civil war, the UNHCR played a large role in the repatriation of Burundi refugees and the rehabilitation of internally displaced people. They began a voluntary repatriation program from Tanzania in March 2002, and since then, more than 158,000 refugees have returned home with UNHCR assistance. Since the beginning of 2005, the UNHCR has helped build 300 classrooms, 24,000 homes, and 19 **health** centers, as well as providing support for income-generating activities. Of the 8,524 refugees who returned home from January to April 2005, UNHCR had assisted 7,776 of them. Amnesty International, however, feels that the UNHCR exerts too much pressure on refugees to return home; the **human rights** group has said that the UNHCR makes refugees feel that they must return, but when they do, they suffer "systematic violations of their basic human rights."

UNITED STATES, RELATIONS WITH. There has actually been very little in the way of a relationship between the United States and Burundi. The United States has been an importer of Burundi coffee and has offered some **international aid** and technical assistance. There was a brief period of time in the early to mid-1960s when the U.S. government saw Burundi as a major concern in East–West relations because of Burundi's relationship with **China**. However, this was short lived, and the United States has, for more than 30 years, paid little attention to Burundi and its **human rights** violations. Following the 1972 massacre, Sen. Edward Kennedy and Sen. John Tunney called for international action to deal with the "situation" in Burundi. In 1995, President Bill Clinton urged Burundi to "say no to violence and extremism." Later, in 2000, Clinton joined other world leaders in a show of strong support to witness the signing of the **Arusha Accord**. Also in 1995, former president Jimmy Carter, former **Tanzanian** president Julius Nyerere, and **South African** archbishop Desmond Tutu served as mediators between factions in Burundi and **Rwanda**. The U.S. Peace Corps and U.S. Agency for International Development (USAID) have both had a sporadic presence in the country, particularly during the peaceful years. USAID continues to work with the people of Burundi on planning and planning for the future. *See also* DUMONT, DONALD; RENCHARD, GEORGE W.

UPRONA (PARTI DE L'UNION ET DU PROGRÈS NATIONAL/ PARTY OF NATIONAL UNION AND PROGRESS). This **political party** spans the entire history of independent Burundi. It was founded in the late 1950s, and Prince **Louis Rwagasore**'s return to Burundi coincided with its beginnings. In 1958, Rwagasore took control of UPRONA, and the party became a strong nationalistic force in the country. In the party's second manifesto, the **Deuxième Manifeste du Parti Politique**, Rwagasore made it clear that, even though he was a *ganwa* and the son of Mwami **Mwambutsa**, and even though the party sought to identify with the Crown while trying to live up to the progressive intentions of its name, he endorsed the monarchy "only insofar as this regime and its dynasty favored the genuine emancipation of the Murundi people." In the same manifesto, it was noted

> that the Burundi monarchy is *constitutional*, and wishes to see the constitution of the realm adapted to a *modern state*. UPRONA favors the democratization of institutions . . . and will firmly and tenaciously combat all forms of social injustice, regardless of the system from which they may come: *feudalism, colonialism,* or *communism*. . . . UPRONA favours the election of the chiefs and subchiefs by the population, and will combat with all its forces those who seek to destroy the *unity* of the country. (italic in original)

This outward show of nationalism was alarming to the **Belgians**, who considered the demands radical.

By the end of 1960, there were approximately 20 recognized political parties; UPRONA was the largest, with its strongest challenge from the **Parti Démocratique Chrétien (PDC)**. When communal elections were held in November and December 1960, Rwagasore was under house arrest and the PDC won 2,004 of the National Assembly seats to UPRONA's 545. However, the following year, after Rwagasore was released, there were general elections that were swept by UPRONA and that named Rwagasore the country's first prime minister following independence. He was assassinated in 1961, and the party separated into factions based on old family and ethnic conflicts. That breach was not reconciled, and there was never again such a strong central political body in Burundi. UPRONA remained somewhat elitist and primarily **Tutsi**.

UPRONA remained the only viable political party until the 1990s (even though it was disbanded between 1987 and 1990) when it was challenged by **Front Démocratique Burundi (FRODEBU)**. In June 1993, FRODEBU's candidate, **Melchior Ndadaye**, won in the first democratic **election** since independence in 1962, taking the majority of the votes against incumbent **Pierre Buyoya**, UPRONA's candidate. The death of Ndadaye just a few months later in an attempted coup led to the most recent long period of ethnic unrest in an even longer series of such events. UPRONA remained a strong force in the political structure of Burundi, considered to be one of the opposition parties in a weak coalition government nominally run by FRODEBU. After the

Arusha power-sharing agreement, in the 2005 series of elections, UP-RONA won only 820 seats in communal elections, behind the **Forces pour la Défense de la Démocratie**'s **(FDD's)** 1,781 seats and FRODEBU's 820 seats. The elections for the Senate and the National Assembly produced similar results.

USUMBURA. *See* BUJUMBURA.

– V –

VAN DER BURGT, JOHANNES-MICHAEL. A Dutch priest who founded a **Catholic** mission in Burundi, arriving in the country in 1896 and leaving in 1908. Van Der Burgt traveled the country extensively, making a number of relief maps of the area. Most notable project, however, was his work on a French–Kirundi dictionary, which was published in 1903. Critics have noted its many digressions, calling them useless, but all note the importance of this monumental task, which included precise information about the history and anthropology of the country in addition to the **language**.

VANSINA, JAN. A historian of oral tradition, Professor Vansina claimed in 1961 that Burundi had no equivalent of the wealth of traditional genres pertaining to the monarchy of **Rwanda**. He further claimed that, because of the circumstances that brought them to power, the *ganwa* were naturally afraid of the verdict of history, leading to a Burundi that was "characteristically prejudiced against history." Vansina pointed out that the field of oral traditions is not completely barren in Burundi; folktales and legends fill the gaps of history, but lack the supplementary memory of the court historians of Rwanda, whose task was to hand down the traditions of the realm as royal ordinance prescribed. In spite of these differences with Rwanda, Burundi's oral tradition has been well studied by Vansina. One of the problems is that traditions are not transmitted by specialists, trained for the task or endorsed by any central body. A result of this lack of specialization is that the approximately 40 primary traditions could potentially be told by almost 9,000 informants, making the task of the researcher nearly impossible.

VOIX DE LA RÉVOLUTION/VOICE OF THE REVOLUTION. During the **Michel Micombero** administration, the government disseminated information to the public through the national radio station, Voix de la Révolution, and the official newspaper, *Unité et Révolution*. Through an agreement between Burundi and the Soviet Union, international news service was supplied to *Unité et Révolution* through TASS, the Soviet news agency, as well as through the French press agency, Agence France Presse. **UPRONA** also periodically sent political teams to all parts of the country to explain official policy and mobilize the population. The radio station continued to be the official government news outlet through several later administrations. *See also* MEDIA.

VURATI (MU-, BA-). The royal rainmakers, traditionally very important during the sorghum and other fertility festivals, such as the *muganuro*. They were traditionally said to own the rain, so they could also prevent rain if they wanted to. They were greatly feared because they were thought to be able to send a thunderbolt to kill anyone who angered them. *See also* GANURO.

VYEYI (BU-, no plural). Another of the qualities that traditionally exists in the ideal Burundi male is this type of parental devotion. This is the basis of respectful relationships between parents and their children. It represents the dignity and respect of a parent and that which is due to a parent. The root with the prefixes designating humans (*umuvyeyi*, *abavyeyi*) means "parent(s)." The word *imvyeye* means "cow who has recently calved."

VYINO (RU-, IM-). Group songs that were popular at reunions of clans. They had refrains comprising short **musical** phrases with strong beats; the singing was often accompanied by dancing. Sometimes, a soloist improvised couplets in the *imvyino*; these were closely related to the present moment or events and were often used to bring news to the group.

VYIVARE (I-). The royal domains within the traditional system. Of interest is that often there were **Hutu** chiefs who held office in these domains. These chiefs had some advantages, because they were not subject to the *ganwa* and the problems involved in the dynastic families; therefore, they could act as independent chiefs. The Hutu chiefs were dismissed by the **Belgian** administration in 1931.

– W –

WHITE FATHERS (PÈRES BLANCS). Although this is the most used name of the **Catholic Church** missionary group, their formal title is the Roman Catholic Order of the Missionaries of Africa. The first mission schools in Burundi are said to have been established in about 1900 by the White Fathers. Traditional **education** before this time was informal in that it primarily focused on providing the children with skills necessary in fulfilling their social and economic responsibilities and becoming productive members of society. The immediate family and the kinship group shared the responsibility for the training of children.

WHITE SISTERS (SOEURS BLANCHES). This group of European nuns came to Ruanda-Urundi during the period from 1898 to 1922 when the **White Fathers** and other missionary groups were becoming well established in the territory. They devoted themselves primarily to teaching **women** and girls, giving medical care in local dispensaries, and organizing a novitiate for members of the population who wanted to become nuns.

WOMEN. In traditional Burundi society, women have had few rights and very little presence in government or civil service, but this has recently begun to change. The ideal woman was fertile and modest, having been trained in silence and reticence. Many women were trained to be such careful listeners that they could repeat whole conversations verbatim. However, husbands also appreciated it when their wives were good at bargaining, negotiating, or managing their property if they had to be away. In this way, intelligent women often became powerful matriarchs.

In spite of this, as well as the great respect mothers receive, women traditionally had very little authority in decision making. A woman's position in the society was mainly determined by the marriage that she contracted. Women of all social classes were expected to act subservient and obedient and to follow the dictates of their husbands and fathers. A few upper-class women were known historically to have achieved considerable independent wealth and authority, but this was very rare in a society in which men virtually monopolized the right to inherit cattle and land. Although voting rights were accorded to women in the 1962 constitution, few women took advantage of them.

Women have had little support from the government institutions of the country, and they have also, in some situations, not supported one another. Wives, for example, have the right to charge their husbands with physical abuse, but they rarely exercise this right. Police seldom intervene in domestic disputes and the **media** seldom report on incidents of violence against women; in fact, there are no known court cases dealing with the abuse of women in at least the last 12 years. A 2000 report by the Amnesty International Committee on the Elimination of Discrimination against Women summarized the following:

> The traditional society is a patriarchal and patrilinear one, in which the woman is constantly under the protection of a father, brother, uncle, husband, or family council. Women have more duties than rights and must subordinate themselves to the customs and practices governing the relations between men.

Burundi's civil war that began in 1993 has brought women into the international arena. Many women joined their husbands, brothers, and fathers as combatants in the war, even keeping their children with them during the fighting. But some of these also were among the first to lay down their arms; one former fighter with a rebel group, upon giving her gun to the **United Nations** peacekeeping force said, "I am tired of fighting and killing." The ex-combatant women were paid a salary for nine months and given money to build houses and buy farming implements and seeds; they were offered basic **education** and were also taught life skills such as how to farm and how to handle money.

The civil war, however, has also brought to light the enormous number of rapes. Like so many other **human rights** abuses in Burundi, rape has become an entrenched feature of the crisis because the perpetrators have largely not been charged with the crime; rapists seem to come from all sectors—government soldiers, armed rebels, and private citizens. The continuing poverty, internal displacement, and a failing **health** system have also contributed to the crime.

Some analysts believe that the scale of rape indicates a deliberate strategy by some to use rape as a weapon of war in order to instill terror and humiliation among civilians. While the status of the average woman in Burundi is low, that of a widow or rape victim is even lower. Several women, for example, told Amnesty International how they had been mocked, humiliated, and rejected by their husbands and families, including women relatives, classmates, friends, and neighbors. One woman living in a camp for internally displaced people, after being raped at gunpoint by a government soldier, was afraid to tell her husband and instead told a woman friend; the friend in turn told the husband. The rape victim said, "I don't know where my husband is. He left me and our children when he heard I'd been raped. I'm still in the camp. I have nowhere to go now. My house was destroyed by soldiers and anyway I think my husband wouldn't allow me to live there. I have no money. The children can't go to school."

The recent peace in Burundi has brought with it more recognition for women as well as of crimes against women. Women are becoming more involved with politics and with development plans. In 2004, a group of **South African** and Burundi women gathered in South Africa to discuss the peace process in Burundi and their roles in it. This meeting was organized by the New Partnership for Africa's Development, an organization based on the belief that Africa's poverty and conflicts will be overcome only by the collective efforts of African countries. Additionally, and very importantly, Burundi's new government has implemented more women's rights and representation. The power-sharing agreement outlined in the **Arusha Accord** guarantees that women have at least a 30 percent representation in government. Under the administration of **Pierre Nkurunziza**, 36 percent of the staffs of all government institutions are women; 7 out of 20 government ministers are women, including the ministers of justice and foreign affairs. One of the two vice presidents is a woman who is a former legislator in the National Assembly and who was reelected in the 2005 election. There is also a woman Speaker of the National Assembly, **Immaculée Nahayo**. Nkurunziza has said, "We did not do this to strike a balance. They deserve it. It is a unique model for Africa. For Burundi this is just the beginning. *See also* ACTION SOCIALE; FOYERS SOCIAUX; *GANURO*; KINIGI, SILVIE; *KORORA*; *KWAHUKANA*; UNION DES FEMMES BURUNDAISES (UFB)/UNION OF BURUNDI WOMEN.

– Y –

YAMUREMYE, JEAN BOSCO. *See* PARTI DE LA RÉCONCILIA-
TION DES PERSONNES (PRP)/PEOPLE'S RECONCILIATION
PARTY.

YANGAYANGA (MU-, BA-). Traveling merchants who traditionally
traversed the country, trading bracelets and other trinkets for cattle.
They were very important to the **economy** of Burundi before the period of European colonization. They were business agents.

YOUTH. Since the country's 1962 independence, the youth of Burundi
have emerged in leadership roles. Many of these people were young
Tutsi who had been **educated** in **Catholic** mission schools. Young
men, especially during precolonial and colonial times, were trained
in oratory skills for leadership roles.

Youth organizations such as the **Jeunesse Nationaliste Rwagasore**,
the **Jeunesse Rwagasore Révolutionnaire**, and the **Union Nationale
des Étudiants Burundi** have long played an important role in the politics of Burundi. Today, in spite of some attempts by the government to
encourage constructive organizations, many of the **Hutu** and Tutsi, including very young men and boys, are militia members. In the case of
the Hutu, this is perhaps not surprising; many older educated and military Hutu have been killed over the years in various massacres. In addition, an estimated 20,000 youths fought alongside the national **army**
in the country's 12-year civil war beginning in 1993. Many of these
children, on both sides, were orphaned and internally displaced. It is reported that some of these children were abducted from the camps. Although the official age for military service is 16, Human Rights Watch
has reported that boys as young as 11 or 12 were seen in uniform carrying arms; one child soldier reported that he was recruited at the age
of 10. Children were also seen in official military training camps. Just
as in the early days of Burundi's independence, youth groups (some
call them gangs) have emerged and been implicated in the country's violence. Among these groups, mostly branches of adult militia, are Sans
Echecs (Without Fail), Sans Défaite (Without Defeat), and Gardiens de
la Paix (Guardians of Peace).

YOYA (KA-, RU-). A newborn infant of either gender was traditionally called *akayoya* or *uruyoya* until the age of two months. The various ages of an individual's life continue to have their own names in Kirundi. Children of both genders are called *igitwengerabarezi* until the age of three months, *igitambambuga* until the age of one year, *umucuko* until the age of two years, and *ingimbi* until the age of 10 years. Boys are called *umwana agimbutse* until the age of 15 years, and girls are called the same thing, but only until the age of 12. After this approximate age of puberty, the names describing an individual's life vary for males and females. A male is *igikwerere* until the age of 20, *umugabo* until the age of 25, *umusore ashitse* until 30, *umuhumure* until 55, *umukambwe* until 60, and *umutama* until 70. A female is *umuyabaga* until 14, *inkumi* until 16, *inkumi sezegeri* until 18, and *igitamba* until 20. After this age, it was traditional to refer to **women** with respect to their child bearing: after she gives birth to the first child, a woman is *avyaye rimwe* (one); after the birth of the second, she is *avyaye kabili* (two), and so on. After her child-bearing years, she is *umutamakazi* until age 50 and *nyogokuru* after that.

– Z –

ZIMU (MU-, MI-). The general traditional name for the spirits of the dead, not particularly benevolent or evil. When Barundi died, their deaths were not considered final. Their bodies decomposed and became dust, but their souls remained and entered other beings. Other derivations of this word are *ubuzimu,* which means "reincarnation," and *kuzima,* which means "to disappear or become extinct."

ZINA (I-, MA-). Literally, this means "names," figuratively, "praise names." In Burundi, the ability to speak well and eloquently is thought to be highly significant both practically and aesthetically. Among the upper classes, speaking well (*imfura*) is a sign of good breeding, and the ideals of oratorical ability are highly stressed. From the age of about 10, aristocratic boys learn speech making, including the composition of these *amazina,* or praise poems.

According to **Ethel Albert**, who researched these speech patterns extensively, the form of these poems is fixed, but the contents are created on an impromptu basis. The naturally alliterative character of Kirundi (as is the case with Bantu **languages** in general) is reinforced by conscious selection of assonant words in the construction of praise names and figures of speech. There are slight modifications in wording and number of verses as authors repeat their increasing store of *amazina* on appropriate occasions. Each composer must demonstrate his own abilities, so nobody borrows the amazina of others except to learn the art of composition.

An interesting aspect of them is that they have a great deal of latitude in terms of truth. **Jan Vansina** tells a story of a teenage boy who recited the amazina verses he had composed in praise of himself; they included the names of enemies he had killed with his lance and his bow, but the boy freely admitted that he had never actually killed anyone. The boy further explained that the purpose of the poem was to boast of heroic deeds, and it did not matter if the deeds were completely imaginary. Again the question of depending on oral traditions for historical facts arises; it is reasonable that the historian might have some doubts. As these grow over the years of a person's life, an elderly man with a long history of bravery, for example, might fill three or four hours with his chanted recitation.

These compositions are primarily for the upper caste; however, there are also farmers' amazina, which praise things of interest to the **agricultural** life. There have even been recorded cases of cow thieves composing amazina in self-praise; because the punishment for stealing cattle was immediate crucifixion if the thief was caught in the act, and because precautions against stealing were elaborate, a cow thief who lived to tell the tale was considered to have earned the right to his amazina. The amazina are divided into four main groups. *Amazina y'ubuhizi* (or *amazina y'urugambo*) are the heroic stories; *amazina y'inka* are pastoral stories; *amazina y'uruhigi* are comical odes; and *amazina y'isuka* are the stories of community farming.

ZIRO (MU-, MI-). This term was employed for a gamut of taboos, the violation of which could bring grave consequences to the perpetrator. These could include hindrances to marriage, prohibitions of mating for both humans and cattle, and dietary prohibitions, among others.

Appendix A:
Kings (*Bami*) of Burundi

Dynastic Name	Given Name	Date of Accession	Date of Death
Ntare I	Rushatsi	c. 1675–1680	c. 1705–1709
Mwezi I	Ndagushimiye	c. 1705–1709	c. 1735–1739
Mutaga I	Seenyamwiiza	c. 1735–1739	c. 1767
Mwambutsa I	Syarushambo	1767	1796
Ntare II	Rugaamba	1796	1850
Mwezi IV	Gisabo	1850	1908
Mutaga II	Mbikije	1908	1915
Mwambutsa IV	Bangiricenge	1915	1977
Ntare V	Charles Ndizeye	1966[a]	1972

Note: [a]Ntare deposed his father Mwambutsa IV while the latter was out of the country. All of the others became *mwami* upon the death of their predecessor.

Appendix B:
Postcolonial Prime Ministers

Prime Ministers	Dates of Office	Ethnic Group	Political Party
Prince Louis Rwagasore	28 September 1961– 13 October 1961	Tutsi	UPRONA
André Muhirwa	20 October 1961– 10 June 1963	Tutsi	UPRONA
Pierre Ngendandumwe	18 June 1963– 6 April 1964	Hutu	UPRONA
Albin Nyamoya	6 April 1964– 7 January 1965	Hutu	UPRONA
Pierre Ngendandumwe (second time)	7 January 1965– 15 January 1965	Hutu	UPRONA
Pié Masumbuko (acting)	15 January 1965– 26 January 1965	Tutsi	UPRONA
Joseph Bamina	26 January 1965– 30 September 1965	Hutu	UPRONA
Léopold Bihumugani (Biha)	13 October 1965– 8 July 1966	Tutsi	UPRONA
Michel Micombero	11 July 1966– 28 November 1966[a]	Tutsi	UPRONA
Albin Nyamoya (second time)	15 July 1972– 5 June 1973	Hutu	UPRONA
Édouard Nzambimana	12 November 1976– 13 October 1978[b]	Tutsi	UPRONA
Adrien Sibomana	19 October 1988– 10 July 1993	Hutu	UPRONA
Sylvie Kinigi[c]	10 July 1993– 7 February 1994	Tutsi	UPRONA

Notes: [a]In 1966, Micombero declared Burundi a republic; from that time on, the president, rather than the prime minister, became the head of state. After that, the office of prime minister became irregular.
[b]The post of prime minister was abolished completely between 13 October 1978 and 19 October 1988.
[c]Kinigi was the first woman to hold a high political post in Burundi.

169

Appendix C:
Postcolonial Presidents

President	Dates of Office	Ethnic Group	Political Party
Michel Micombero	28 November 1966– 1 November 1976	Tutsi	UPRONA (military)
Jean-Baptiste Bagaza	2 November 1976– 3 September 1987	Tutsi	UPRONA (military)
Pierre Buyoya	3 September 1987– 10 July 1993	Tutsi	UPRONA (military)
Melchior Ndadaye[a]	10 July 1993– 21 October 1993	Hutu	FRODEBU
François Ngeze[b]	21 October 1993– 27 October 1993	Tutsi	UPRONA (military)
Sylvie Kinigi (acting)	27 October 1993– 5 February 1994	Tutsi	UPRONA
Cyprien Ntaryamira	5 February 1994– 6 April 1994	Hutu	FRODEBU
Sylvestre Ntibantunganya (acting until 1 October 1994)	6 April 1994– 25 July 1996	Hutu	FRODEBU
Pierre Buyoya (second time)	25 July 1996– 30 April 2003	Tutsi	UPRONA
Domitien Ndayizeye	30 April 2003– 26 August 2005	Hutu	FRODEBU
Pierre Nkurunziza[c]	26 August 2005–	Hutu	CNDD-FDD

Notes: [a]Ndadaye was the first democratically elected president, the first Hutu president, and the first civilian president; his assassination was the catalyst to 12 years of civil war.
[b]Ngeze was a member of the military and the chairman of the Committee of National Salvation; he declared himself president in the rebellion.
[c]Nkurunziza's party won the legislative elections and appointed him president in the country's first democratic election since 1993.

171

Bibliography

CONTENTS

I. INTRODUCTION

This bibliography is an attempt to list as many sources on Burundi as possible, but it is by no means exhaustive. Since Burundi's independence in 1962, there have been slightly more sources in English than there were before, and since 1990, there have been even more—but this is not to say that there are many. Most of the primary sources describing the history, culture, and language of the country are in untranslated French, and, sadly, many of the English sources have emerged only because of Burundi's several periods of civil unrest since its independence. During Burundi's most recent civil war (1993–2005), there was increased intervention and interest from other countries in the region and throughout the world, explaining the increase of English sources. Some publications that regularly cover Burundi news and political analysis include *Africa Report*, *Issue*, and *Africa Today*; in addition, occasional articles appear in such general news periodicals as *Time*, *Newsweek*, *The Nation*, *The Economist*, *The New Yorker*, and *The New York Times*.

With the increased international interest has also come increased, specialized responses to the Burundi conflict and its resolution. Such human rights organizations as Human Rights Watch and Amnesty International regularly publish reports and analyses of the country and the region. These are available both in print and electronically. Other international organizations such as the United States Institute for Peace and the Nelson Mandela Foundation have also covered Burundi's emergence from civil unrest. The United Nations Integrated Regional and International News Network (IRIN) is a wealth of current news, covering a wide range of political analyses, profiles of political leaders, and personal stories. People of Burundi operate a website specifically designed to keep the world current on national issues; this can be accessed at www.abarundi.org and is updated regularly. The popular search engine Google provides a valuable service to researchers: one can register with them at no cost to receive daily news on any designated subject. Each day provides current news from publications around the world, including many mentioned here.

There are very few comprehensive bibliographies on Burundi and very few collections of primary materials. Some useful sources, however, include the Africa Library in Brussels and the Museum for Central Africa in Tervuren, Belgium. In North America, there is the Hoover Institution at Stanford University, where part of the historical Derscheid Collection is available. This collection is probably still one of the best known primary collections on Burundi. Fortunately, the modern researcher has the advantage of highly efficient interlibrary loan systems throughout the world.

There have been several general histories of Burundi written in English, and some of these have been especially useful in compiling this dictionary and bibliography. Listed in this bibliography are numerous books and articles by two prolific Africa researchers, René Lemarchand

and Warren Weinstein. Professor Lemarchand's *Rwanda and Burundi* (1970) is an excellent source of information on the general details of history and culture of the two countries up until that time; it also includes a limited but very useful bibliography. Thirty-five years later, Lemarchand is still examining the intricacies of the country and the motivations behind its political and social development. Weinstein's books and articles spanning the last 30 years provide insight into Burundi's international relations.

Sources on Burundi's economy remain scarce, as do sources specifically dealing with the language and literature of the country. A few researchers are prominent in these narrower areas: Jan Vansina for cultural anthropology and oral literary history, and Ethel Albert, F. Rodegem, A. A. Trouwborst, R. Bourgeois, and Jean-Pierre Chrétien for sociology, cultural anthropology, and literary and language history. Few of these are current; the modern researcher will find more information in these areas in some of the electronic sources listed above.

This bibliography is divided into 14 sections in an attempt to make it useful to readers with different purposes; other researchers might divide the sources differently, but these are the categories that seemed to emerge naturally as the dictionary was being formed. The first two sections include the general history of Burundi specifically and of the region, because so much of Burundi's development is entwined with other countries in the region (particularly Rwanda, the Democratic Republic of the Congo, Tanzania, Uganda, and South Africa). The next three sections of the bibliography divide Burundi's history temporally: precolonial history, which includes some works on the early exploration of the region; colonial history, which includes works on both the German and Belgian occupations of the region; and postcolonial history, which covers Burundi's history and political affairs up to the present time. The following section covers economics and development. Section VIII is on linguistics and covers language issues falling under the current definition of the field: all issues of language, including its discourse structure and influence on social aspects of a people. The next two sections cover verbal, musical, visual, and written arts and general sociology. Section XI is on religion and includes works on traditional as well as imported religion. The remaining sections cover international relations, education, geography, geology, agriculture, health, and medicine.

II. GENERAL HISTORY

Botte, Roger. "Burundi: De Quoi Vivait l'État." *Cahiers d'Études Africaines* 22, nos. 3–4 (1988): 277–317.

Bourgeois, R. *Banyarwanda et Barundi*. 3 vols. Brussels: Académie Royale des Sciences Coloniales, 1954–1957.

Camus, C. "Le Ruanda et l'Urundi." *Congo* 6, no. 1 (1924): 105–11.

Carpenter, Allan, and Matthew Maginnis. *Burundi*. Chicago: Children's Press, 1973.

Chrétien, Jean-Pierre. "Le Burundi." *Documentation Française*, no. 3364 (1967).

Derkinderen, G. *Atlas du Congo Belge et du Ruanda-Urundi*. Paris: Elsevier, 1956.

Gann, L. H., and P. Duignan. *The Rulers of Belgian Africa, 1884–1914*. Princeton, N.J.: Princeton University Press, 1979.

Gildea, R. Y., and A. Taylor. "Rwanda and Burundi." *Focus* 13, no. 6 (February 1963).

Hakizimana, Deo. *Burundi: Le Non-dit*. Geneva: Éditions Remesha, 1992.

Jamoulle, A. "Le Ruanda-Urundi." *Expansion Belge* 8 (1927): 18–23.

Laurenty, Jean-Sebastien. *Les Cordophones de Congo Belge et du Ruanda-Urundi*. Tervuren, Belgium: Musée du Congo Belge, 1968.

Legum, Colin. *Congo Disaster*. Baltimore: Penguin, 1961.

Lemarchand, René. *Rwanda and Burundi*. New York: Praeger, 1970.

Louis, William Roger. *Ruanda-Urundi, 1884–1919*. Oxford: Clarendon Press, 1963.

Maes, J. "Ruanda-Urundi." *Afrika* 2 (1947): 1037–47.

Maquet, J. J. "Ruanda-Urundi, Lands of the Mountains of the Moon." In *The Belgian Congo from Wilderness to Civilization*. Brussels: Les Beaux Arts, 1956.

Marzorati, A. "The Belgian Congo and Ruanda-Urundi." *Civilisations* 1 (1951): 149–54.

McDonald, Gordon C., et al. *Area Handbook for Burundi*. Washington, D.C.: American University, 1969.

Meyer, Hans. *Die Barundi*. Leipzig: Otto Spamer, 1916. English translation: *The Barundi*. Translated by Helmut Handzik. Human Relations Area Files, 1954. French translation: *Les Barundi*. Paris: Société Française d'Histoire d'Outre-Mer, 1984.

Mulago, Vincent. "L'Union Vitale Bantu, ou le Principe de la Cohésion et de la Communauté chez les Bashi, les Nabyarwanda et les Barundi." *Annali Lateranensi* 20 (1956): 261–63.

Mworoha, Emile. *Histoire du Burundi*. Paris: Hatier, 1987.

Nahayo, Simon. "Contribution à la Bibliographie des Ouvrages Relatifs au Burundi." *Geneva Africa* 10, nos. 1–2 (1971): 92–99, 100–111; 11, no. 1 (1972): 94–104.

Rodegem, F. M. *Documentation Bibliographique sur le Burundi.* Bologna: Editrice Missionaria Italiana, 1978.

Roucek, Joseph. "Rwanda and Burundi." *African Trade and Development* 4 (1962): 12–15.

Rozier, R. *Le Burundi, Pays de la Vache et du Tambour.* Paris: Presses du Palais Royal, 1972.

Sandrart, Georges. *Ruanda-Urundi.* Brussels: Dessart, 1953.

Schumacher, P. "Urundi." *Æquatoria* 12, no. 4 (1949): 129–32.

Sohier, J. *Répertoire Géneral de la Jurisprudence et de la Doctrine Coutumière du Congo et du Ruanda-Urundi.* Brussels: Ferdinand Larcier, 1957.

Steinhart, Edward. "Vassal and Fief in Three Lacustrine Kingdoms." *Cahiers d'Études Africaines* 7, no. 4 (1967): 606–23.

Straunard, S. A. "Le Ruanda-Urundi." *Revue Nationale* 191 (1949): 193.

Verger, Pierre. *Congo Belge et Ruanda-Urundi.* Paris: P. Harmann, 1952.

Weinstein, Warren. *Historical Dictionary of Burundi.* Metuchen, N.J.: Scarecrow Press, 1976.

Weinstein, Warren, and Robert Schrire. *Political Conflict and Ethnic Strategies: A Case Study of Burundi.* Syracuse, N.Y.: Maxwell School of Citizenship, 1976.

Whitaker, P., and J. Silvey. "A Visit to the Congo, Rwanda and Burundi." *Makerere Journal*, no. 9 (1964): 71–82.

Wolbers, Marian F. *Burundi.* New York: Chelsea House, 1989.

III. REGIONAL HISTORY

Arnold, Guy. *Historical Dictionary of Civil Wars in Africa.* Lanham, Md.: Scarecrow Press, 1999.

Barns, A. *The Wonderland of the Eastern Congo.* New York: Putnam, 1922.

Burkitt, M. C. "Prehistory in the Congo." *Nature* 155 (1945): 585.

Cervenka, Zdenek. *Land-locked Countries of Africa.* Uppsala, Sweden: Scandinavian Institute of African Studies, 1973.

——. *The Unfinished Quest for Unity.* New York: Africana, 1977.

Chrétien, Jean-Pierre. "Echanges et Hiérarchies dans les Royaumes des Grands Lacs de l'Est Africain." *Annales* 29, no. 6 (1974): 1327–37.

——, ed. *Histoire Rurale de l'Afrique des Grands Lacs.* Paris: Diffusion Karthala, 1983.

Clark, J. Desmond, et al. *The Cambridge History of Africa.* Vols. 1–8. Cambridge: Cambridge University Press, 1975.

Cole, S. *The Prehistory of East Africa*. New York: New American Library, 1963.

Decalo, Samuel. *Coups and Army Rule in Africa*. New Haven, Conn.: Yale University Press, 1975.

Dorsey, Learthen. *Historical Dictionary of Rwanda*. Lanham, Md.: Scarecrow Press, 2000.

Emerson, Rupert. "Nation-Building in Africa." In *Nation-Building*, edited by K. Deutsch and W. Folz. New York: Atherton, 1963.

Foster, F. Blanche. *East Central Africa: Kenya, Uganda, Tanzania, Rwanda, and Burundi*. New York: Watts, 1981.

Frederick, A. *In the Heart of Africa*. London: Cassel, 1910.

Gann, L. H., and P. Duignan, eds. *Colonialism in Africa, 1870–1960*. Cambridge: Cambridge University Press, 1975.

Gluckman, Max. *Order and Rebellion in Tribal Africa*. London: Cohen & West, 1963.

Gourevitch, Philip. "Letter from Rwanda: After the Genocide." *The New Yorker* (18 December 1995): 78–94.

————. *We Wish to Inform You That Tomorrow We Will Be Killed with Our Families: Stories from Rwanda*. New York: Picador USA, 1998.

Gray, Richard, and David Birmingham, eds. *Pre-Colonial African Trade*. London: Oxford University Press, 1970.

Hochschild, Adam. *King Leopold's Ghost*. Boston: Houghton Mifflin, 1998.

Hunter, G. *The Best of Both Worlds? A Challenge on Development Policies in Africa*. London: Oxford University Press, 1967.

————. *The New Societies of Tropical Africa*. London: Oxford University Press, 1962.

Hunton, W. Alphaeus. *Decision in Africa: Sources of Current Conflict*. New York: International Publishers, 1960.

Ilunga, A. "Crise Politique: Concept et Application à l'Afrique." *Cahiers Économique et Sociaux* 3, no. 3 (1965): 321–38.

Lemarchand, René, ed. *African Kingdoms in Perspective: Political Change and Modernization in Monarchical Settings*. London: F. Cass, 1977.

Leys, C., and C. Pratt, eds. *A New Deal in Central Africa*. New York: Praeger, 1960.

Maquet, J. J. *Africanité*. New York: Oxford University Press, 1972.

————. *Aide Mémoire d'Ethnologie Africaine*. Brussels: Institut Royal Colonial Belge, 1954.

————. "Institutionalisation Féodale des Relations de Dépendance dans Quatre Cultures Interlacustres." *Cahiers d'Études Africaines* 9, no. 35 (1968): 402–14.

————. *The Premise of Inequality in Ruanda*. Oxford: Oxford University Press, 1961.

Martin, Jane J. *Africa*. Guildford, Conn.: Dushkin, 1985.

Mazrui, Ali A. *The African Condition: A Political Diagnosis*. Cambridge: Cambridge University Press, 1980.

Murphy, E. Jefferson. *History of African Civilization*. New York: Delta, 1972.

Parkin, D. J. *Town and Country in Central and Eastern Africa*. London: Oxford University Press, 1975.

Phillipson, David. *African Archaeology*. Cambridge: Cambridge University Press, 1993.

Pierce, Julian R. *Speak Rwanda*. New York: Picador USA, 1999.

Posnansky, M., ed. *Prelude to East African History*. London: Oxford University Press, 1966.

Suret-Canale, J. *Afrique Noire, Occidentale et Centrale*. Translated from the 1961 edition. New York: Pica Press, 1971.

Taylor, Bayard. *The Lake Regions of Central Africa*. New York: Negro Universities Press, 1969.

Van Noten, Francis. *The Archaeology of Central Africa*. Graz, Austria: Akademische Druck, 1982.

Vansina, Jan. "The Use of Process Models in African History." In *The Historian in Tropical Africa: Studies Presented and Discussed*, edited by Jan Vansina, R. Mauny, and L. V. Thomas, 375–90. London: Oxford University Press, 1964.

Voices of Rwanda. Pretoria, South Africa: JAM International, 2003.

Wakano, Katambo. *Coups d'Etat, Revolutions and Power Struggles in Post-Independence Africa*. Nairobi: Afriscript, 1985.

Wallerstein, I. *Africa: The Politics of Independence*. New York: Vintage, 1961.

IV. PRECOLONIAL HISTORY AND EARLY EXPLORATION

Bennett, Norman, ed. *Henry Stanley's Despatches to the* New York Herald, *1871–1872, 1874–1877*. Boston: Boston University Press, 1970.

Bloch, Marc. *Feudal Society*. London: Routledge and Kegan Paul, 1965.

Botte, Roger. "Burundi: La Relation Ubugabire dans la Tête de Ceux qui la Décrivent." *Cahiers d'Études Africaines* 9 (1969): 363–71.

Burton, Richard F. *The Nile Basin*. 2 vols. London: Tinsley, 1864.

———. "On Lake Tanganyika: Ptolemy's Western Lake-Reservoir of the Nile." *Journal of the Royal Geographic Society* (1865): 1–15.

Chrétien, Jean-Pierre. "Du Hirsute au Hamite: Les Variations du Cycle de Ntare Rushatsi du Burundi." *History in Africa* 8 (1981): 3–41.

———. "Le Passage de l'Expédition d'Oscar Baumann au Burundi." *Cahiers d'Études Africaines* 8 (1968): 48–95.

Cohen, Daniel. *Henry Stanley and the Quest for the Source of the Nile.* New York: M. Evans, 1985.

Eisenstadt, S. N., and René Lemarchand. *Political Clientelism, Patronage and Development.* London: Sage, 1981.

Ghislain, Jean. *Le Féodalité au Burundi.* Brussels: Académie Royale des Sciences d'Outre-Mer, 1970.

Grant, James A. *A Walk across Africa: Domestic Scenes from My Nile Journal.* London: William Blackwood and Sons, 1864.

Guillet, Claude, and Pascal Ndayishinguje. *Légendes Historiques du Burundi: Les Multiples Visages du Roi Ntare.* Paris: Karthala, 1987.

Hertefelt, M. d', A. A. Trouwborst, and J. H. Scherer. *Les Anciens Royaumes de la Zone Interlacustre Méridionale: Ruanda, Burundi, Buha.* London: International African Institute, 1962.

———. "Cultures Préhistoriques de l'Âge des Métaux au Ruanda-Urundi et au Kivu." *Bulletin de l'Académie Royale Scientifique Coloniale* 6 (1956): 1126–49.

Leroy, F. J. "Archéologie Préhistorique au Burundi, Mugera, 1926." *Revue de l'Université Officielle de Bujumbura* 2, no. 7 (1966): 165–71.

Leroy, P. "Stanley et Livingstone en Urundi." *Lovania* 44 (1957): 23–24.

Nenquin, Jacques. *Contributions to the Study of the Prehistoric Cultures of Rwanda and Burundi.* Tervuren, Belgium: Musée Royal de l'Afrique Centrale, 1967.

———. "Notes on the Protohistoric Pottery Cultures in the Congo Ruanda-Burundi Region." In *Background to Evolution in Africa,* edited by W. W. Bishop and J. D. Clark. Chicago: University of Chicago Press, 1967.

Nsanze, Augustin. *Un Domaine Royal au Burundi: Mbuye.* Bujumbura: Université du Burundi Centre de Civilisation Burundaise, 1980.

Rice, Edward. *Captain Sir Richard Francis Burton.* New York: HarperCollins, 1990.

Speke, John Hanning. *Journal of the Discovery of the Source of the Nile.* London: Blackwood and Sons, 1863.

Stanley, Henry M. *The Exploration Diaries of H. M. Stanley, from the Original Manuscripts.* New York: Vanguard, 1961.

———. *How I Found Livingstone: Travels, Adventures and Discoveries in Central Africa.* New York: Scribner, Armstrong, 1872.

———. *My Kalula, Prince, King, and Slave: A Story of Central Africa.* 1874. Reprint, New York: Negro Universities Press, 1969.

———. *Through the Dark Continent.* New York: Harper, 1878.

Thomson, J. *To the Central African Lakes and Back.* 2 vols. London: Sampson Low, 1881.

Trouwborst, Albert. "La Base Territoriale de l'État du Burundi Ancien." *Revue Universitaire du Burundi* 1, nos. 3–4 (1973): 245–55.

———. "Le Barundi." In *Les Anciens Royaumes de la Zone Interlacustre Méridionale: Rwanda, Burundi, Buha*, edited by J. Vansina. Tervuren, Belgium: Musée de l'Afrique Centrale, 1962.

Van Grunderbeek, Marie-Claude. *Le Premier Age du Fer au Rwanda et au Burundi: Archéologie et Environnement*. Butare, Rwanda: Institut National de Recherche Scientifique, 1983.

Vansina, Jan. "Note sur la Chronologie du Burundi Ancien." *Académie Royale des Sciences d'Outre-Mer Bulletin des Séances* 3 (1967): 429–44.

Wauters, A. *Exploration du Dr. Baumann dans la Région Située entre le Lac Victoria et le Tanganyika*. Brussels: Le Mouvement Géographique, 1893.

———. *Les Montagnes de la Lune: Exploration du Dr. Oscar Baumann*. Brussels: Le Mouvement Géographique, 1893.

Zangrie, L. "Quelques Traces Ethnologiques de l'Origine Égyptienne des Batutsi." *Jeune Afrique* 15 (1951): 9–15.

V. COLONIAL HISTORY

Anstey, Roger. *King Leopold's Legacy*. London: Oxford University Press, 1966.

Berlage, Jean. *Repertoire de la Presse du Congo Belge, 1884–1954, et du Ruanda-Urundi, 1920–1954*. Brussels: Commission Belge de Bibliographie, 1955.

Botte, Roger. "Rwanda and Burundi, 1889–1930: Chronology of a Slow Assassination." *International Journal of African Historical Studies* 18, no. 1 (1985): 53–91.

Bragard, Lucie. "Vers l'Indépendence du Ruanda-Urundi." *Les Dossiers de l'Action Sociale Catholique* 8 (1959): 643–76.

Brausch, E. J. *Belgian Administration in the Congo*. London: Oxford University Press, 1961.

Buhrer, J. *L'Afrique Orientale Allemande et la Guerre 1914–1918*. Paris: Fournier, 1923.

Bustin, Edouard. *Lunda under Belgian Rule: The Politics of Ethnicity*. Cambridge, Mass.: Harvard University Press, 1975.

Cauvin, André, and Bwana Kitoko. *Un Livre Réalisé au cours du Voyage du Roi des Belges au Congo et dans le Ruanda-Urundi*. Brussels: Elsevier, 1956.

Chauleur, P. "Les Étapes de l'Indépendence du Ruanda-Urundi." *Études* 314 (September 1962): 225–31.

Comhaire, J. "Au Ruanda-Urundi: Faits, Programmes, Opinions." *Zaire* 10 (1952): 1051–68.

Delacauw, A. "Droit Coutumier des Barundi." *Congo* 3 (1935), 332–57; 4 (1936): 481–522.

——. "Emigration des Barundi." *Grands Lacs* 64, nos. 4–6 (1949): 41–44.

Durieux, André. *Institutions Politiques, Administratives et Judiciaires du Congo Belge et du Ruanda-Urundi*. Brussels: Éditions Bieleveld, 1957.

Engels, A. "La Conquête du Ruanda-Urundi." *Bulletin de l'Institut Royal Colonial Belge* (1935): 359–60.

Gahama, Joseph. *Le Burundi sous Administration Belge*. Paris: Karthala, 1983.

Gelders, V., and J. Biroli. "Native Political Organization in Ruanda-Urundi." *Civilisations* 4 (1954): 125–32.

Gille, Albert. "Histoire du Muname." *Jeune Afrique* 4 (1948): 17–27.

Goebel, C. "Mwambutsa, Mwami de l'Urundi." *Revue Coloniale Belge* 115 (1950): 510–11.

Gorju, Mgr. *En Zigzags à Travres l'Urundi*. Namur: Missionaires d'Afrique (Pères Blancs), 1926.

Halewyck de Heusch, Michel. *Les Institutions Politiques et Administratives des États Africains soumis à l'Autorité de la Belgique*. Brussels: Bolyn, 1938.

Harroy, Jean-Paul. *Burundi: 1955–1962*. Brussels: Hayez, 1987.

Hertefelt, Marcel d'. "Le Ruanda et le Burundi vers l'Indépendence." *Archives Diplomatiques et Consulaires* 27 (August–September 1962): 372–73.

Jentgen, P. *Les Frontières du Ruanda-Urundi et le Régime International de Tutelle*. Brussels: Académie Royale des Sciences d'Outre-Mer, 1957.

——. "Ruanda-Urundi: The Mandate and International Trusteeship." *Geographical Review* 49 (January 1959): 120–22.

Jesman, Czeslaw. "Ruanda-Urundi in Transition." *British Survey Main Services* (August 1961): 1–21.

Jewsiewicki, Bogumil. "The Formation of the Political Culture and Ethnicity in the Belgian Congo, 1920–1959." In *The Creation of Tribalism in Southern Africa*, edited by Leroy Vail. London: James Currey, 1989.

Lechat, Michel. "La Réforme de l'Organisation des Jurisdictions Indigènes du Ruanda-Urundi." *Journal de Tribunes d'Outre-Mer* 40 (1961): 141–42.

——. *Le Burundi Politique*. Bujumbura: Service de l'Information du Ruanda-Urundi, 1961.

"Les Institutions Féodales de l'Urundi." *Revue de l'Université de Bruxelles* 1 (1949): 101–12.

Maquet, J. J. "Ruanda et Burundi: Évolutions Divergeantes ou Parallèles?" *Afrique Contemporaine* 5, no. 25 (1960): 21–25.

——. "Ruanda-Urundi: The Introduction of an Electoral System for Councils in a Caste Society." In *From Tribal Rule to Modern Government*, edited by R. Apthorpe. Lusaka, 1960.

Maquet, J. J., and M. d'Hertefelt. *Élections en Société Féodale: Une Étude sur l'Introduction du Vote Populaire au Ruanda-Urundi*. Brussels: Académie Royale des Sciences Coloniales, 1959.

Maus, Albert. "Le Statut Politique du Ruanda-Urundi et la Situation des Bahutu." *Eurafrica* 3 (1959): 19.

———. "Ruanda-Urundi: Terre d'Invasions." *Société Belge d'Études et Expansion* 178 (1957): 1023–27.

Meyer, Roger. *Introducing the Belgian Congo and Ruanda-Urundi.* Brussels: Office of Publicity, 1958.

Michiels, A., and N. Laude. *Congo Belge et Ruanda-Urundi.* Brussels: Universelle, 1958.

Moulaert, G. "La Conquête du Ruanda-Urundi." *Bulletin de l'Institut Royal Colonial Belge* (1935): 361–71.

Mworoha, Émile. "La Cour du Roi Mwezi Gisabo (1852–1908) du Burundi à la Fin du XIXᵉ Siècle." *Études d'Histoire Africaine* 7 (1985): 39–58.

———. *Peuples et Rois de l'Afrique des Lacs: Le Burundi et les Royaumes Voisins au XIXᵉ Siècle.* Dakar: Les Nouvelles Éditions Africaines, 1977.

Neesen, V. "Le Premier Recensement par Échantillonnage au Ruanda-Urundi." *Zaire* 5 (1953): 469–88.

———. "Quelques Donnés Démographiques sur la Population du Ruanda-Urundi." *Zaire* 7, no. 10 (1953): 1011–25.

Orts, P. "Le Mandat de la Belgique sur le Ruanda-Urundi." *Bibliothèque Coloniale Internationale. Proceedings, The Hague Session* (1927): 385–89.

———. "Le Ruanda-Urundi Devant l'Organisation des Nations Unies." *Revue Coloniale Belge* 88 (1949): 333–56.

Papy, L. "Un Pays d'Afrique Centrale: Le Ruanda-Urundi d'Après le Travaux Récents." *Cahiers d'Outre-Mer* 24 (1953): 399–407.

Perraudin, J. "L'Oeuvre Civilisatrice de la Belgique au Ruanda-Urundi." *Grands Lacs* 121 (1949): 53–65.

Pétillon, L. "Le Ruanda-Urundi et le Conseil de Tutelle." *Revue Coloniale Belge* 106 (1950): 151–54.

Postiaux, H. "La Colonisation du Territoire du Ruanda-Urundi." *Les Cahiers Colonioux de l'Institut Colonial de Marseilles*, nos. 551–52 (1929): 332.

Rousseau, R. "La Dernière Année de la Tutelle Belge au Rwanda-Burundi." *Vie Économique et Sociale* 33 (1962): 306–12.

Ryckmans, Pierre. "La Conquête Politique de l'Urundi." *Grands Lacs* (1936): 305.

———. "Le Probleme Politique au Ruanda-Urundi." *Congo* 1, no. 3 (1925): 407–13.

———. "Le Régime Juridique au Ruanda-Urundi." *Journal de Tribunes d'Outre-Mer* 59 (1955): 68–9.

———. "Le Ruanda-Urundi et l'ONU." *Revue Coloniale Belge* 76 (1948): 749–53.

———. "Note sur les Institutions, Moeurs et Coutumes de l'Urundi." In *Rapport sur l'Administration Belge au Ruanda-Urundi.* Brussels Resident Report 1936, 34–58.

Sandrart, George. "La Justice Indigène au Ruanda-Urundi." *Servir* 2 (1940): 26–28.

Sasserath, Jules S. *Le Ruanda-Urundi: Un Étrange Royaume Féodal au Coeur de l'Afrique*. Brussels: Germinal, 1948.

Schlippé, P. de. *Vers un Progrès Social Planifié: Rapport d'une Mission au Ruanda-Urundi (20 Février–20 Mai 1957)*. Usumbura: Vice-Gouvernement Général, 1958.

Simon, M. "L'Oeuvre Civilisatrice de la Belgique au Ruanda-Urundi." *Revue Coloniale Belge* 8 (1946): 9–11.

Slade, Ruth. *King Leopold's Congo*. London: Oxford University Press, 1962.

Taquet, J. "Deux Questions Intéressant la Location des Terres Domaniales dans le Ruanda-Urundi." *Revue Juridique du Congo Belge* (October 1934): 192–98.

United Nations Report on Ruanda-Urundi. Trusteeship Council 26th Session, Supplement No. 3, Document T/1551. 14 April to 30 June 1960.

Vallotton, H. *Voyage au Congo Belge et au Ruanda-Urundi*. Brussels: Weissenbruch, 1955.

Van Bilsen, A. A. J. *Vers l'Indépendance du Congo et du Ruanda-Urundi*. Kinshasa: Presses Universitaires du Zaire, 1977.

Van der Kerken, Georges. "L'Évolution de la Politique Indigène au Congo Belge et au Ruanda-Urundi." *Revue de l'Institut de Sociologie* 1 (1953): 25–62.

Van der Stickelen, A. "Régime Juridique au Ruanda-Urundi." *Journal de Tribunes d'Outre-Mer* 57 (1955): 33–34.

Van Grieken-Taverniers, Madeleine. *La Colonisation Belge en Afrique Centrale: Guide des Archives Africaines du Ministère des Affaires Africaines, 1885–1962*. Brussels: Ministère des Affaires Étrangeres, du Commerce Extérieur et de la Coopération au Développement, 1981.

Vanhove, J. *Histoire du Ministère des Colonies*. Brussels: Académie Royale des Sciences d'Outre-Mer, 1968.

Vansina, Jan. "Notes sur l'Histoire du Burundi." *Æquatoria* 1 (1961): 1–10.

VI. POSTCOLONIAL HISTORY

Anjo, J. "L'Affaire Ngendendumwe." *Remarques Africaines* 306 (1968): 46–47.

Aupens, Bernard. "Burundi: Le Massacre Érigé en Politique." *Revue Française d'Études Politiques Africaines* 78 (1972): 7–11.

———. "L'Engrenage de la Violence au Burundi." *Revue Française d'Études Politiques Africaines* 9 (July 1973): 48–69.

Bacamurwanko, J. "Burundi: Which Way Out? (Perspective of the Crisis)." Washington, D.C., 1994.

———. "Crisis in Burundi: The Agony of the Text." Washington, D.C., 1994.

Batungwanayo, Charles. "Burundi, le Pourquoi d'un Génocide." *Remarques Africaines* 407 (1972): 19–21.

Batururimi, Elias. "Le Pari du Mwami Mwambutsa IV." *Remarques Africaines* 7, no. 247 (1965): 3–5.

———. "Où Va le Pays?" *Remarques Africaines* 7, no. 252 (1965): 5–7.

Bentley, Kristina A., and Roger Southall. *An African Peace Process: Mandela, South Africa, and Burundi*. Cape Town, South Africa: Nelson Mandela Foundation, 2005.

Bernard, René. "The Constitutional Crisis in Burundi." *Nationalist* (Dar es Salaam), 17 August 1966.

Bertenel, Paul. "Burundi: Pourquoi." *Jeune Afrique* 597 (1972): 18.

Bimazubute, Gilles. "L'Uprona: Du Parti Indépendantiste au Parti-État." *Le Réveil*, 7–13 June 1991.

Boyer, Allison. "Unity at Last?" *Africa Report* (March–April 1992): 37–40.

Brooke, James. "In Burundi Minority Persists in Control of Nation." *New York Times*, 5 June 1987.

Buname, Emmanuel. "Burundi: Régime d'Opression." *Journal du Centre International des Étudiants Étrangers de Louvain* 4 (1971): 28–29.

"Burundi: Génocide ou Massacre?" *Jeune Afrique* 596 (1972): 16–17.

"Burundi: No End in Sight." *Africa Confidential* 13, no. 12 (1972): 1–2.

"Burundi: Sursis pour les Tutsis." *Jeune Afrique* 256 (1965): 24–25.

"Burundi: Time for International Action to End a Cycle of Mass Murder." *Amnesty International Bulletin*, 1994.

"Burundi at Close Range." *Africa Report* (March 1965): 19–24.

Cart, Henri-Philippe. "Conceptions des Rapports Politiques au Burundi." *Études Congolaises* 9 (1966): 1–22.

Ceulemans, Jacques. "Burundi: La Gestion Douleureuse de l'Indépendence." *Remarques Africaines* 8, no. 275 (1966): 520–22.

Chrétien, Jean-Pierre, and André Guichaoua. "Burundi, d'une République à l'Autre: Bilan et Enjoux." *Politique Africaine* 29 (1988): 87–100.

Christiansen, Hanne. *Refugees and Pioneers: History and Field Study of a Burundian Settlement in Tanzania*. Geneva: United Nations Research Institute for Social Development, 1985.

Coalition for Peace and Justice in Burundi. *Newsletter* 1, no. 1 (1994).

———. Response to Ambassador Bacamurwanko's Document "Burundi: Which Way Out? (Perspective of the Crisis)," 1994.

Dejemeppe, B. *Le Nauirage au Burundi*. Louvain, Belgium: Ligue Belge pour la Défense des Droits de l'Homme, 1972.

Evans, Glynne. *Responding to Crises in the African Great Lakes*. Oxford: Oxford University Press, for the International Institute for Strategic Studies, 1997.

Forscher, Romain. "Les Massacres au Burundi." *Esprit* (July–August 1972): 123–31.

Gahungu, Pierre. "Où Va le Royaume du Burundi?" *Remarques Africaines* 7, no. 248 (1965): 8–9.

Greenland, Jeremy. "Black Racism in Burundi." *New Blackfriars* (October 1973): 443–51.

Halberstam, D. "Rwanda and Burundi Become Independent African States." *New York Times*, 1 July 1962.

Hammer, Joshua. "Fears of Another Rwanda." *Newsweek* (10 April 1995): 38–39.

Howe, Marvine. "Slaughter in Burundi." *New York Times*, 11 June 1972.

Hoyt, Michael. "Messages Concerning the Burundi Massacres to and from the American Embassy in Bujumbura." Evanston, Ill.: Melvill Herskovits Library, Northwestern University, 1972.

Human Rights Watch. *Proxy Targets: Civilians in the War in Burundi*. New York: Human Rights Watch, 1998.

Hutu Students of Burundi. "Manifeste des Étudiants du Burundi." Mimeo, 1969.

International Commission of Jurists. "Events in Burundi." Press release, 2 November 1965.

International Labor Organization. "Les Violations de la Liberté Syndicale et des Droits de l'Homme au Burundi." Press release, 1966.

Kay, Reginald. *Burundi since the Genocide*. London: Minority Rights Group, 1987.

Kidwingira, Bonaventure. "Le Vrai Visage de l'UNEBA." *Remarques Africaines* 9, no. 285 (1967): 121–24.

Kiraranganiya, Boniface. *La Vérité sur le Burundi*. Sherbrooke, Que.: Éditions Naaman, 1985.

Latham-Koening, A. L. "Ruanda-Urundi on the Threshold of Independence." *World Today* 18 (July 1962): 288–95.

"Le Burundi." *Bulletin d'Information de la Coopération au Développement* 11 (1966): 29–36.

"Le Burundi à la Recherche d'une Stabilité." *Présence Africaine* 47 (1963): 235.

"Le Climat Politique au Burundi: L'Affaire Ngendendumwe." *Remarques Africaines* 8, no. 265 (1966): 221–26.

Lemarchand, René. *Burundi: Ethnic Conflict and Genocide*. Cambridge, Mass.: Woodrow Wilson Center Press, 1996.

———. "Burundi: Ethnicity and the Genocidal State." In *State Violence and Ethnicity*, edited by Pierre van den Berghe. Niwot: University Press of Colorado, 1990.

———. *Burundi: Ethnocide as Discourse and Practice*. New York: Woodrow Wilson Center Press, 1994.

———. "Managing Transition Anarchies: Rwanda, Burundi, and South Africa in Comparative Perspective." *Journal of Modern African Studies* 32, no. 4 (1994): 581–604.

———. "The Military in Former Belgian Africa." In *Political-Military Systems: Comparative Perspectives*, edited by C. M. Kelleher. Beverly Hills, Calif.: Sage, 1974.

———. "The Passing of Mwamiship in Burundi." *Africa Report* (January 1967): 14–24.

———. "Political Instability in Africa: The Case of Rwanda and Burundi." *Civilisations* 16 (1966): 1–29.

———. *Selective Genocide in Burundi*. London: Minority Rights Group, 1973.

———. "Social and Political Changes in Burundi." In *Five African States: Responses to Diversity*, edited by G. Carter. Ithaca, N.Y.: Cornell University Press, 1963.

———. "Social Change and Political Modernisation in Burundi." *Journal of Modern African Studies* 4, no. 4 (1966): 14–24.

Madirisha, Juvenal. "Le Burundi, ses Leaders et l'UNEBA." *Remarques Africaines* 8, no. 277 (1966): 562–64.

———. "L'UNEBA Devient une Milice Républicaine." *Remarques Africaines* 9, no. 290 (1967): 272–75.

"Manifeste des Étudiants Barundi en Belgique." *Remarques Africaines* 8, no. 261 (1966): 119–26.

Manirakiza, Marc. *Burundi: De la Révolution au Régionalisme, 1966–1976*. Brussels: Le Mat de Misaine, 1992.

———. *La Fin de la Monarchie Burundaise, 1962–1966*. Brussels: Le Mat de Misaine, 1990.

Martin, David, and René Lemarchand. *Selective Genocide in Burundi*. London: Minority Rights Group, 1974.

Melady, Thomas Patrick. *Burundi: The Tragic Years*. Maryknoll, N.Y.: Orbis, 1974.

Morris, Roger, et al. *Passing By: The United States and the Genocide in Burundi, 1972*. Washington, D.C.: Carnegie Endowment for International Peace, 1973.

Mpozagara, Gabriel. *La République du Burundi*. Paris: Éditions Berger-Levrault, 1971.

Munene, Mbenga. "Burundi: L'Oeuvre des Mercenaires." *Remarques Africaines* 419 (1973): 6.

Ndabakwaje, Libère. "L'Histoire de l'UNEBA." *Remarques Congolaises et Africaines* 6, no. 8 (1964): 184–88.

Ndaje [pseud. for a group of Hutu students of Burundi]. "Le Masque de l'UNEBA." *Remarques Africaines* 8, no. 276 (1966): 551–54.

——. "L'Impérialisme, la Féodalité et la Persécution du Peuple au Burundi." *Remarques Africaines* 8, no. 268 (1966): 324–26.

Ndarubagiye, Léonce. *Burundi: The Origins of the Hutu-Tutsi Conflict.* Nairobi: University of Nairobi Press, 1995.

Nelan, Bruce. "A Recurring Nightmare." *Time* (10 April 1995): 50–51.

Newbury, David. "Burundi without Peasants." *Journal of African History* 31, no. 3 (1990): 509–10.

Ngabissio, N. N. "Burundi Pourquoi?" *Jeune Afrique* (17 June 1972): 18–20.

Nicayenzi, Zénon. "Note des Éveques sur le Danger qui Menace le Burundi." *Remarques Congolaises et Africaines* 6, no. 20 (1964): 470–72.

Niqueaux, Jacques. "Le Burundi à l'Épreuve." *Revue Nouvelle* 43, no. 2 (1966): 176–81.

——. "Rwanda et Burundi, les Frères Ennemis aux Sources du Nil." *Revue Nouvelle* 43, no. 5 (1966): 466–81.

Niyonzima, David, and Lon Fendall. *Unlocking Horns: Forgiveness and Reconciliation in Burundi.* Newbury, Ore.: Barclay Press, 2001.

"Nouveaux Témoignages sur le Burundi." *Remarques Africaines* 15, nos. 430–31 (1973): 34.

Nsanze, Térence. "Burundi: Tableau Authentique des Faits et Événements Récents." *Remarques Africaines* 8, no. 268 (1966): 321–23.

——. *L'Édification de la République du Burundi au Carrefour de l'Afrique.* Brussels: Remarques Africaines, 1970.

Nyangoma, Gervais. Letter to the editor. *Reporter* (9 April 1964): 8–9.

Nyankanzi, Edward L. *Genocide: Rwanda and Burundi.* Rochester, Vt.: Schenkman Books, 1998.

Nzeyimana, Laurent. "Burundi: Aux Nouveaux Hommes, au Nouveau Régime, de Nouvelles Institutions." *Remarques Africaines* 9, no. 283 (1967): 61–65.

Nzisabira, Benoit. "Le Multipartisme et la Politique de l'Unité Nationale au Burundi." *Le Réveil*, June 1991, 31–38.

Nzohabanayo, C. "La Possession d'État de National au Burundi." *Revue Juridique et Politique* 25, no. 4 (1971): 445–70.

Ould-Abdallah, Ahmedou. *Burundi on the Brink, 1993–1995.* Washington, D.C.: United States Institute of Peace Press, 2000.

"Out of Africa: Burundi." *Africa Report* (June 1962): 8–9.

Pabenel, Jean-Pierre. "Statistiques Tribales au Burundi en 1986." *Politique Africaine* 32 (1988): 111–16.

Pereira, C. C. "Décentralisation et Développement National au Burundi." *Bulletin de l'Institut International d'Administration Publique* 21 (1972): 55–62.

Perlez, Jane. "The Bloody Hills of Burundi." *New York Times Magazine*, 6 November 1988, section 6, pp. 90ff.

"A Political Trial in Burundi." *Bulletin of the International Commission of Jurists* (July 1963): 5–15.

Ragoen, J. "Il n'y Aura pas de Printemps Burundais." *Zaire* 24 (15 May 1972): 8.

———. "Rébellion au Burundi." *Zaire* 24 (29 May 1972): 26–29.

République du Burundi: IIe Republique Respect des Engagements. Bujumbura: Ministère de l'Information, 1984.

Reyntjens, Filip. *Again at the Crossroads: Rwanda and Burundi, 2000–2001.* Current African Issues series. Antwerp: Nordiska Afrikainstitutet, 2001.

———. *Talking or Fighting? Political Evolution in Rwanda and Burundi, 1998–1999.* Current African Issues series. Antwerp: Nordiska Afrikainstitutet, 1999.

Rodegem, F. M. "Burundi: La Face Cachée de la Rébellion." *Intermédiare* 4 (1973): 15–19.

Sabimbona, Simon. "Une République Révolutionnaire?" *Remarques Africaines* 9, no. 285 (1967): 127–29.

Sebiva, Gatti. "Burundi: Détente entre le Parlement et le Gouvernement." *Études Congolaises* 8 (October 1963): 42–44.

Semahuna, Charles. "Aux Aveugles du Burundi." *Remarques Congolaises et Africaines* 6, no. 21 (1964): 498–99.

Soulik, S. "Interview du Colonel Michel Micombero." *Remarques Africaines* 305 (1968): 6–9.

Staub, Irvin. *The Roots of Evil: The Origins of Genocide and Other Group Violence.* Cambridge: Cambridge University Press, 1989.

Tannenwald, Paul. "Burundi: Le Prix de l'Ordre." *Revue Française d'Études Politiques Africaines* 58 (1970): 69–87.

Ugeux, E. Xavier. "Après Sept Ans de République: Le Bilan d'une Tragèdie." *Remarques Africaines* 429 (1973): 14–16.

———. "Génocide au Burundi." *Remarques Africaines* 400 (1971): 3–6; 401 (1972): 11–12.

———. "Parodie Judiciare au Burundi." *Remarques Africaines* 393 (1972): 9–10.

Ugeux, E. Xavier, and J. Wolf. "Une Interview Exclusive de Mwambutsa IV, Ancien Roi du Burundi." *Remarques Africaines* 403 (1973): 8–11.

"The United Nations Findings on Rwanda and Burundi." *Africa Report* 9, no. 4 (1964): 7–8.

United States. House Committee on Foreign Affairs. Subcommittee on Human Rights and International Organizations. "Recent Violence in Burundi: What Should Be the U.S. Response?" 1988.

UPRONA. "Compte-rendu de la Conférence au Sommet de Kitéga du 8 Septembre au 6 Octobre." Bujumbura, 1964. Mimeographed. Burundi, Africa: Burundi National Archives.

Watson, Catharine. "After the Massacre." *Africa Report* (January–February 1989): 51–55.

———. "Burundi." *Africa Report* (September–October 1993): 58–61.

———. "Death of Democracy." *Africa Report* (January–February 1994): 26–31.

Webster, John. *The Constitutions of Burundi, Malagasy, and Rwanda*. Syracuse, N.Y.: Syracuse University Maxwell Graduate School of Public Affairs, 1964.

———. *The Political Development of Rwanda and Burundi*. Syracuse, N.Y.: Syracuse University Program of Eastern African Studies, 1966.

Weinstein, Warren. "Burundi: Alternatives to Violence." *Issue* 5, no. 2 (1975): 17–22.

———. "Burundi: Political and Ethnic Powderkeg." *Africa Report* (November 1970): 18–20.

———. "Burundi: Racial Peace and Royalty." *Africa Today* 12, no. 6 (1965): 12–15.

———. "Conflict and Confrontation in Central Africa: The Revolt in Burundi, 1972." *Africa Today* 19, no. 4 (1972): 17–37.

———. "Ethnicity and Conflict Regulation: The 1972 Burundi Revolt." *Afrika Spectrum* 9, no. 1 (1974): 42–49.

———. "Humanitarian Aid and Civil Strife: Politics vs. Relief in Burundi." In *Civil Wars and the Politics of International Relief*, edited by Morris Davis. New York: Praeger, 1975.

———. "Human Rights in Jeopardy: Burundi and Uganda." *Africa Today* 22, no. 1 (1975): 75–80.

———. "Rwanda and Burundi: Enemy Brothers Coming Together." *Pan African Journal* 5, no. 1 (1972): 39–44.

———. "Rwanda-Burundi: An Aborted Putative Nation." In *Divided Nations in a Divided World*, edited by J. Stoessinger, N. Lebow, et al. New York: McKay, 1974.

———. "Tensions in Burundi." *Issue* 2, no. 4 (1972): 27–29.

Williams, Roger. "Slaughter in Burundi." *World* (21 November 1972): 20–24.

Wingert, Norman. *No Place to Stop Killing*. Chicago: Moody Press, 1974.

Wolf, J. "Le Destin Tragique du Roi Ntare V." *Remarques Africaines* 400 (1972): 7–8.

Zarembo, Alan. "Standing on the Brink." *Africa Report* (March–April 1995): 24–29.

Ziegler, Jean. "Un Royaume en Crise: Le Burundi." *Le Monde*, 19 November 1965.

VII. ECONOMICS AND DEVELOPMENT

Aerts, L. *L'Évolution Économique du Ruanda-Urundi de 1949 à 1955*. Usumbura: Vice-Gouvernement Général, 1957.

Bell, Philip W., ed. *African Economic Problems: A Collection of Published and Unpublished Works*. Kampala, Uganda: Makaere University College, 1964.

Blakey, K. A. *Economic Development of Burundi*. Cairo: Institute of National Planning, 1964.

Botte, Roger. "Qui Mangeait Quoi? L'Alimentation au Burundi à la Fin du XIXième Siècle." *Cultures et Développement* 15, no. 3 (1983): 455–69.

Chrétien, Jean-Pierre. "La Fermeture du Burundi et du Rwanda aux Commerçants de l'Extérieur (1905–1906)." *Entreprises et Entrepreneurs en Afrique, XIXe-XXe Siècles* 2 (1983): 25–47.

Cierfayt, Albert. *Le Développement Énergétique du Congo Belge et du Ruanda-Urundi*. Brussels: Académie Royale des Sciences d'Outre-Mer, 1960.

Declerk, L. "Note sur le Droit Foncier Coutumier au Burundi." *Revue Juridique du Rwanda et du Burundi* 1 (1965): 38–42.

Durant, A. "Structure Économique du Ruanda-Urundi." *Bulletin de la Chambre de Commerce du Ruanda-Urundi* (2nd trimestre, 1957): 13–18.

Heyse, T. *Bibliographie des Problèmes Fonciers et du Régime des Terres: Afrique, Congo Belge, Ruanda-Urundi*. Brussels: Centre de Documentation Economique et Sociale, 1960.

International Labor Organization. "Rapport au Gouvernement de la République du Burundi sur l'Administration du Travail." Geneva: International Labor Organization, 1970.

Jaspar, H. "Le Ruanda-Urundi: Pays à Disettes Périodiques." *Congo* 2 (1929): 1–21.

Kayitare, Tharcisse. "Congo-Rwanda-Burundi: Un Nouvel Ensemble Économique en Gestation." *Remarques Africaines* 355 (1970): 151–52.

Lefebvre, Jacques. *Structures Économiques du Congo Belge et du Ruanda-Urundi*. Brussels: Treuvenberg, 1955.

Mottoule, L. "Equilibre de l'Alimentation chez l'Indigène du Congo Belge et du Ruanda-Urundi." *Servir* 1–2 (1945): 25–32, 77–81.

Neesen, V. "Aspects de l'Économie Démographique du Ruanda-Urundi." *Bulletin de l'Institut de Recherches Économiques et Sociales de l'Université de Louvain* 22, no. 5 (1956): 473–504.

Nicayenzi, Zénon. "Le Dévéloppement Économique: Processes Continu ou Discontinu; Le Cas du Burundi." *Synthèses* (Kinshasa), no. 5 (1970): 69–80.

"Régime des Investissements au Burundi." *Industries et Travaux d'Outre-Mer* (November 1969): 957–58.

Robatel, J. P. "La Condition Ouvrière à Bujumbura." *Cultures et Dévéloppement* 2, no. 2 (1970): 427–34.

Steward, C. C., and D. Crummey. *Modes of Production in Precolonial Africa*. Beverly Hills, Calif.: Sage, 1981.

Trouwborst, Albert. "L'Accord de Clientèle et Organisation Politique au Burundi." *Anthropologica* 4 (1962): 9–43.

——. "L'Organisation Politique en Tant que Système d'Échange au Burundi." *Anthropologica* 3, no. 1 (1961): 1–17.

Van Asbroek, J. J. "La Structure Démographique et l'Évolution Économique du Ruanda-Urundi." *Bulletin de la Société Royale Belge de Géographie*, no. 4 (1956): 15–32.

Van de Walle, E. "Chômage dans un de Petite Ville d'Afrique: Usumbura." *Zaire* 14 (1960): 341–59.

——. "Facteurs et Indices de Stabilisation et d'Urbanisation à Usumbura." *Recherches Economiques de Louvain* 27, no. 2 (1961): 97–121.

Van Tichelen, H. E. "Problèmes du Développement Économique du Ruanda-Urundi." *Zaire* 11 (1957): 451–74.

Wagner, Michele D. "Trade and Commercial Attitudes in Burundi before the Nineteenth Century." *International Journal of African Historical Studies* 26, no. 1 (1993).

VIII. LINGUISTICS

Albert, Ethel M. "Cultural Patterning of Speech Behavior in Burundi." In *Directions in Sociolinguistics*, edited by John Gumperz and D. Hymes. New York: Holt, Rinehart & Winston, 1972.

——. "Rhetoric, Logic, and Poetics in Burundi: Cultural Patterning of Speech Behavior." *American Anthropologist* 66, no. 6 (1964).

Alexandre, P. *Langues et Langage en Afrique Noire*. Paris: Payot, 1970.

Bagein, E. *Petite Grammaire Kirundi*. Bujumbura: Presses Lavigerie, 1951.

Barakana, Gabriel. "L'Unification des Langues au Ruanda-Urundi." *Civilisations* 2, no. 1 (1952): 67–78.

Bigangara, Jean-Baptiste. *Elements de Linguistique Burundaise*. Bujumbura: Ministry of Youth, Sports and Culture, 1982.

Bonneau, H. *Dictionnaire Français–Kirundi et Kirundi–Français*. Bujumbura: Presses Lavigeries, 1950.

Bonvini, E., and P. Durant. "L'Enregistrement Sonore dans l'Enquête Linguistique." *Afrique et Langage* 1 (1974): 21–34.

Coupez, André. "Langues Secrètes au Ruanda-Urundi." *Folia Scientifica Africae Centralis* 4, no. 3 (1958): 69.

Coupez, André, and A. E. Mecussen. "Notation Pratique de la Quantité Vocalique et de la Tonalité en Rundi et Rwanda." *Orbis* (Louvain) 10, no. 2 (1962): 428–33.

Eggers, Ellen K. "Temporal Anaphora in Discourse." Ph.D. diss., University of Washington, 1990.

Guthrie, Malcolm. *The Classification of the Bantu Languages*. London: Oxford University Press, 1948.

——. "Linguistic Evidence Regarding Bantu." *Journal of African History* 2 (1962): 189–216.

——. "Linguistics." In *The African World: A Survey of Social Research*, edited by R. A. Lystad. New York: Praeger, 1965.

——. "Some Developments in the Pre-history of Bantu Languages." *Journal of African History* 2 (1962): 273–82.

Homberger, L. "Les Langues Bantou." In *Les Langues du Monde*, edited by M. Meillet. Paris: Éd. Champion, 1924.

——. *Les Langues Négro-Africaines et les Peuples qui les Parlent.* Paris: Payot, 1941.

Kimenyi, Alexandre. *Kinyarwanda and Kirundi Names: A Semiolinguistic Analysis of Bantu Onamastics.* Lewiston, N.Y.: E. Mellen Press, 1988.

Kirundi Basic Course. Washington, D.C.: Foreign Service Institute.

Meeussen, A. E. *Essai de Grammaire Rundi.* Tervuren, Belgium: Musée Royal du Congo Belge, 1959.

——. *Notes de Grammaire Rundi.* Tervuren, Belgium: Musée Royal du Congo Belge, 1952.

Menard, F. *Dictionnaire Français–Kirundi, Kirundi–Français.* Roulers: De Meester, 1909.

——. *Grammaire Kirundi.* Algiers: Maison-Carrée, 1908.

——. *Guide de Conversation Kirundi.* Algiers: Maison-Carrée, 1910.

Mioni, A. *Problèmes de Linguistique d'Orthographe et de Coordination Culturelle au Burundi.* Naples: Istituto Universitario Orientale, 1970.

Mvuyekure, Augustin. "Ijambo, ou le Discours au Burundi." *Que Vous en Semble?* 4, nos. 14–15 (1971): 75–97.

Ntahokaja, J. B. "La Litérature Orale du Burundi." *Études Scientifiques* (March 1979): 19–28.

——. "Le Kirundi: Instrument de Développement Politique, Économique et Culturel." *African Languages* 5, no. 2 (1979): 87–94.

Phillipson, D. W. "Archaeology and Bantu Linguistics." *World Archaeology* 8, no. 1 (1976): 65–82.

——. "The Spread of the Bantu Language." *Scientific American* 256, no. 236 (1977): 106–16.

Rodegem, F. M. *Dictionnaire Rundi–Français.* Tervuren, Belgium: Annales du Musée Royal de l'Afrique Centrale, 1970.

——. *Essai de Dictionnaire Explicatif Rundi.* Bujumbura: Les Presses Lavigerie, 1961.

——. "Le Poker Verbal: Réflexions sur un Colloque." *Cultures et Développement* 7, no. 2 (1975): 369–97.

——. *Précis de Grammaire Rundi.* Brussels: E. Story-Scientia, 1967.

Van Bulck, G. *Mission Linguistique, 1949–1951.* Brussels: Institut Royal Colonial Belge, 1954.

IX. LITERATURE, MUSIC, AND VISUAL ARTS

Belinga, M. S. Eno. *Littérature et Musique Populaires en Afrique Noire*. Paris: Association pour la Coopération Franco-Africaine, 1965.

Boone, Olga. *Les Tambours du Congo Belge et du Ruanda-Urundi*. Tervuren, Belgium: Musée Royal du Congo Belge, 1951.

Boyayo, A. "Importance de la Poésie Guerrière Rundi dans la Reconstitution de l'Histoire Nationale." *Revue Nationale d'Éducation du Burundi* 3, no. 5 (1966): 4–8.

Bozzini, G., et al. *Proverbi Rundi*. Milan: Pime, 1980.

Carrington, J. F. *Talking Drums of Africa*. London: Carey Kingsgate Press, 1949.

Chrétien, Jean-Pierre. "Des Légendes Africaines Face à des Mythes Européens." *Cultures et Développement* 3 (1974): 579–87.

Chrysostome, Jean. "Fabrication de Poterie en Urundi." *Trait d'Union* 21, nos. 3–4 (1953): 15–18.

Clifford, Mary Louise. *Bisha of Burundi*. New York: Thomas Y. Crowell, 1973.

Collaer, P. "Notes sur la Musique d'Afrique Centrale." *Problèmes d'Afrique Centrale*, no. 26 (1964): 267–71.

Curtis-Burlin, N. *Songs and Tales from the Dark Continent*. New York: Schirmer, 1920.

Dechaume, P. "Proverbes de l'Urundi." *Grands Lacs*, no. 78 (1940): 36–37.

Finnegan, Ruth. *Oral Literature in Africa*. Oxford: Oxford University Press, 1970.

Gérard, Albert S. *African Language Literatures*. Washington, D.C.: Three Continents Press, 1981.

Heusch, Luc de. *Le Roi Ivre ou l'Origine de l'État: Mythes et Rites Bantous*. Paris: Gallimard, 1972.

Hockett, Betty M. *What Will Tomorrow Bring?* Newberg, Ore.: George Fox Press, 1985.

Jadot, J. M. "Les Arts Populaires au Congo Belge, au Ruanda et dans l'Urundi." *Zaire* 2 (1950): 181–88.

——. *Les Écrivains Africains du Congo Belge et du Ruanda-Urundi*. Brussels: Académie Royale des Sciences d'Outre-Mer, 1959.

Lord, A. B. *The Singer of Tales*. Cambridge, Mass.: Harvard University Press, 1964.

Louipas, P. "Tradition et Légende des Batutsi sur la Création du Monde et Leur Éstablissement au Ruanda." *Anthropos* 3 (1908): 1–13.

MacGaffey, W. "Oral Tradition in Central Africa." *International Journal of African Historical Studies* 7, no. 3 (1975): 417–26.

Makarkiza, André. *La Dialectique des Barundi*. Brussels: Académie Royale des Sciences Coloniales, 1959.

Merriam, Alan P. "Les Styles Vocaux dans la Musique du Ruanda-Urundi." *Jeune Afrique* 7 (1953): 16.

Ndoricimpa, L., and C. Guillet. *L'Arbre-Mémoire: Traditions Orales du Burundi*. Bujumbura: Centre de Civilisation Burundaise, 1984.

Nsuka, Y. M. "Littératures Traditionnelles au Congo Kinshasa, au Rwanda et au Burundi: Bibliographie Commentée." *Cahiers Congolais* 14, no. 2 (1970): 87–153.

Ntahokaja, J. B. "La Musique des Barundi." *Grand Lacs*, nos. 4–6 (1948–49): 45–49.

———. "Proverbes et Sentences." *Grand Lacs*, nos. 4–6 (1948–49): 36–38.

Otten, Rik, and Victor Bachy. *Le Cinema dans les Pays des Grands Lacs: Zaire, Rwanda, Burundi*. Paris: L'Harmattan, 1984.

Propp, V. "Morphology of the Folktale." *International Journal of American Linguistics: Bulletin*, no. 24 (1958): 4.

Ramirez, Francis, and Christian Rolot. *Histoire du Cinema Colonial au Zaire, au Rwanda et au Burundi*. Tervuren, Belgium: Musée Royal de l'Afrique Centrale, 1985.

Risselin, J. P. "La Chanson Savante chez les Watousis." *Jeune Afrique*, no. 6 (1949): 24–25.

Rodegem, F. M. *Anthologie Rundi*. Paris: A. Colin, 1973.

———. "Le Style Oral au Burundi: Interview d'un Troubadour aux Sources du Nil." *Congo-Tervuren* 6 (1960): 119–27.

———. *Paroles de Sagesse au Burundi*. Louvain, Belgium: Peeters, 1983.

———. *Sagesse Kirundi*. Tervuren, Belgium: Musée Royal de l'Afrique Centrale, 1961.

———. "Syntagmes Complétifs Spéciaux en Rundi." *Annales du Musée Royal de l'Afrique Centrale* 68 (1970): 181–207.

———. "Une Forme d'Humour Contestataire au Burundi: Les Wellérismes." *Cahiers d'Études Africaines* 14, no. 3 (1974): 521–42.

Sartiaux, P. "Aspects Traditionnels de la Musique au Ruanda-Urundi." *Jeune Afrique* 21 (1954): 19–26.

Soyinka, W. *Myth, Literature, and the African World*. London: Cambridge University Press, 1976.

Vansina, Jan. *De la Tradition Orale: Essai de Methode Historique*. Tervuren, Belgium: Musée Royal de l'Afrique Centrale, 1961.

———. *La Légende du Passé*. Tervuren, Belgium: Musée Royal de l'Afrique Centrale, 1972.

———, ed. *Les Anciens Royaumes de la Zone Interlacustre Méridionale: Rwanda, Burundi, Buha*. Tervuren, Belgium: Musée Royal de l'Afrique Centrale, 1962.

———. *Oral Tradition: A Study in Historical Methodology*. Chicago: Aldine, 1965.

Werner, Alice. *Myths and Legends of the Bantu*. London: Cass, 1933.
Zuure, Bernard. "Poésies chez les Barundi." *Africa* 5, no. 3 (1932): 344–54.

X. SOCIETY

Albert, Ethel M. "Socio-Political Organization and Receptivity to Change: Some Differences between Ruanda and Urundi." *Southwestern Journal of Anthropology* 16 (1960): 46–74.

———. "A Study of Values in Urundi." *Cahiers d'Études Africaines* 2 (1960): 148–60.

———. "Women of Burundi: A Study of Social Values." In *Women of Tropical Africa*, edited by Denise Paulme. Berkeley: University of California Press, 1960.

Amselle, Jean-Loup, and Elikia M'bokolo, eds. *Au Coeur de l'Ethnie*. Paris: Découverte, 1985.

Anastase, Frère. "Le Nom et ses Implications dans la Culture Bantoue." *Servir* 22, no. 4 (1961): 129–35.

Arnoux, A. "Quelques Notes sur les Enfants au Ruanda et à l'Urundi." *Anthropos* 26 (1918): 341–51.

Aupens, Bernard. "La Culture Française au Burundi: Analyse Historique et Sociologique." *Culture Française* 2 (1967): 9–18.

Baeck, L. "Quelques Aspects Sociaux de l'Urbanisation au Ruanda-Urundi." *Zaire* 10 (1956): 1 15–45.

Bahenduzi, Michel. "Les Stéréotypes Idéologiques de la Description de l'Ancien Burundi." In *Culture et Société, Revue de Civilisation Burundaise*. Vol. 4. Bujumbura: Ministère de la Jeunesse, des Sports et de la Culture, 1981.

Barth, F. *Ethnic Groups and Boundaries: The Social Organization of Culture Difference*. London: Allen & Unwin, 1969.

Blankoff-Scarr, Goldie, trans. *Ruanda-Urundi: Social Achievements*. Brussels: Belgian Congo and Ruanda-Urundi Information and Public Relations Office, 1960.

Boone, Olga. "Carte Ethnique du Congo Belge et du Ruanda-Urundi." *Zaire* 8 (1954): 451–66.

Bourgeois, R. *L'Évolution du Contrat de Bail à Cheptel au Ruanda-Urundi*. Brussels: Académie Royale des Sciences d'Outre-Mer, 1958.

———. "Rituel du Marriage Coutumier au Ruanda-Urundi." *Bulletin de Juridictions Indigènes et du Droit Coutumier Congolais*, no. 6 (1955): 133–46.

Boyayo, A. "La Polygamie en Droit Coutumier Rundi." *Revue Nationale d'Éducation du Burundi* 4, no. 5 (1967): 16–17.

Brain, James L. "The Tutsi and the Ha: A Study in Integration." *Journal of African and Asian Studies* 8, no. 1–2 (1973): 39–49.

Chrétien, Jean-Pierre. "La Société du Burundi: Des Mythes aux Réalités." *Revue Françaises d'Études Politiques Africaines*, nos. 163–64 (1979): 94–118.

Chrétien, Jean-Pierre, and Émile Mworoha. "Les Tombeaux des Bami du Burundi: Un Aspect de la Monarchie Sacrée en Afrique Orientale." *Cahiers d'Études Africaines* 1 (1970): 40–79.

Chrysostome, Soeur Jean. "L'amour Maternel chez les Barundi." *Trait d'Union* 39, no. 5 (1956): 5–9.

Cleene, N. de. *Introduction à l'Ethnographie du Congo Belge et du Ruanda-Urundi*. 2nd ed. Antwerp: Éditions de Sikkel, 1957.

Clerck, Louis de. *Introduction à l'Étude du Droit Coutumier*. Bujumbura: Université Officielle, 1968.

Coupez, André. "Texte Ruundi: Les Rois du Pays." *Zaire* 11, no. 6 (1957): 623–36.

———. "Texte Ruundi, 2." *Æquatoria* 21, no. 3 (1958): 81–97.

Delhaise, C. "Chez les Warundi et les Wohorohoro." *Bulletin de la Société Royale Belge de Géographie* (1908): 386–421, 429–50.

Dickerman, Carol. "City Women and the Colonial Regime: Usumbura, 1939–1962." *African Urban Studies* 18 (1984): 33–48.

Elam, Yitzchak. *The Social and Sexual Roles of Hima Women*. Manchester: Manchester University Press, 1973.

Gerkens, G. *Les Batutsi et les Bahutu*. Brussels: Institut Royal de Sciences Naturelles Belge, 1949.

Gille, Albert. "L'Umuganuro ou Fête du sorgho en Urundi." *Bulletin des Juridictions Indigènes et du Droit Coutumier Congolais* 14, no. 11 (1946): 368–71.

———. "Notes sur l'Organisation des Barundi." *Bulletin de Juridictions Indigènes et du Droit Coutumier Congolais*, no. 3 (1938): 75–81.

Goffin, J. "Le Rôle Joué par le Gros Bétail en Urundi." *Bulletin des Juridictions Indigènes et du Droit Coutumier Congolais* 19 (1951): 31–53, 61–86, 100–21.

Gourou, Pierre. *La Densité de la Population au Ruanda-Urundi*. Brussels: Institut Royal Colonial Belge, 1953.

Guillaume H. "Peuplement Indigène, Institutions et Régime des Biens au Ruanda-Urundi." *Athenation* (Usumbura), nos. 2–3 (1956): 27–42, 36–53.

Gulliver, P. H. *The Family Herds*. London: Routledge, 1955.

Hiernaux, Jean. *Analyses de la Variation des Caractères Physiques Humains en une Région de l'Afrique Centrale: Ruanda-Urundi et Kivu*. Tervuren, Belgium: Annales du Musée Royal du Congo Belge, 1956.

———. *Les Caractères Physiques des Populations du Ruanda et de l'Urundi*. Brussels: Institut Royal Colonial Belge, 1954.

———. "Note sur l'Homme de la Ruzizi." *Zaire* 8 (1957): 845–46.

———. "Note sur une Ancienne Population du Ruanda-Urundi: Les Renge." *Zaire* 10 (1956): 351–60.

———. "Racial Properties of the Natives of Ruanda-Urundi." *Anthropos* 50, nos. 4–6 (1955): 967.

Jeffreys, M. "The Batwa: Who Are They?" *Africa* 1 (1953): 45–54.

Kagame, Alexis. "Les Hamites du Ruanda et du Burundi, sont-ils des Hamites?" *Bulletin des Séances, Académie Royale des Sciences Coloniales* 2 (1956): 341–63.

Kahombo, Mateene. "Quelques Principes du Choix des Noms Individuels dans Certaines Sociétés Bantu." *Cahiers d'Études Africaines*, no. 50 (1972): 357–61.

Kisyeti, Gérard. "Le Tribalisme au Burundi." *Remarques Africaines* 10, no. 326 (1968): 539–41.

"La Chasse aux Hutu au Burundi." *Revue Française d'Études Politiques Africaines* 81 (1972): 103–5.

Lemarchand, René. "L'Influence des Systèmes Traditionnels sur L'Évolution Politique du Rwanda et du Burundi." *Revue de l'Institut de Sociologie* 2 (1962): 333–57.

———. "Status Differences and Ethnic Conflict: Rwanda and Burundi." In *Ethnicity and Nation Building*, edited by W. Bell and W. E. Freeman. Beverly Hills, Calif.: Sage, 1974.

Leurquin, Philippe. "L'Actif Mobilier des Habitants des Sous-Chefferies Kigoma (Ruanda) et Nyangwa (Urundi)." *Bulletin de l'Institut de Recherches Économiques et Sociales de l'Université de Louvain* 23, no. 2 (1957): 67–94.

———. *Le Niveau de Vie des Populations Rurales du Ruanda-Urundi*. Louvain, Belgium: Éditions Nauwelaerts, 1960.

Lowie, R. H. *Social Organization*. London: Routledge, 1950.

Maquet, Emma. *Outils de Forges du Congo, du Rwanda, et du Burundi*. Tervuren, Belgium: Musée Royal de l'Afrique Centrale, 1965.

Maquet, J. J. "Le Problème de la Domination Tutsi." *Zaire* 6 (1952): 1011–16.

Maus, Albert. "Batutsi et Bahutu au Ruanda-Urundi." *Europe-Afrique* (Bukavu) (April 1954): 8–10.

Muhirwa, A. "Une Fille peut-elle Hériter au même Titre que ses Fréres?" *Servir* 1 (1946): 41–42.

Murray, H. J. R. "The Game of the Kubuguza among the Abatutsi." *Man* 53 (December 1953): 194.

Nkezabera, J. "Le Choix d'un Nom." *Servir* 2 (1953): 49–50.

Nkundikije, André. "Problèmes Ethniques Face à la Revolution Burundaise." *Remarques Africaines* 9, no. 290 (1967): 275–77.

Ntahokaja, J. B. "La Dot au Burundi: L'Institution, ses Avatars, les Tendences Actuelles." *Revue de l'Université Officielle de Bujumbura* 2, no. 7 (1968): 141–49.

Ntahombaye, Philippe. *Des Noms et Des Hommes: Aspects Psychologiques et Sociologiques du Nom au Burundi*. Paris: Éditions Karthala, 1983.

———. "Le Nom Individuel, Support Matériel de Message: Le Cas du Burundi." *Culture et Société*, no. 1 (1978): 12–34.

Perraudin, J. "Mort et Funérailles chez les Anciens Barundi." *Missions*, no. 3 (1952): 46–47.

Possoz, E. "Batoa, Batwa, Batswa." *Africa*, no. 3 (1954): 237–59.

Rhodius, George. "The Evolution of the Native Woman in the Belgian Congo and Ruanda-Urundi." *African Woman* 1 (1955): 73–74.

Rodegem, F. M. "La Fête des Prémices au Burundi." *Africa Linguistica* 5 (1971): 207–54.

———. "Nanga Yivuza: Un Secte Synchrétique au Burundi." *Cultures et Dévéloppement* 2, no. 2 (1970): 427–34.

———. "Sens et Rôle des Noms Propres en Histoire du Burundi." *Études d'Histoire Africaine* 7 (1975): 77–87.

Rozier, Raymond. "Structures Sociales et Politiques au Burundi." *Revue Française d'Études Politiques Africaines*, no. 91 (1973): 70–78.

Rutynx, J. "Ethique Indigène et Problèmes d'Acculturation en Afrique Centrale Belge." *Revue de l'Institut de Sociologie Solvay*, no. 2 (1958): 309–33.

Ryckmans, Pierre. "L'Organisation Politique et Sociale dans l'Urundi." *Revue Générale Belge* (15 April 1921): 460–84.

Schumacher, P. "Les Batwa." *Congo*, no. 1 (1931): 555–58.

———. "Les Batwa, sont-ils des Pygmées Authentiques?" *Æquatoria* 10, no. 4 (1947): 130–33.

Seruvumba, J. N. "A Propos de la Rupture du Mariage." *Bulletin de Juridictions Indigènes et du Droit Coutumier Congolais*, no. 12 (1947–48): 317–74.

———. "Propriété Vente et Bail de Vaches." *Bulletin de Juridictions Indigènes et du Droit Coutumier Congolais*, no. 5 (1947–48): 171–72.

Simons, Eugene. "Coutumes et Institutions des Barundi." *Bulletin des Juridictions Indigènes et du Droit Coutumier Congolais*, nos. 7–12 (1943–44): 137–60, 163–79, 181–222, 237–65, 269–82.

———. *Coutumes et Institutions des Barundi*. Elisabethville: Revue Juridique du Congo Belge, 1944.

———. "Note sur les Coutumes Indigènes Relatives aux Dommages-Intérêts dans l'Urundi." *Bulletin de Juridictions Indigènes et du Droit Coutumier Congolais*, no. 1 (1933–34): 3–5.

Smets, G. "Commerce, Marchés et Spéculations chez les Barundi." *Congo* 5 (1938): 568–74.

———. "Funérailles et Sépultures des Bami et Bagabekazi de l'Urundi." *Bulletin de l'Institut Royal Colonial Belge* 12, no. 2 (1941): 210–34.

———. "La Eschyle et les Barundi." *Bulletin de l'Académie Royale Belge*, no. 3 (1949): 141–58.

———. "Le Régime Successoral en Urundi." *Congo* 4 (1937): 453–54; 5 (1938): 297–307.

———. "Les Institutions Féodales de l'Urundi." *Revue de l'Université Bruxelles* 1 (February–April 1949): 101–12.

———. "L'Umuganuro chez les Barundi." *Congrés International Scientifique, Anthropologique, et Ethnologique.* Copenhagen, 1928.

———. "Quelques Observations sur les Usages Successoraux des Batutsi de l'Urundi." *Bulletin des Séances* 18 (1937): 729–40.

———. "Quelques Remarques sur les Techniques des Barundi." *Archelon* 1 (1937): 56–66.

———. "The Structure of the Barundi Community." *Man* 46, no. 6 (1946): 12–16.

Sohier, A. "La Réforme de la Dot et la Liberté de la Femme Indigène." *Bulletin de Juridictions du Ruanda-Urundi*, no. 9 (1950): 79–87.

———. "Le Droit de la Vache." *Journal de Tribunes d'Outre-Mer*, no. 9 (1951): 105.

Sousberghe, L. de. "Cousin Croisés et Descendants: Les Systèmes du Rwanda et du Burundi Comparés à ceux du Bas-Congo." *Africa* 35 (1965): 396–420.

Townshend, Philip. *Le Jeux de Mankala au Zaire, au Rwanda et au Burundi.* Brussels: Centre d'Étude et de Documentation Africaines, 1977.

Trouwborst, Albert. "Kinship and Geographical Mobility in Burundi." *International Journal of Comparative Sociology* 6, no. 1 (March 1965): 166–82.

———. "La Mobilité de l'Individu en Fonction de l'Organisation Politique des Barundi." *Zaire* 18 (1959): 787–800.

Turner, Victor. *The Drums of Affliction.* Oxford: Clarendon Press, 1968.

Van Bulck, G. "La Promotion de la Femme au Congo Belge et au Ruanda-Urundi." *Zaire* 15, no. 10 (1956): 1068–74.

———. "Le Troupeau de Vaches est-il un Placement de Capital en Afrique Orientale." *Zaire* 15, no. 5 (1956): 17–23.

Van Mal, G. "Note sur la Coutume Indigène en Fait de Dommages Intérêts et Droit de Vengeance (Territoire de Ruyigi, Urundi)." *Bulletin de Juridictions Indigènes et du Droit Coutumier Congolais*, no. 1 (1935–36): 13–14.

Verbrugghe, A. "Introduction Historique au Problème de la Nationalité au Burundi." *Revue Juridique et Politique* 25, no. 4 (1971): 435–38.

———. "La Responsabilité Civile des Commettants du Fait de leurs Préposés en Droit Burundais et Belge." *Revue Juridique et Politique* 27, no. 4 (1973): 563–68.

———. "La Situation de la Feffe Divorcée en Droit Traditionnel Burundais." *Revue Juridique et Politique* 28, no. 4 (1974): 593–99.

Vincent, Marc. *L'Enfant au Ruanda-Urundi.* Brussels: Institut Royal Colonial Belge, 1954.

Waleffe, F. "La Sécurité Sociale au Congo Belge et au Ruanda-Urundi." *Revue Belge de Sécurité Sociale*, nos. 5–6 (1954): 186–220.

Walhin, F. "Dommages et Intérêts dus en Vertu des Usages Locaux." *Bulletin de Juridictions du Ruanda-Urundi*, no. 8 (1950): 444–49.

———. "La Situation des Métis au Ruanda-Urundi en Matière Repressive." *Bulletin de Juridictions du Ruanda-Urundi*, no. 9 (1950): 469–75.

———. "Note à Propos de la Rupture du Mariage." *Bulletin de Juridictions du Ruanda-Urundi*, no. 5 (1948): 265–66.

Ziégler, Jean. "L'intégration Sociale et Politique entre Batutsi et Bahutu dans la Région Extra-Coutumière de Bujumbura." In *Travaux Sociologiques*, edited by P. Atteslander and R. Girod, vol. 1. Bern: Huber, 1966.

———. "Structures Ethniques et Partis Politiques au Burundi." *Le Mois en Afrique*, no. 18 (1967): 54–68.

XI. RELIGION

Arnoux, R. P. *Les Pères Blancs aux Sources du Nil*. Paris: Édition Saint-Paul, 1948.

Berger, Iris. *Religion and Resistance: East African Kingdoms in the Precolonial Period*. Tervuren, Belgium: Musée Royal de l'Afrique Centrale, 1981.

Bigangara, Jean-Baptiste. *Le Fondement de l'Imanisme: Religion Traditionnelle au Burundi*. Bujumbura: Ministére de la Jeunesse, des Sports et de la Culture, 1984.

Chrétien, Jean-Pierre. "Eglise et État au Burundi: Les Enjeux Politiques." *Afrique Contemporaine* 142, no. 2 (1987): 63–71.

———. *Pouvoir d'État et Autorité Mystique: L'Infrastructure Religieuse des Monarchies des Grands Lacs*. Paris: Société Française d'Histoire d'Outre-Mer, 1981.

Claver, Rév. Mère. "Traditions des Batusi." *Missions des Pères Blancs d'Afrique* (1907): 177–84.

Dechaume, P. "Imana, le Dieu des Paiens Barundi." *Grands Lacs*, nos. 5–6 (1936): 348–52.

Garnier, C., and J. Fralon. *Le Fétichisme en Afrique Noire*. Paris: Payot, 1951.

Greenland, Jeremy. "The Reform of Education in Burundi: Enlightened Theory Faced with Political Reality." *Comparative Education* 10, no. 1 (1974): 57–63.

Guillebaud, Rosemary. "The Doctrine of God in Ruanda-Urundi." In *African Ideas of God: A Symposium*, edited by Edwin Smith. London: Edinburgh House Press, 1950.

Heyse, T. *Associations Religieuses au Congo Belge et au Ruanda-Urundi*. Brussels: Institut Royal Colonial Belge, 1948.

Janssens, R. "Sur les Coutumes et Croyances de l'Urundi." *Bulletin de Juridictions Indigène et du Broit Coutumier Congolais*, nos. 9–10 (1953–54): 205–21, 229–40.

Kayoya, M. "Un Problème Très Urgent: L'Orientation de l'Action Catholique au Burundi." *Théologie et Pastoral au Rwanda et au Burundi*, no. 3 (1968): 106–13.

Keuppens, J. "Les Pères Blancs au Ruanda-Urundi." *Bulletin de l'Union Missionaire Clergé* (January 1956): 15–25.

MacGaffey, W. "Comparative Analysis of Central African Religions." *Africa* 17, no. 1 (1972): 21–31.

Mbiti, John. *African Religions and Philosophy*. New York: Praeger, 1969.

Péroncel-Hugoz, Jean-Pierre. "Burundi: Le Bras de Fer entre l'Eglise et l'État." *Le Monde*, 27 August 1987.

Perraudin, J. "Imana, Le Dieu des Barundi." *Missions*, no. 1 (1952): 11–12.

———. "Le Culte des Morts Chez les Anciens Barundi." *Missions*, no. 4 (1952): 55–56.

———. *Naissance d'une Église: Histoire du Burundi Chrétien*. Bujumbura: Presses Lavigerie, 1963.

Radner, Ephraim. "Breaking the Power of the Church in Burundi." *Christian Century* 102 (1985): 915–18.

Rodegem, F. M. "La Motivation du Culte Initiatique au Burundi." *Anthropos* 66 (1971): 863–930.

Roy, R. "Notes sur les Banyabungu: Description de l'Initiation au Culte de Ryangombe." *Congo*, no. 2 (1924): 327–47; no. 1 (1925): 83–108.

Tempels, Placide. *Bantu Philosophy*. Translated from *Banto Filosofie*. Paris: Présence Africaine, 1946. Reprint, Antwerp, 1969.

Zuure, Bernard. *Croyances et Pratiques Religieuses des Barundi*. Brussels: Bibliothèque Congo, 1929.

———. "Immâna, le Dieu des Barundi." *Anthropos* 21 (1926): 733–76.

———. *L'Ame du Murundi*. Paris: Beauchesne, 1931.

———. "Les Croyances de l'Urundi Révelées par les Usages et Pratiques." *Grands Lacs*, no. 9 (1948–49): 66–69.

XII. INTERNATIONAL RELATIONS

Balfour, Patrick. "Tanganyika and Ruanda-Urundi." *Geographical Magazine* 8 (1938): 42–48.

Bascom, W., and M. Herskovits, eds. *Continuity and Change in African Cultures*. Chicago: University of Chicago Press, 1959.

Bowman, Michael, et al. "No Samaritan: The U.S. and Burundi." *Africa Report* (July–August 1973).

"Burundi: China's Hand in Spiel." *Internationales Afrika Forum* 3, nos. 9–10 (1967): 439–40.

Larkin, Bruce. *China and Africa, 1949–1970*. Berkeley: University of California Press, 1971.

Ogunsanwo, Alaba. *China's Policy in Africa, 1958–1971*. Cambridge: Cambridge University Press, 1974.

Reuss, Conrad. "La Coopération Internationale au Burundi, 1962–1966." *Revue de l'Université Officielle de Bujumbura* 2, no. 5 (1968): 5–48.

———. "Réflexions sur l'Aide de la Belgique au Burundi." *Études Congolaises* 12, no. 2 (1969): 8196.

Reynolds, Quentin. "Interview with Tung Chi-ping." *Look* (1 December 1964): 24.

Sterling, Claire. "Chou En-lai and the Watusi." *The Reporter* (12 March 1964): 22–23.

Weinstein, Warren. "The Limits of Military Dependency: The Case of Belgian Aid to Burundi, 1961–1973." *Journal of African Studies* 2, no. 3 (1975): 419–31.

———, ed. *Soviet and Chinese Aid to Africa*. New York: Praeger, 1975.

XIII. EDUCATION

Chrétien, Jean-Pierre. "L'Enseignement au Burundi." *Revue Française d'Études Politiques Africaines*, no. 76 (1972): 61–81.

Greenland, Jeremy. *Western Education in Burundi, 1916–1973: The Consequences of Instrumentalism*. Brussels: Centre d'Étude et de Documentation Africaines, 1980.

"L'Éducation des Enfants chez les Baganwa de l'Urundi." *Grands Lacs*, nos. 10–11 (1949): 17–22.

Poelmans, R. "Vers un Enseignement plus Efficient au Ruanda-Urundi." *Actualité Congolaise* (Léopoldville), no. 22 (1952): 4.

Van der Meulen, F. "L'Organisation de l'Enseignement pour Indigènes au Ruanda-Urundi." *Servir*, no. 5 (1953): 171–79.

Vanhove, Julien. "L'Oeuvre d'Éducation au Congo Belge et au Ruanda-Urundi." In *L'Encyclopédie Belge*. Brussels: 1953.

XIV. GEOGRAPHY, GEOLOGY, AND AGRICULTURE

Adamantidis, D. *Monographie Pastorale du Ruanda-Urundi*. Brussels: Ministère des Colonies, 1956.

Aderca, Bernard M. *La Gisement de Terres Rares de la Karonge*. Brussels: Académie Royale des Sciences d'Outre-Mer, 1971.

Adriaens, E., and F. Lozet. "Contribution à l'Étude des Boissons Indigènes du Ruanda-Urundi." *Bulletin Agricole du Congo Belge* 42, no. 4 (1951): 933–50.

Blankoff-Scarr, Goldie, trans. *Ruanda-Urundi: Geography and History*. Brussels: Belgian Congo and Ruanda-Urundi Information and Public Relations Office, 1960.

Chrétien, Jean-Pierre. "Les Années de l'Éleusine, du Sorgho et du Haricot dans l'Ancien Burundi." *African Economic History*, vol. 7. Madison: University of Wisconsin, 1979.

Deuse, Paul. *Contribution à l'Étude des Tourbières du Ruanda et du Burundi*. Butare, Rwanda: Institut pour la Recherche Scientifique en Afrique Centrale, 1966.

Everaerts, E. "Monographie Agricole du Ruanda-Urundi." *Bulletin Agricole du Congo Belge* 30, no. 3 (1939): 343–94; no. 4 (1939): 581–615.

Fontaines, Paul. *Les Exploitations Minières de Haute Montagne au Ruanda-Urundi*. Brussels: M. Hayez, 1939.

Gevers, Marie. *Des Mille Collines aux Neuf Volcans*. Paris: Stock, Delamain et Boutelleau, 1953.

Guillaume, H. "Monographie de la Plaine de la Ruzizi." *Bulletin des Juridictions Indigènes et du Droit Coutumier Congolais* 18 (1950): 33–66.

Harroy, Jean-Paul. "La Lutte Contre la Dissipation des Ressources Naturelles au Ruanda-Urundi." *Civilisations* 4 (1954): 363–74.

Harroy, J.-P., J. Lebrun, et al. *Le Ruanda-Urundi: Ses Ressources Naturelles, ses Populations*. Brussels: Les Naturalistes Belges, 1956.

Hiernaux, Jean. "Problèmes d'Anthropologie Physique en Afrique Centrale." *Folio Scientifica Africae Centralis* (Institut pour la Recherche Scientifique en Afrique Centrale), no. 4 (1955): 6–8.

Jones, William I. *Farming Systems in Africa: The Great Lakes Highlands of Zaire, Rwanda, and Burundi*. Washington, D.C.: World Bank, 1984.

Jungers, E. "L'Agriculture Indigène au Ruanda-Urundi." *Société Belge d'Études et Expansion*, no. 123 (1946): 323–27.

Kayondi, C. "Murunga: Colline du Burundi." *Les Cahiers d'Outre-Mer* 25, no. 98 (1972): 164–204.

Lejoune, J. B. "L'Agriculture Indigène au Ruanda-Urundi." *Courrier Agricole d'Afrique* 4, no. 1 (1940): 1–4.

Lismont, J., and S. Gabungu. "La Toponymie au Service de la Géographie et du Kirundi." *Revue Nationale d'Éducation au Burundi*, no. 4 (1971–72): 12–18.

Maquet, J. J., and Jean Hiernaux. "Les Pasteurs de l'Itombwe." *Science et Nature*, no. 8 (1955): 3–12.

Marchi, F. "L'Élévage du Gros et du Petit Bétail au Ruanda-Urundi." *Bulletin Agricole du Congo Belge* 30, no. 4 (1939): 619–61.

Muhirwa, A. "Opinions d'un Murundi sur les Poisons et l'Anthropologie." *Servir* 8, nos. 4–5 (1947): 198–200, 240–48.

Nicaise, Joseph. "Applied Anthropology in the Congo and Ruanda-Urundi." *Human Organization* 19 (1960): 112–17.

Nicolai, H. "Progrès de la Connaissance Géographique au Zaire, au Rwanda et au Burundi en 1967, 1968 et 1970." *Bulletin de la Société Belge d'Études Géographiques*, no. 2 (1971): 263–317.

Peeters, Leo. "Le Rôle du Milieu Géographique dans l'Occupation Humaine du Rwanda-Burundi." *Bulletin de la Société Royale de Géographie d'Anvers* 74 (n.d.): 29–47.

Schantz, Homer L. "Urundi: Territory and People." *Geographical Review* 12 (1922): 329–59.

Schlippe, P. de. "Enquête Préliminaire du Système Agricole des Barundi de la Région Bututsi." *Bulletin Agricole du Congo Belge* 48, no. 4 (1957): 827–82.

Schouteden, H. *Faune du Congo Belge et du Ruanda-Urundi*. Tervuren, Belgium: Musée Royal du Congo Belge, 1948.

Skinner, Snider W. *The Agricultural Economy of the Belgian Congo and Ruanda-Urundi*. Washington, D.C.: Foreign Agricultural Service, U.S. Department of Agriculture, 1960.

Van der Velpen, C. *Géographie du Burundi*. Brussels: de Boeck, 1970.

Vervloet, G. "Aux sources du Nil." *Bulletin de la Société Royale Belge de Géographie*, no. 34 (1910): 108–37.

Waleffe, A. *Étude Géologique du sud-est Burundi: Régions du Mosso et du Nkoma*. Tervuren, Belgium: Musée Royal de l'Afrique Centrale, 1965.

XV. HEALTH AND MEDICINE

Hooper, Edward. *The River: A Journey to the Source of HIV and AIDS*. Boston: Little, Brown, 1999.

L'Epine, C. de. "Histoire des Famines et Disettes de l'Urundi." *Bulletin Agricole du Congo Belge* 20, no. 3 (1929): 440–42.

May, Jacques M. *The Ecology of Malnutrition in Middle Africa*. New York: Hafner, 1965.

Vyncke, J. *Psychoses et Névroses en Afrique Centrale*. Brussels: Académie Royale des Sciences Coloniales, 1957.

Waleffe, Fernand, Jr. *La Réparation des Accidents du Travail et des Maladies Professionnelles au Congo Belge et au Ruanda-Urundi*. Brussels: G. van Campenhout, 1948.

About the Author

Ellen K. Eggers teaches English and linguistics at California State University, Chico. She has a M.A. in applied linguistics from the Pennsylvania State University and a Ph.D. in linguistics from the University of Washington. Eggers lived in Bujumbura, Burundi, from 1985 to 1986, where she taught English and linguistics at the University of Burundi and collected Kirundi data for an earlier research project and several papers and articles on the language's discourse structure. She has lectured on the language and history of Burundi at the University of Nebraska and at California State University, Chico.